HOPE IN A SECULAR AGE

This book argues that hope is the indispensable precondition of religious practice and secular politics. Against dogmatic complacency and despairing resignation, David Newheiser argues that hope sustains commitments that remain vulnerable to disappointment. Since the discipline of hope is shared by believers and unbelievers alike, its persistence indicates that faith has a future in a secular age.

Drawing on premodern theology and postmodern theory, Newheiser shows that atheism and Christianity have more in common than they often acknowledge. Writing in a clear and engaging style, he develops a new reading of deconstruction and negative theology, arguing that, despite their differences, they share a self-critical hope. By retrieving texts and traditions that are rarely read together, this book offers a major intervention in debates over the place of religion in public life.

DAVID NEWHEISER is a Research Fellow in the Institute for Religion and Critical Inquiry at Australian Catholic University. His work has appeared in *The Journal of the American Academy of Religion*, *The Journal of Religious Ethics*, and *Theory, Culture & Society*. He is also the editor of numerous collections, including *Desire, Faith, and the Darkness of God* (2015).

HOPE IN A SECULAR AGE

*Deconstruction, Negative Theology, and
the Future of Faith*

DAVID NEWHEISER

Australian Catholic University

CAMBRIDGE
UNIVERSITY PRESS

University Printing House, Cambridge CB2 8BS, United Kingdom

One Liberty Plaza, 20th Floor, New York, NY 10006, USA

477 Williamstown Road, Port Melbourne, VIC 3207, Australia

314–321, 3rd Floor, Plot 3, Splendor Forum, Jasola District Centre, New Delhi – 110025, India

79 Anson Road, #06–04/06, Singapore 079906

Cambridge University Press is part of the University of Cambridge.

It furthers the University's mission by disseminating knowledge in the pursuit of education, learning, and research at the highest international levels of excellence.

www.cambridge.org
Information on this title: www.cambridge.org/9781108498661
DOI: 10.1017/9781108595100

© Cambridge University Press 2019

This publication is in copyright. Subject to statutory exception and to the provisions of relevant collective licensing agreements, no reproduction of any part may take place without the written permission of Cambridge University Press.

First published 2019

Printed in the United Kingdom by TJ International Ltd. Padstow Cornwall

A catalogue record for this publication is available from the British Library.

Library of Congress Cataloging-in-Publication Data
NAMES: Newheiser, David, 1982– author.
TITLE: Hope in a secular age : deconstruction, negative theology, and the future of faith / David Newheiser.
DESCRIPTION: Cambridge, United Kingdom ; New York, NY : Cambridge University Press, 2019. | Includes bibliographical references and index.
IDENTIFIERS: LCCN 2019020562 | ISBN 9781108498661 (hardback) | ISBN 9781108724395 (paperback)
SUBJECTS: LCSH: Hope. | Hope–Religious aspects. | Hope–Political aspects. | Negative theology. | Christianity and atheism. | Religion and politics.
CLASSIFICATION: LCC BD216 .N49 2019 | DDC 190–dc23
LC record available at https://lccn.loc.gov/2019020562

ISBN 978-1-108-49866-1 Hardback

Cambridge University Press has no responsibility for the persistence or accuracy of URLs for external or third-party internet websites referred to in this publication and does not guarantee that any content on such websites is, or will remain, accurate or appropriate.

*with gratitude for my family:
both the family I was born with
and the family I have found*

Contents

Acknowledgments		*page* viii
Introduction		1
1	Deconstruction: The Need for Negativity	17
2	Negative Theology: Critique and Commitment	40
3	The Discipline of Hope	63
4	Beyond Indeterminacy and Dogma	85
5	Atheism and the Future of Faith	108
6	Negative Political Theology	132
Conclusion		154
Bibliography		157
Subject Index		171

Acknowledgements

During the long evolution of this book, I have learned that, although hope is a discipline that we each take on for ourselves, no one hopes alone. The work you find here has been sustained by the companionship of many people – too many, really, to name.

I owe a particular debt to my teachers, each of whom formed my work in ways that would surprise them: Fritz Hinrichs, Wade Bradshaw, Lad Sessions, Alexandra Brown, Eduardo Velasquez, Morwenna Ludlow, Philip Endean, George Pattison, Arnold Davidson, Kevin Hector, Denys Turner, and Kathryn Tanner.

My work is marked by the colleagues I found at the institutions I have passed through: Oxford, Yale, the University of Chicago, Princeton, the University of Texas at Austin, Brown, and l'Institut Mémoires de l'édition contemporaine. I am especially grateful to Paul Wilmot, Brandon Gallagher, Saara Folini-Kaipainen, Devin Singh, Rick Elgendy, Joshua Daniel, Barnaby Reidel, Emily Dumler-Winkler, Leora Batnisky, Eric Gregory, Stacy Johnson, Lorraine Pangle, Patricia Roberts-Miller, Stephen Bush, Daniel Vaca, and Andre Willis. I have also relied on the administrative staff at each of these institutions; without their work, I couldn't do mine.

For the last four years I have benefited from the support of the Institute for Religion and Critical Inquiry at Australian Catholic University. My colleagues in Melbourne are generous and engaging, and I feel fortunate to be part of such a vibrant community. I have come to rely on my partners in a project I lead on the topic of atheism: Rachel Davies, Christiaan Jacobs-Vandegeer, Robyn Horner, Charles Lockwood, Henning Tegtmeyer, Denys Turner, and Stephan van Erp. I have also learned a great deal from Vincent Lloyd and Linn Tonstad, with whom I have discussed the themes of this book over a period of years and through whom my thinking has been repeatedly transformed.

A number of people read substantial portions of the manuscript and offered feedback that I continue to mull, among them Gil Anidjar, Teresa

Brown, Stephen Bush, Sylvia Clark, Sarah Coakley, Emily Dumler-Winckler, Lexi Eikelboom, Paul Fiddes, Kali Handelman, Robyn Horner, Carl Hughes, Christiaan Jacobs-Vandegeer, Stacy Johnson, Tamsin Jones, Mark Jordan, Scott Kirkland, Adam Kotsko, Vincent Lloyd, Andrew Prevot, Marika Rose, Mary-Jane Rubenstein, Joeri Schrijvers, Ted Smith, Sarah Stewart-Kroeker, Jeffrey Stout, Daniel Vaca, Nehama Verbin, Nathaniel Warne, and Andre Willis. Every time I have contact with Beatrice Rehl of Cambridge University Press, I am grateful that she is my editor. Thanks to Kate Mertes for preparing the index and to Jill Hobbs for copyediting the text.

There are several people whose companionship throughout this project has been extraordinary: Alda Balthrop-Lewis, Joshua Daniel, Rick Elgendy, Martin Kavka, Bradley Onishi, Devin Singh, Kathryn Tanner, and Denys Turner. Without them, my work and my life would poorer. For feeding me, diverting me, and enduring me, especially in the final push, I thank Owen, Rebekah, Chris, Jennifer, Mary, Jim, Caroline, and above all Alda.

Portions of Chapters 5 and 6 previously appeared in print: David Newheiser, "Derrida and the Danger of Religion," *Journal of the American Academy of Religion* 86, no. 1 (2018): 42–61; and David Newheiser, "Desacralizing Political Theology: Dionysius the Areopagite and Giorgio Agamben," DOI:10.1111/moth.12506. I thank the publishers for permission to reuse this material.

Introduction

I wrote this book because I believe it is hard to hope.

We invest in the people we love and the causes we care about, but people and projects may fail us. At the extreme, despair is an ordeal: physical suffering can compress attention within a present that has become unbearable, and psychological suffering may prevent a person from seeing any way forward. Although some people assert that everything will be alright, the reality of grief, anxiety, and exhaustion cannot be brushed away. Frustrated hopes are painful to maintain, so we are sometimes brought to abandon them.

Despair is directly opposed to hope, but complacency presents a more insidious challenge. Italo Calvino recounts the following story:

> A sibyl, questioned about Marozia's fate, said: "I see two cities, one of the rat, one of the swallow." This was the interpretation of the oracle: Today Marozia is a city where all run through leaden passages like packs of rats ... but a new century is about to begin in which all the inhabitants of Marozia will fly like swallows in the summer sky.[1]

Years later, on returning to the city, the narrator finds that its inhabitants believe that the prophecy has been fulfilled. However, he comments, "The wings I have seen moving about are those of suspicious umbrellas under which heavy eyelids are lowered; there are people who believe they are flying, but it is already an achievement if they can get off the ground flapping their batlike overcoats." Those who see themselves as the oracle's fulfillment are proud of their parody of the swallow's wings. Their confidence is closed to anything other than their grim, gray reality.

I see this story as a parable of hope. The citizens of Marozia move through the city with their eyelids lowered, immune to anything beyond

---

[1] Italo Calvino, *Invisible Cities*, trans. William Weaver (New York: Harcourt Brace Jovanovich, 1978), 154–55.

what is before them. Because they believe that the swallow's prophecy has been fulfilled, they have no need for the future, and they are numb to the possibility of something different from what they already possess. This indifference is more prosaic than the drama of despair, but it is equally hopeless. Where suffering and satisfaction constrain imagination within an enveloping present, hope is directed toward a future that remains unfulfilled. In Marozia, it would seem, there is no room for hope.

However, Calvino continues, "It also happens that, if you move along Marozia's compact walls, when you least expect it, you see a crack open and a different city appear." The Marozia of self-interested commerce is all that its inhabitants can imagine, but life remains capable of surprise. "It is enough for someone to do something for the sheer pleasure of doing it, and for his pleasure to become the pleasure of others: at that moment, all spaces change, all heights, distances; the city is transfigured, becomes crystalline, transparent as a dragonfly." This other Marozia flickers within a fracture in the existing order, vibrating for an instant before disappearing. "Everything must happen as if by chance, without attaching too much importance to it, ... remembering clearly that at any moment the old Marozia will return and solder its ceiling of stone, cobwebs, and mould over all heads." The first Marozia continually reasserts itself, but its monopoly is incomplete: the prospect of transformation shimmers beneath the surface of everyday life. This suggests that hope remains possible even when the world seems to exclude it.

Human experience strings together a series of surprises, from unpredictable minutiae – the timing of the bus, the texture of a cloud – to major events. For this reason, even those whose existence is generally regular find themselves destabilized by unpredictable tragedy or delight. This represents both a challenge and an opportunity for resilience. From the minute we wake, we are propelled by desires that may not be fulfilled, but this incompletion throws us into motion. Because every relationship eventually confronts disappointment, love must endure vulnerability, but vulnerability is also what lends love its energy. From individual desires to political movements, every project we pursue is not certain to succeed, but this same uncertainty energizes action against the odds. As Calvino describes, even the most monotonous life feels the force of the future.

Disappointment is always possible – and yet people persist. This book is premised on the conviction that both the disappointment and the persistence are real, and neither should be forgotten. In my understanding, hope constitutes a disciplined resilience that enables desire to endure without denying its vulnerability. Daily life depends on a hundred small hopes, and this is doubly true of our deepest commitments. Because complacency and despair exert a constant pull, hoping is hard, but it is also indispensable.

A Secular Age

Like every word, *hope* has a history. In European languages, it carries connotations associated with Judaism and Christianity.[2] Hope is a central theme in the Bible, from the messianic expectations described in the Hebrew Scriptures to the florid imagery of the Apocalypse of John. The most widely recited Christian creeds include the hope for the resurrection of the body, and expectations for the future (both personal and cosmic) are central to Christian commitment. For this reason, medieval theologians identified hope as one of three virtues that are central to relationship with God. In cultures that are marked by a Judeo-Christian past, it is possible to detect echoes of this tradition when people talk about hope, even among those who no longer identify as religious. This makes hope an important site for reflection on the place of religion in secular societies.

The character and significance of secularization are hotly contested. In the 1960s and 1970s, many scholars assumed that religion was in decline, but by the end of the century most recognized that the situation was more complex.[3] Charles Taylor's book *A Secular Age* (2007) represents a landmark attempt to develop a more nuanced narrative. According to Taylor, secularization signifies a change in the conditions for religious commitment rather than the loss of religion altogether. Taylor notes that many people remain committed to a religious tradition, but they do so surrounded by a dizzying range of alternatives. He writes, "We cannot help looking over our shoulder from time to time, looking sideways, living our faith also in a condition of doubt and uncertainty."[4] Because modernity is many-layered, this experience is culturally and geographically specific, but I think Taylor is right that (among certain people and in certain places) it is widely shared. In many communities, religious commitment has become

---

[2] To take one example, the *Oxford English Dictionary*'s earliest entry for "Hope (n.)" is from a Christian commentary on the book of Isaiah: "Ne bepæce Ezechias eow mid leasum hopan, þæt God eow..ahredde" [Ælfric Homilies (c. 1000)].

[3] Compare, for instance, Peter L. Berger, *The Sacred Canopy; Elements of a Sociological Theory of Religion* (Garden City, NY: Doubleday, 1967); and Peter L. Berger, "Secularism in Retreat," *The National Interest*, no. 46 (1996): 3–12.

[4] Charles Taylor, *A Secular Age* (Cambridge, MA: Belknap Press of Harvard University Press, 2007), 11.

one option among many, a source of anxiety rather than a site of consensus.⁵

In key respects, the secular age that Taylor describes resembles Calvino's Marozia. According to Taylor, modern science made it possible to describe the world as an order that could be understood on its own terms, without reference to anything more. Whereas the world was once porous to the supernatural, it has become self-sufficient. At the same time, religious rhythms of festival and fasting have been supplanted by the uniform time that is measured by clocks, and contemplative reflection has been displaced by the dominance of instrumental rationality. Much as the inhabitants of Marozia have lost the sense of anything beyond their daily business, many people assume that what Taylor calls "the immanent frame" excludes transcendence.⁶

Where Taylor suggests that modern science and market capitalism have banished the gaps and crevices through which something otherworldly used to appear, Calvino indicates that immanence is never entirely closed. In Marozia, the regularity of daily commerce can collapse at any time. Unexpected delight can crack the dull regularity of ordinary time, suddenly transfiguring everything. Because the old Marozia remains in force, this crystalline city is not a place that can be inhabited, but its possibility qualifies the authority of the present. In my understanding, hope unsettles the secular in precisely this way.

There is a lively debate among philosophers concerning whether religious beliefs are justified, but I think this issue is secondary: in my view, religious commitment hinges on ethics rather than epistemology. The view that beliefs ought to be justified is a judgment about how people should live, not a fact that can be demonstrated. One never knows whether one's love for another person will be a source of suffering or delight, nor can one know whether one's goals will come to fruition. Nevertheless, love sometimes endures, and people pursue desires that are vulnerable to

---

⁵ As I discuss at greater length in Chapter 5, scholars such as Talal Asad have argued that the concept of religion was constructed in the modern era as a term of contrast to the secular state; from the outset, it was an abstraction designed to bolster the state's monopoly on violence. Similarly, before "secular" came to name a sphere distinct from religion, it referred to (Christian) clergy who lived among the laity, whereas "religious" clergy withdrew to cloistered life. Where some assume that the secular and the religious are discrete identities that stand opposed, the boundary between them is under constant negotiation, and the meaning of both is marked by the legacy of Christianity (see Talal Asad, *Genealogies of Religion: Discipline and Reasons of Power in Christianity and Islam* [Baltimore: Johns Hopkins University Press, 1993], 191–92; Saba Mahmood, "Religious Reason and Secular Affect: An Incommensurable Divide?," *Critical Inquiry* 35, no. 4 [2009]: 836–62).

⁶ Taylor, *A Secular Age*, 15, 542.

disappointment. The persistence of hope indicates that, although rational deliberation is an important dimension of human existence, it is not the only one. On account of hope, it remains possible to hold commitments that transcend the immanent frame. For this reason, I will argue, reflection on hope illuminates the future of faith in a secular age.

The Problem with Hope

At the same time, I aim to show that taking secularization seriously clarifies the character of hope. In *The Myth of Sisyphus* (1942), Albert Camus argues that hope no longer holds purchase in a universe divested of illusions.[7] In his view, religious hope imposes meaning upon a meaningless world, and so is unsustainable. Camus claims that any comfort hope provides is prone to collapse, and I think he is correct. Perhaps there were once communities in which everyone expected a life after death, but within pluralized societies religious hopes are no longer self-evident. Those who are suffering are sometimes told that God has a plan, but when trauma is intense, easy comfort can seem obscene. Even the faithful must confront a world in which God appears to be silent; in this context, faith is premised upon endurance of doubt. Once the world is demystified, the confidence claimed by some seems like a denial of present realities and a distraction from things as they are.

Camus is committed to resolute lucidity as an individual practice, but his point also applies to politics. Attention to an outcome one desires can congeal into unjustified confidence, and this feeling of security may displace attention from improvement in the present. Along these lines, Karl Marx argues that the promise of heaven distracts people from injustice on earth; as he describes it, otherworldly hopes are imaginary flowers that hide the chain of oppression. More recently, afro-pessimists such as Calvin Warren claim that hope undercuts the critique of present injustice by positing a realization that is never satisfied. There is therefore reason to worry that hope is politically debilitating.[8]

Some Christians defend a form of hope that confirms these criticisms. In a recent book, David Elliot argues that Christian hope constitutes a confident expectation that is grounded in the promises of God. He writes,

---

[7] Albert Camus, *The Myth of Sisyphus, and Other Essays* (New York: Knopf, 1955). I discuss Camus's critique of hope in Chapter 3.

[8] Cf. Karl Marx, *Critique of Hegel's "Philosophy of Right,"* trans. Joseph O'Malley (Cambridge: Cambridge University Press, 1970); Calvin L. Warren, "Black Nihilism and the Politics of Hope," *CR: The New Centennial Review* 15, no. 1 (April 1, 2015): 215–48.

"Theological hope ... provides an ultimate meaning and transcendent purpose to our lives; and it rejoices and refreshes us 'on the way' (*in via*) with the prospect of ultimate reconciliation and lasting beatitude."[9] According to Elliot, whereas secular hope is fragile, Christian hope supplies life with a significance that it would otherwise lack, and it offers the guarantee of eternal life. This corresponds to the security that concerns Warren, Marx, and Camus. Where they claim that the world does not provide assurance of this sort, Elliot writes that Christian hope is "supremely confident and triumphal."[10] There is reason to worry that such confidence ignores what it is like to live in a world where religious commitment is no longer obvious.

Elliot represents one strand of Christian reflection on hope, but there are others. In the New Testament, the Apostle Paul identifies hope as central to salvation – "in hope we were saved" – but this does not entail that it is certain (Rom. 8:24). He continues, "Now hope that is seen is not hope. For who hopes for what is seen? But if we hope for what we do not see, we wait for it with perseverance [*hypomonēs*]" (Rom. 8:24–25, translation modified). Where Elliot claims that Christian hope consists in confident expectation, Paul suggests that hope concerns the invisible; because this hope remains unrealized, Paul explains, Christians are suspended in a state of unfulfilled desire. Paul is attentive to the ambivalence of this situation. Immediately before this passage he writes, "We know that the whole creation has been groaning in labor pains until now; and not only the creation, but we ourselves" (Rom. 8:22–23). This suggests that, rather than representing a triumphal confidence, Christian hope is a discipline that endures the pain of incompletion.

Because Christians believe in an invisible God, they have had ample opportunity to practice perseverance in response to disappointment. Revisiting this strand of Christian tradition in conversation with Camus's austere lucidity underscores the fact that Christian faith was always uncertain. Like modern revolutionaries, the biblical prophets are oriented by the desire for something more; for both, this hope sustains resistance to present injustice. Although the content of these hopes are different, they share the same form. Where theologians like Elliot argue that Christian hope is unique, I will argue that religious and secular hopes are both

---

[9] David Elliot, *Hope and Christian Ethics*, 2017, 2.   [10] Ibid., 61.

vulnerable to disappointment, and so they both require the same resilience.[11]

The Discipline of Hope

To clarify the character of hope, my argument draws on a tradition of Christian thought that foregrounds the hiddenness of God. The Torah insists that God alone should be worshipped, and so it proscribes the representation of God in graven images (cf. Exodus 20:4). Although Christians believed that Jesus Christ was "the image of the invisible God" (Col. 1:15), this paradoxical phrase suggests that God remains obscure. The Apostle Paul writes that "now we see through a glass, darkly" (1 Cor. 13:12). On this view, Christian knowledge of God is imperfect – at least for now, it fumbles in the dark. Some theologians therefore insist that every attempt to represent God, in images or in words, must be accompanied by a disciplined negativity.

In the second century, theologians such as Justin Martyr and Clement of Alexandria placed this biblical tradition into conversation with Platonic philosophy to underscore that God is beyond understanding.[12] Where they called God "incomprehensible," "ineffable," "ingenerate," etc., fourth-century theologians such as Gregory of Nyssa situated this negativity within a sustained ethical practice. Gregory argues that every concept drawn from a comprehensible image only approximates the divine, and so it risks becoming an idol.[13] For this reason, he says, intimacy with God requires passage from the light of knowledge into the darkness of the divine.[14]

This tradition was given systematic expression by Dionysius the Areopagite, a fifth-century theologian – sometimes called "Pseudo-Dionysius" or "Pseudo-Denys" – who had an enormous influence on medieval theology, from Thomas Aquinas and Meister Eckhart in the West to Maximus the Confessor and Gregory Palamas in the East. Dionysius argues that God is beyond human understanding, and so everything humans say

---

[11] Since the category of religion is notoriously unstable, I do not assume that Christianity stands for every religious tradition. Nevertheless, I believe the example is suggestive – not least because, in many contexts, Christian history has shaped the categories with which this debate has been framed.

[12] See D. W. Palmer, "Atheism, Apologetic, and Negative Theology in the Greek Apologists of the Second Century," *Vigiliae Christianae* 37, no. 3 (1983): 234–59; Henny Fiskå Hägg, *Clement of Alexandria and the Beginnings of Christian Apophaticism: Knowing the Unknowable* (New York: Oxford University Press, 2006).

[13] Gregory of Nyssa, *The Life of Moses* (New York: Paulist Press, 1978), 96.   [14] Ibid., 97.

about God falls short. On this view, even if Christians are right that there is a God, their understanding of God's promises and intentions remains unreliable. Since, as Dionysius says, "the mysteries of God's Word lie ... in the brilliant darkness of a hidden silence," they cannot be appropriated for the purpose of possessing certainty.[15] Instead, he affirms Christian practice as an experiment that may be mistaken.

In the twentieth century, a number of theorists with no religious commitments of their own found that this tradition – which they called "negative theology" – helped to clarify the negativity of their own work.[16] My argument focuses on Jacques Derrida, an apparently godless philosopher who engaged negative theology repeatedly throughout his career. Derrida discusses Dionysius directly at several points, but I am more interested in the implicit connections between them. Precisely because they are different in so many respects, their similarity is striking and instructive. In Derrida's account, the claim to possess metaphysical certainty serves to stave off anxiety by reinforcing the subject's present understanding. In response, Derrida's deconstructive negativity functions as an ethical practice of persistence in the face of vulnerability. In this way, like Dionysius, Derrida's negativity is inseparable from an affirmation that resists false assurance.

Dionysius and Derrida rarely speak explicitly about hope, but I think hope is implicitly at the center of their work. They come from very different times and hold very different commitments, but both authors underscore that every attempt at speech is provisional. For both of them, self-critique preserves the possibility of development beyond what the self can foresee. In contrast to bare negation, they proliferate paradoxical juxtapositions to encourage ethical transformation. Neither author takes the impossibility of knowledge to preclude speech; on the contrary, they

---

[15] MT 997B, 135. References to the Dionysian corpus are abbreviated as follows: DN, The Divine Names; MT, The Mystical Theology; CH, The Celestial Hierarchy; EH, The Ecclesiastical Hierarchy; Ep, Epistles. Because it is the most widely available translation, page references correspond to the translation of Colm Luibhéid: *Pseudo-Dionysius: The Complete Works*, The Classics of Western Spirituality, trans. Colm Luibhéid (New York: Paulist Press, 1987). Because this translation is somewhat free, I have modified it where noted. I have referred for comparison to the translations of John Parker (*The Works of Dionysius the Areopagite*, trans. John Parker [Merrick, NY: Richwood, 1976]); and John D. Jones (*The Divine Names and Mystical Theology*, Mediaeval Philosophical Texts in Translation, no. 21, trans. John D. Jones [Milwaukee, WI: Marquette University Press, 1980]).

[16] For reasons I discuss at length in Chapter 2, this tradition requires both affirmation and negation, so to call it "negative theology" is somewhat misleading. I use that name here because it is more common than the cumbersome alternative, "apophatic theology." Nevertheless, the reader should consider the name negated (as well as affirmed).

both say a great deal about justice (in the case of Derrida) and about God (in the case of Dionysius). Insofar as they affirm experimental commitments that are fundamentally uncertain, Derrida and Dionysius exemplify the disciplined persistence of hope.

Although their positions are opposed, Elliot and Camus both suggest that we must choose between certitude and hopelessness. Derrida and Dionysius offer an alternative: in my reading, they describe a hope that acknowledges its uncertainty, sustaining affirmation without sacrificing self-critique. A hope of this kind does not diminish the present through unjustified confidence. Instead, insofar as it holds a longing that remains unfulfilled, hope highlights the gap between present reality and the desired future. Because hope is vulnerable to disappointment, it encourages a restless dissatisfaction with the status quo. In my view, such a hope avoids the complacent fantasy that Camus criticizes, and it is available to the religious and the irreligious alike.

Acknowledging the affinity between secular and religious hope clarifies hope's character. Analytic philosophers such as Adrienne Martin claim that hope must have an object that the hoper understands to be possible, but I will argue that this is a mistake.[17] On my account, because hope represents a discipline of the will, it may persist even when one believes the desired outcome cannot occur. For this reason, I think hope is consistent with a profound pessimism. Hope is decision added to desire, and as such it is unconstrained by calculation. A hope untethered from the rational evaluation of probabilities is perilous, for there is no guarantee that it will be fulfilled. Nevertheless, it remains an indispensable dimension of human life.

Keeping Faith in the Dark

Dionysius and Derrida do not share the same commitments, nor do they affirm the same hopes. Where Dionysius was a premodern monk, thoroughly immersed in Christian worship, Derrida was formed by a Jewish upbringing and the secularism of the French academy. However, these differences throw their affinity into sharper relief. Although Derrida does not affirm a religious identity, he draws on religious texts to describe a politics that is motivated by messianic expectation. Conversely, Dionysius

---

[17] Adrienne Martin, *How We Hope: A Moral Psychology* (Princeton, NJ: Princeton University Press, 2013).

argues that Christian commitment requires self-critique; in his view, there can be no knowledge concerning the object of faith. Since religious and political commitments both exceed the available evidence, Dionysius and Derrida suggest that they both require a leap of faith, and so both must be sustained by an unknowing hope.

Following Derrida's lead, the relation between deconstruction and negative theology has served as a crucial site for reflection on religion and postmodernism.[18] Unfortunately, this literature tends to reinforce stereotypes about religion that I aim to unsettle. According to John Caputo, whereas Dionysius affirms a determinate conception of transcendence (as "God"), Derrida affirms an indeterminate orientation. Like Caputo, Jean-Luc Marion claims that Derrida repudiates negative theology; according to Marion, Dionysius secures a knowledge of God that Derrida lacks. Martin Hägglund claims that determinate faith circumscribes transcendence, and so he concludes that Derrida defends an atheism that excludes religious commitment. All three commentators claim that Derrida's indeterminacy is opposed to the content of Christian doctrine, they simply differ over which side is better.[19]

This consensus misconstrues both authors. Whereas Caputo claims that Derrida rejects the particularity of determinate religious traditions, I will argue that deconstruction is consistent with Christian commitment. (That is not to say that Derrida himself affirmed a religious identity: the point is simply that his project does not preclude it.) This is evident from Derrida's published engagement with Dionysius, but the case becomes even clearer when unpublished archival material is taken into account. Although Derrida sometimes worries that Dionysian negativity is too limited, he is clear that this concern applies to his own work as well. From the outset to the end of his career, Derrida argues that pure indeterminacy is a state that cannot be achieved. For this reason, he does not prohibit the affirmation of particular commitments, religious or otherwise. Instead, he aims to encourage an ethics of uncertainty in relation to that which is beyond oneself.

---

[18] Because the term "postmodernism" is frequently misleading, Derrida generally avoids it (see Jacques Derrida, "No (Point of) Madness: Maintaining Architecture," in *Psyche: Inventions of the Other*, Vol. II, ed. Peggy Kamuf and Elizabeth Rottenberg (Stanford, CA: Stanford University Press, 2008), 87.

[19] John D. Caputo, *The Prayers and Tears of Jacques Derrida: Religion without Religion* (Bloomington: Indiana University Press, 1997); Jean-Luc Marion, "In the Name," in *God, the Gift, and Postmodernism*, ed. John D. Caputo and Michael J. Scanlon (Bloomington: Indiana University Press, 1999), 20–42; Martin Hägglund, *Radical Atheism: Derrida and the Time of Life* (Stanford, CA: Stanford University Press, 2008).

Most commentators agree that negative theology maintains a confidence that Derrida disavows. This reading is reinforced by specialist interpreters such as Andrew Louth and Alexander Golitzin, who claim that Dionysius exempts Christian practice from critique. In response, I will argue that Dionysian *apophasis* (Greek for "unsaying") comprises a discipline of dispossession that opens the subject to transformation. Like Derrida, Dionysius believes that people tend to project themselves onto that which is different, so he insists that talk of transcendence requires self-critique. On his account, Christian discourse is a provisional attempt that is relativized by the unforeseeable future. Rather than surreptitiously asserting certainty, Dionysius describes a hope that endures darkness.

On the basis of their shared misreading, Caputo recommends an indeterminate spirituality, Marion asserts a confident traditionalism, and Hägglund rejects religion altogether. Insofar as each commentator represents a common response to secularization, my retrieval of deconstruction and negative theology opens another possibility. Although Dionysius does not display Derrida's melancholic inclination, he exhibits a negativity that is equally rigorous, while Derrida affirms a faith that differs from religious commitment in content but not in kind. Attending to their affinity shows that religious commitment can be resolutely undogmatic, and that religious traditions can contribute to reflection in a secular context. In this way, Dionysius and Derrida demonstrate that it is possible to keep faith in the dark through the discipline of hope.

A Reading Method

For reasons of principle, my argument unfolds through the interpretation of particular texts. Dionysius and Derrida suggest that people think by reading, and I believe they are right. On their account, the future comes in the context of the present, the other is inseparable from the same, and the unknown beckons from behind the known. For this reason, they both suggest that a revolution in thought does not require pure novelty; instead, we can uncover unexpected possibilities in familiar traditions. Derrida and Dionysius explore new horizons by reworking the text they had at hand, and I do the same. Because this approach is creative, my conclusions might surprise the authors themselves, but that does not mean that the reading is wrong. On the contrary, I think my work should be judged by the standard on which they rely – which is to say, by its fidelity to the texts themselves rather than some reconstruction of the author's inner life.

Jorge Luis Borges describes a scrupulosity that bedevils some interpreters: "In that Empire, the Art of Cartography attained such Perfection that the map of a single Province occupied the entirety of a City, and the map of the Empire, the entirety of a Province. In time, those Unconscionable Maps no longer satisfied, and the Cartographers Guilds struck a Map of the Empire whose size was that of the Empire, and which coincided point for point with it."[20] Some readers are guided by the longing for an interpretation that would perfectly correspond to the original text, point for perfect point. Where premodern readers played upon a range of interpretive methods, scholars since the Enlightenment have tended to identify the significance of a text with the meaning it held in its original context. However, just as a full-scale map is useless for navigation, a reading that attempts to reproduce a text's historical sense constrains its significance for the questions that confront us today.

Borges reports that "in the Deserts of the West, still today, there are Tattered Ruins of that Map,"[21] and Derrida suggests that ruins are where reading thrives. Although some suppose that philosophy may surpass the past in one leap, Derrida claims that "it is necessary still to inhabit the metaphor in ruins, to dress oneself in tradition's shreds and the devil's patches."[22] This decay opens the possibility of creative interpretation. Derrida continues, "One can, by using them, use up tradition's words, rub them like a rusty and devalued old coin."[23] Some suggest that tradition demands either repetition or rejection, but Derrida argues that fidelity involves invention, not mere repetition. As we shall see, his practice of reading opens surprising avenues for thought precisely because it is characterized by painstaking care.

In similar fashion, Dionysius engages the past by actively transforming it. He adopts the name of a convert of the Apostle Paul, and he claims to have witnessed the eclipse that accompanied the crucifixion of Christ (though he lived centuries after the fact). Early modern interpreters, unfamiliar with ancient practices of authorship and interpretation, saw this gesture as a simple forgery, but this misunderstands the significance of the pseudonym. By taking the name, "Dionysius" recontextualizes apostolic tradition with dramatic effect, collapsing the distance between

---

[20] Jorge Luis Borges, "On Exactitude in Science," in *Collected Fictions*, trans. Andrew Hurley (New York: Viking, 1998), 325.
[21] Ibid.
[22] Jacques Derrida, "Violence and Metaphysics: An Essay on the Thought of Emmanuel Levinas," in *Writing and Difference*, trans. Alan Bass (Chicago: University of Chicago Press, 1978), 112.
[23] Ibid.

fifth-century Neoplatonic philosophy and first-century Christian communities. In this way, he displays a fidelity that reinterprets its sources in light of contemporary concerns. Like Derrida, Dionysius models a constructive method that works through careful and creative interpretation. If I read their work in ways that would surprise them, it is because I am following their lead.

The Arc of the Argument

In Chapter 1 I argue that, despite its reputation, deconstruction constitutes an ethical practice that preserves the possibility of unpredictable transformation. Theorists such as Rita Felski and Eve Kosofsky Sedgwick claim that critique corrodes the capacity to make affirmative judgments in particular contexts. They echo those commentators who associate deconstruction with a pure play that precludes responsible rationality. I argue instead that deconstruction constitutes a discipline of openness to the unexpected. According to Derrida's diagnosis, metaphysical certainty aims to assuage the anxiety that arises in an unstable world; his concern is that this buys some comfort while closing the individual to others. In contrast, deconstructive negativity enables another kind of affirmation – uncertain, subject to revision, and sustained by hope.

In Chapter 2 I argue that Christian thought inhabits an unresolved tension between negativity and affirmation. Whereas commentators such as Stathis Gourgouris claim that religion asserts a certainty that excludes critique, negative theology unsettles every claim to represent the divine. Dionysius the Areopagite argues that Christian discourse must be simultaneously affirmed and negated. Although this seems like simple contradiction on the level of logic, it becomes the means of ethical transformation when enacted in time. In my reading, negative theology is not mainly a matter of linguistic technique; on the contrary, it destabilizes the self through thoroughgoing self-critique. Insofar as Dionysius continues to affirm practices that are directed toward an unknowable God, he models a hope that persists despite its uncertainty.

Chapter 3 draws upon my reading of Derrida and Dionysius to clarify the character of hope. Although Dionysius and Derrida rarely use the word, I argue that the uncertain affirmation that I describe in the first two chapters is predicated upon the discipline of hope. Where Albert Camus claims that hope posits a confidence that distracts from life here and now, Derrida and Dionysius describe a hope that claims no assurance concerning what is to come. On my account, rather than projecting desire onto a fantasized future, a self-critical hope energizes efforts to improve the present. A hope of this kind is a practice, not the conclusion of a proof; it depends upon decision, which inevitably goes beyond the evidence. For this reason, it cannot guarantee a good result, but that does not mean that it must be abandoned. On the contrary, hope is what enables us to acknowledge our vulnerability while pressing forward nonetheless.

Chapter 4 addresses two common responses to secularization: dogmatic retrenchment and indeterminate spirituality. Commentators such as John Caputo and Jean-Luc Marion claim that deconstruction and negative theology are incompatible; as they observe, Dionysius affirms Christian commitment while Derrida does not. In my reading, however, deconstruction and negative theology share a hope that is identical in kind, though not in content. Although Derrida and Dionysius affirm different commitments and express different hopes, they both rely on a hope that incorporates self-critique. They suggest that it is necessary neither to assert an impossible certainty nor to attempt an unsustainable indeterminacy. Instead, they model a hope that affirms particular beliefs and practices while acknowledging that every commitment is radically uncertain.

In light of my account of hope, Chapter 5 argues that it is both impossible and unnecessary to exclude religion from secular politics. Political theorists such as Mark Lilla claim that religion is a source of violence, and so they conclude that religion and politics should be strictly separated. In my reading, Derrida's work entails that a secularism of this kind is both impossible (because religion remains influential in the wake of secularization) and unnecessary (because religious traditions are diverse and multivalent). Where Martin Hägglund claims that deconstruction entails a radical atheism; Derrida suggests that political commitments are formally indistinguishable from religious faith insofar as both are directed toward the unforeseeable future. Although Derrida admits that religion is dangerous, he demonstrates that one may endure instability for the sake of something more important than safety. Where secularism and theocracy both promise an impossible clarity, Derrida suggests that believers and unbelievers both share an uncertain hope.

In Chapter 6 I develop a negative political theology that addresses the problem posed by the persistence of the sacred. Giorgio Agamben argues that, whether it derives from religious worship or national identity, reverence for the sacred functions to neutralize resistance. My account of hope indicates on the contrary that a concern for transcendence can intensify critique. Dionysius demonstrates that, rather than affirming the sacred uncritically or disavowing it altogether, communities can acknowledge the special significance of particular texts and traditions while maintaining an ethical discipline that loosens their authority.

Hope Today

The present state of global politics is troubling. In the United States, which I know best, the rise of right-wing populism has cast a cold light on the deep-seated racism and xenophobia that distorts American society. In the United States, as in other parts of the world, inequalities of race, class, and gender are deeply entrenched, and popular resistance is undermined by manipulation, suppression, and deprivation. For this reason, the question of hope is urgent today – not because hope has diminished, but because it is so widespread.

Donald Trump's 2016 presidential campaign was premised on a grim vision of "American carnage," but this pessimism was linked to the hope that American greatness would return.[24] Similarly, in the 2016 referendum in which Britain voted to leave the European Union, widespread despair over the value of international institutions was the backdrop for hope in a nationalist future. There is good reason to think this hope was misplaced, but it was hope nonetheless. For this reason, I disagree with those who say that our world is distinctively hopeless.[25]

However, the pervasive importance of hope is often occluded. Some political leaders present their policies as if success were guaranteed, but this neglects the uncertainty of political action. Others find it difficult to combine critique of the prevailing regime with constructive proposals; in this case, the failure to fulfill an imagined ideal can impede the pursuit of imperfect improvement. Against both tendencies, hope offers a way to affirm particular policies while subjecting them to ongoing critique. In itself, hope is not enough to solve the issues that face us today, but I believe it is required for democratic politics to flourish.

---

[24] Donald Trump, "Inaugural Address," Washington, DC, January 20, 2017, accessed June 28, 2019, https://www.whitehouse.gov/briefings-statements/the-inaugural-address/. Much earlier, Ronald Reagan made the link explicit: "For those who have abandoned hope, we'll restore hope and we'll welcome them into a great national crusade to make America great again" (Ronald Reagan, "Presidential Nomination Acceptance Speech," Republican National Convention, Detroit, MI, July 17, 1980, accessed June 28, 2019, https://www.reaganlibrary.gov/7-17-80).

[25] Some theologians claim that secularism undermines hope, while some leftist theorists worry that hope is eroded by neoliberal consumerism (Elliot, 110; Mary Zournazi, *Hope: New Philosophies for Change* [New York: Routledge, 2003], 14). In my view, both tendencies underestimate the ambivalence of hope.

On my account, hope constitutes a disciplined resilience that allows us to admit that our cherished assumptions may be misguided and that familiar institutions may be unjust. For this reason, it nurtures the work of attentive reflection and democratic debate – open, undetermined, and honest. In many parts of the world, these practices appear to be breaking down, and in some cases (it would seem) the damage to civil society may be irreparable. However, hope is also the precondition for action in the face of overwhelming odds. Although hope does not determine what we should do, it empowers us to address problems that appear intractable.

Because we are shaped by the world as it is, transformation is difficult to envision. It requires that we stretch past our present understanding, and this a difficult thing to do. However, hope is what enables us to persist when things are difficult. Insofar as it is oriented toward what does not yet exist, hope loosens our grip on what is comfortable and familiar, pressing us to imagine unpredictable possibilities. Hope is nourished when rays from a crystalline future glimmer in the fissures of everyday reality, but it can persist even when, with a turn of the head, it seems that nothing was there after all. Hope does not assume that it will bring the future into being, but it refuses to give up the struggle simply because the situation is bleak.

CHAPTER I

Deconstruction
The Need for Negativity

At the age of twenty-two, as a student at l'École normale supérieure, Jacques Derrida wrote an essay titled "The Idea of Simplicity." In a handwritten note, his teacher commented dryly: "You seem to be on good terms with complication."[1] This is a complaint that any reader of Derrida can confirm. His writing rapidly shifts between punning play and dense exegesis, and it demands mastery of a web of textual references ranging from classic philosophy to contemporary literature. This elusiveness is partly a matter of principle. According to Derrida, the concepts that guide his work – *différance*, play, justice, and so on – cannot be defined or identified. For this reason, his writing displays a compulsive reflexivity that constantly strains to escape itself. Because this commitment to complication makes Derrida difficult to read, some readers dismiss his work as nihilism or nonsense.[2]

I think Derrida has more to offer than this response allows. In my reading, from the beginning of his career to the end, he addresses a

---

[1] Jacques Derrida, "L'idée de Simplicité (École normale supérieure)" 219DRR/337/3, Fonds Jacques Derrida, IMEC, Saint-Germain-la-blanche herbe, Normandie (translation my own). The teacher in question was Louis Althusser.

[2] See John Milbank, *Theology and Social Theory: Beyond Secular Reason*, 2nd ed. (Oxford; Malden, MA: Blackwell, 2006), 278, 311; John Milbank, *Truth in Aquinas* (London; New York: Routledge, 2001), 77; John Milbank, "The Sublime in Kierkegaard," in *Post-Secular Philosophy: Between Philosophy and Theology*, ed. Phillip Blond (London; New York: Routledge, 1998), 76; Catherine Pickstock, *After Writing: On the Liturgical Consummation of Philosophy*, Challenges in Contemporary Theology (Oxford; Malden, MA: Blackwell, 1998), 77; Catherine Pickstock, "Reply to David Ford and Guy Collins," *Scottish Journal of Theology* 54, no. 3 (2001): 416; Conor Cunningham, *A Genealogy of Nihilism: Philosophies of Nothing and the Difference of Theology* (London; New York: Routledge, 2002), 155ff. Guy Collins argues persuasively that such critiques are grounded in a basic ignorance of Derrida's texts ("Thinking the Impossible: Derrida and the Divine," *Literature and Theology* 14, no. 3 [September 1, 2000]: 313–34; and "Defending Derrida: A Response to Milbank and Pickstock," *Scottish Journal of Theology* 54, no. 3 [2001]: 344–65). I have responded to Milbank's reading of Derrida in David Newheiser, "Eckhart, Derrida, and the Gift of Love," in *Desire, Faith, and the Darkness of God: Essays in Honor of Denys Turner*, ed. David Newheiser and Eric Bugyis (Notre Dame, IN: University of Notre Dame Press, 2015), 430–56.

problem that has profound significance for ethical life. In his diagnosis, people claim to possess certainty in an attempt to assuage their anxiety at the volatility of human life. Because this buys comfort at the cost of closing the subject to that which is different, Derrida responds by arguing that every conceptual and political system is constitutively open to radical otherness. To this end, his project – which he sometimes calls "deconstruction" – highlights the instability of texts and institutions (despite attempts to stabilize them). This negativity is needed, in his view, to resist the danger of complacency.

In my view, reading Derrida in terms of ethics clarifies the significance of his complicated oeuvre, but it remains that Derrida's analysis may be misguided. Where Derrida worries that people are tempted to assert an impossible certainty, others argue that the problem of precarity is more urgent today. Eve Kosofsky Sedgwick and Rita Felski claim that critique is a theoretical technique with limited utility.[3] In their view, the tendency to valorize suspicion and exposure excludes affirmation and support. In a similar vein, Bruno Latour suggests that, in the face of poverty and war, critique is a perverse response, and one that is liable to demagogic abuse. He writes, "Is it really the task of the humanities to add deconstruction to destruction?"[4] As Latour's comment implies, this complaint echoes concerns that many readers have about Derrida's work. Whereas critique often styles itself as politically indispensable, these theorists suggest that we need a politics of relation, not negation.

I think Sedgwick, Felski, and Latour are right to claim that negativity is not enough. However, Derrida suggests that critique becomes hegemonic only if it is insufficiently critical. Crucially, his negativity is reflexive: by acknowledging that negation is inadequate, Derrida opens the possibility of florid affirmation. Thus, to take an important example, Derrida argues that justice is elusive and incalculable, but at the same time he acknowledges that it remains necessary (by calculating as best we can) to identify some things as unjust. On his account, deconstruction functions as a reminder that every claim with respect to justice remains subject to revision, but that does not entail that all claims must cease. On the

---

[3] Although Felski and Sedgwick do not discuss Derrida at length, there are indications that he is one of the critics they have in mind (cf. Rita Felski, *The Limits of Critique* [Chicago: University of Chicago Press, 2015], 28, 31, 42; Eve Kosofsky Sedgwick, *Touching Feeling: Affect, Pedagogy, Performativity* [Durham, NC; London: Duke University Press, 2006], 93–94, 125).

[4] Bruno Latour, "Why Has Critique Run out of Steam? From Matters of Fact to Matters of Concern," *Critical Inquiry* 30, no. 2 (January 1, 2004): 225.

contrary, Derrida indicates that a rigorous negativity is the precondition for an affirmation that endures without assurance.

My argument focuses on four texts that I see as key to Derrida's corpus: "Structure, Sign, and Play" (1966), "Différance" (1968), "Force of Law" (1990), and *Rogues* (2003). Where some readers assume that Derrida turned toward ethics in his later work, I argue that his earliest writings are motivated by an ethics of uncertainty that becomes increasingly explicit throughout his career. In my reading, Derrida holds negativity and affirmation in tension to encourage a persistence that acknowledges its vulnerability. Rather than foreclosing concrete judgements, Derrida opens a space for unpredictable improvement by insisting that every judgment is uncertain. Because Derrida's negativity encourages a form of commitment that refuses complacency, he exemplifies the discipline of hope, which presses forward despite its uncertainty.

An Ethics of Uncertainty

Although it is not immediately apparent, Derrida's early work responds to an ethical problem. At the outset of his career, in "Structure, Sign, and Play (1966)," Derrida portrays the history of philosophy as a series of attempts to found a conceptual system upon a stable point of reference. In his view, this search for stability is consistently thwarted, for every element in a system is constituted by its relation to other elements. Because these relations are complex and unstable, every structure involves some degree of play. Although the philosophers Derrida has in mind were aware of this dynamic, Derrida claims that they sought to contain it. Derrida calls the fundamental ground that philosophers sought the transcendental signified, a pure point of presence that holds the structure as a whole together. Many concepts have served this function: "*eidos, archē, telos, energeia, ousia* (essence, existence, substance, subject) *aletheia*, transcendentality, consciousness, God, man, and so forth."[5] In this way, according to Derrida, philosophy asserts a security that transcends the play of meaning.

Derrida argues that this attempt at security ends in contradiction. He writes, "The center is at the center of the totality, and yet, since the center does not belong to the totality (is not part of the totality), the totality has its center elsewhere. The center is not the center."[6] Because the pure

---

[5] Jacques Derrida, "Structure, Sign, and Play in the Discourse of the Human Sciences," in *Writing and Difference*, trans. Alan Bass (Chicago: University of Chicago Press, 1978), 279–80.
[6] Ibid., 279.

presence of the transcendental signified must be insulated from the play of meaning that characterizes structure, it lies outside the structure. At the same time, however, to organize the structure it must lie within the structure as its center. With the rise of structuralism in the twentieth century, Derrida writes, "it was necessary to begin thinking that there was no center, that the center could not be thought in the form of a present-being, that the center had no natural site, that it was not a fixed locus but a function."[7] This conclusion was linked to the claim that language is itself a system of differential relationships whereby the meaning of each unit is determined by its relation to others. If nothing is exempt from this system of differences, there cannot be a pure point of meaning that would secure the coherence of the whole.

Derrida writes that "the absence of the transcendental signified extends the domain and the play of signification infinitely."[8] On his account, without a stable foundation, the movement of meaning cannot be controlled in advance. Some have taken this to mean that Derrida favors play to the exclusion of order.[9] Richard Rorty enthusiastically endorses an idea of total play that he identifies with Derrida, while Jürgen Habermas argues that Derrida's play is politically irresponsible.[10] In response to such readings, Derrida writes, "I never proposed 'a kind of "all or nothing" choice between pure realization of self-presence and complete freeplay or undecidability.' I never believed in this and I never spoke of 'complete freeplay or undecidability.' ... There can be no 'completeness' where freeplay is concerned."[11] On Derrida's terms, the idea of total play is

---

[7] Ibid., 280.   [8] Ibid.
[9] John R. Searle, "The Word Turned Upside Down," *The New York Review of Books*, October 27, 1983, 79. Searle is not the only one to hold this view; cf. Peter Barry, *Beginning Theory: An Introduction to Literary and Cultural Theory* (Manchester: Manchester University Press, 1995), 66–68; James Hans, *The Play of the World* (Amherst: University of Massachusetts Press, 1981), 10.
[10] Richard Rorty, *Consequences of Pragmatism: Essays, 1972–1980* (Minneapolis: University of Minnesota Press, 1982), 96; Jürgen Habermas, *The Philosophical Discourse of Modernity: Twelve Lectures* (Cambridge, MA: MIT Press, 1987), 210. Cf. T. K. Seung, *Structuralism and Hermeneutics* (New York: Columbia University Press, 1984), xii.
[11] Jacques Derrida, *Limited Inc* (Evanston, IL: Northwestern University Press, 1988), 115. He immediately adds, "Greatly overestimated in my texts in the United States, this notion of 'freeplay' is an inadequate translation of the lexical network connected to the word *jeu*, which I used in my first texts, but sparingly and in a highly defined manner. Above all, no completeness is possible for undecidability" (115–16). Nicholas Royle claims that "[Geoffrey] Hartman's *Saving the Text* can certainly be seen as culpable" in what Royle calls "the widespread misconception of Derrida's work as practising and promoting 'free play'" (Nicholas Royle, *After Derrida* [Manchester: Manchester University Press, 1995], 49). There, Hartman comments exuberantly on an essay of Derrida's: "Freeplay reaches here a methodical craziness" (Geoffrey Hartman, *Saving the Text: Literature, Derrida, Philosophy* [Baltimore: Johns Hopkins University Press, 1981], 22).

nonsensical, for play is always the interplay of the elements within a structure.[12] This intertwining tension is central to the ethical significance of Derrida's project.

Although this essay is framed in terms of the coherence of conceptual systems, what is at stake is the human desire for safety. Derrida writes, "The concept of centered structure is in fact the concept of a play based on a fundamental ground, a play constituted on the basis of a fundamental immobility and a reassuring certitude, which itself is beyond the reach of play. On the basis of this certitude anxiety can be mastered, for anxiety is invariably the result of a certain mode of being implicated in the game."[13] In Derrida's analysis, the claim that some structures are stabilized expresses a latent desire. Philosophers tend to present their arguments in abstract terms, but Derrida reads their appeal to a fundamental ground as an attempt to reassure themselves. As he observes, it is unsettling to find oneself caught in a game that one did not choose and that one does not control. In response, although it is understandable to seek a stable point of reference, Derrida argues that such security is illusory.

By denying false assurance, Derrida does not leave people in despair. Instead, he describes the possibility of an affirmation that acknowledges its uncertainty. The recognition that structures are decentered is sometimes melancholic, colored by loss, but it is also possible to affirm play (rather than seeing it as a threat). He explains, "This affirmation then determines the noncenter otherwise than as loss of the center. And it plays without security. For there is a sure play: that which is limited to the substitution of given and existing, present, pieces."[14] Whereas some forms of play attempt to preserve their security by limiting disruption, the affirmation Derrida has in mind persists without any promise of safety. This is not the total play that Rorty imagines, nor is it the indiscriminate politics that Habermas fears. Insofar as we cannot manage without determinate structures, rational deliberation on particular cases is indispensable. However, in response to the anxiety that colors human life, Derrida imagines an affirmation that acknowledges the need to remain always in motion.

---

[12] I think Kevin Hart is correct: "Deconstruction is accordingly a critique of 'ground' as such, though not an affirmation of groundlessness" (Kevin Hart, *The Trespass of the Sign: Deconstruction, Theology, and Philosophy*, 1st paperback ed. [New York: Cambridge University Press, 1991], 74).
[13] Derrida, "Structure, Sign, and Play," 279.
[14] Ibid., 292. A few lines earlier Derrida contrasts this ethic with another: "If Levi-Strauss, better than any other, has brought to light the play of repetition and the repetition of play, one no less perceives in his work a sort of ethic of presence, an ethic of nostalgia for origins, an ethic of archaic and natural innocence, of a purity of presence and self-presence in speech."

Derrida's interpretive method displays this principled commitment to play. In a line that crystalizes his program and approach, Derrida writes that "the passage beyond philosophy does not consist in turning the page of philosophy (which usually amounts to philosophizing badly), but in continuing to read philosophers *in a certain way*."[15] Whereas it might be tempting to surpass the errors of earlier philosophers in a single leap, Derrida argues that this gesture allows problematic concepts to persist undetected, and in any case such a desire is predicated upon a nostalgia for purity that Derrida does not share.[16] Rather than assuming that one must either endorse the past or oppose it, Derrida seeks to forge a passage beyond that is also a passage through, amplifying the latent tendencies of classic texts so as to highlight the ways in which they surpass themselves.[17] In this way, Derrida's negativity is implicitly affirmative, working from within to open unexamined possibilities.

Destabilizing Subjectivity

In "Différance," two years after "Structure, Sign, and Play," Derrida elaborates on the significance of this disruption for human subjectivity. Once again, he initially frames the point in relation to language, describing the contrast between the structuralist understanding of differential signification and earlier attempts to constrain play. He writes, "The sign is usually said to be put in the place of the thing itself, the present thing ... The sign represents the present in its absence."[18] The ideal, from this perspective, is to be in an immediate relation with the thing, to be able to grasp or show it directly; failing that, the sign represents the presence of the thing it signifies in its absence. Derrida continues, "The sign, which defers presence, is conceivable only on the basis of the presence that it defers and moving toward the deferred presence that it aims to reappropriate."[19] The representational function of the sign points to a presence that is not properly its own, but for this reason the presence it promises is deferred.

---

[15] Ibid., 288.   [16] Ibid., 284.
[17] In *Of Grammatology*, Derrida writes, "The movements of deconstruction do not destroy structures from the outside. They are not possible and effective, nor can they take accurate aim, except by inhabiting those structures. Inhabiting them *in a certain way,* because one always inhabits, and all the more when one does not suspect it" (*Of Grammatology*, 1st U.S. ed. [Baltimore: Johns Hopkins University Press, 1976], 24).
[18] Jacques Derrida, "Différance," in *Margins of Philosophy*, trans. Alan Bass (Chicago: University of Chicago Press, 1982), 9.
[19] Ibid.

Like the classical account of structure, this interpretation of the sign grounds signification in a foundational presence.

Derrida contrasts this view with that of Ferdinand de Saussure, who argues that every sign takes its meaning from its relation to other signs. Derrida comments, "The first consequence to be drawn from this is that the signified concept is never present in and of itself, in a sufficient presence that would refer only to itself. Essentially and lawfully, every concept is inscribed in a chain or in a system within which it refers to the other, to other concepts, by means of the systematic play of differences."[20] Whereas the classical account implies that signs refer directly to a given concept (which would be exempt from signification), Saussure suggests that the concept signified by a given signifier is never fully present; on the contrary, it too is woven into the web of relationships that constitutes signification. Derrida names this play *différance* (with an "a") to differentiate it from *différence* (with an "e"), which denotes the difference of one thing from another. *Différance* joins the twin senses of the French verb *différer*, "to differ" and "to defer." The classical understanding of the sign relies on the second sense of *différer* insofar as it takes the signifier as the deferred presence of the signified, whose absence is a temporary delay. However, Derrida suggests that this underestimates the importance of the first sense of *différer*, whereby everything (including the signified) takes its meaning from its relation to others.

Derrida claims that *différance* is originary – which is to say that there is no point of presence exempt from play. Insofar as *différence* is primordial, spatial presence always refers elsewhere, and temporal presence is always compromised by the past and the future. This entails that presence is never self-sufficient; instead, Derrida says, presence is inescapably constituted by that which it is not. He continues, "It is because of *différance* that the movement of signification is possible only if each so-called 'present' element ... is related to something other than itself, thereby keeping within itself the mark of the past element, and already letting itself be vitiated by the mark of its relation to the future element."[21] Derrida claims that every signifier refers to others, ahead and behind, and each of those refers elsewhere in turn. In this way, according to Derrida, everything is related to that which is different.

Although it could seem that Derrida valorizes absence over and against presence, Derrida explains that his treatment of the sign "puts into question the authority of presence, or of its simple symmetrical opposite,

[20] Ibid., 11. [21] Ibid., 13.

absence or lack."²² The two poles relate reciprocally, for both presence and absence take their meaning in relation to the other, and so neither is primary. Derrida explains that *différance* consists neither in pure presence nor in pure absence; he writes, "It differs from, and defers itself; which doubtless means that it is woven of differences, and also that it sends out delegates, representatives, proxies; but without any chance that the giver of proxies might 'exist,' might be present, be 'itself' somewhere."²³ In Derrida's account, *différance* differs and defers, neither present nor absent, playing within determinate structures without promising that it will at some point be fully present. In this way, *différance* exemplifies an otherness that verges upon consciousness while remaining elusive.

Like "Structure, Sign, and Play," "Différance" (1968) addresses the operation of symbolic systems, but its argument carries ethical implications. Derrida's deconstruction of presence responds to Edmund Husserl, who argues that consciousness in the present is always inflected by the past and the future, that which is retained in memory and that which is anticipated.²⁴ This resembles Derrida's claim that every presence is related to that which is different, but there is a crucial distinction: where Husserl takes consciousness as a pure and undifferentiated presence, Derrida does not.²⁵ Derrida comments, "The privilege granted to consciousness therefore signifies the privilege granted to the present; and even if one describes the transcendental temporality of consciousness, and at the depth at which Husserl does so, one grants to the 'living present' the power of synthesizing traces, and of incessantly reassembling them."²⁶ In Derrida's reading, Husserl acknowledges that consciousness is related to that which is different, but he subordinates the otherness of the past and the future to the self-contained presence of consciousness.

Derrida imagines a Husserlian objection to his account of *différance*: "Can one not conceive of a presence, and of a presence to itself of the subject before speech or signs, a presence to itself of the subject in a silent and intuitive consciousness?"²⁷ It might seem that the subject enters the play of difference only when they attempt communication. Even if one

---

[22] Ibid., 10.   [23] Ibid., 20–21.   [24] Ibid., 13.
[25] Dan Zahavi suggests that Derrida's critique of Husserl is unfair (see Dan Zahavi, *Self-Awareness and Alterity: A Phenomenological Investigation* [Evanston, IL: Northwestern University Press, 1999], 82ff). Zahavi may be right, but Husserl does construe all transcendence as internal to transcendental subjectivity (*Cartesian Meditations: An Introduction to Phenomenology* [The Hague: M. Nijhoff, 1960], 83–84), and he construes memory and expectation as the presentification of past and future (*Analyses Concerning Passive and Active Synthesis: Lectures on Transcendental Logic* [Dordrecht; Boston: Kluwer Academic Publishers, 2001], 110).
[26] "Différance," 16.   [27] Ibid.

grants that signs are constituted in relation to each other, one could think that the subject is transparent to itself, prior to speech. However, in Derrida's view, we never have access to pure presence, even in relation to our own self. He writes, "A certain alterity – to which Freud gives the metaphysical name of the unconscious – is definitively exempt from every process of presentation."[28] On this view, the unconscious is not even potentially present, for it is not a presence that is simply hidden, waiting to be uncovered. Where Husserl claims that consciousness stabilizes the individual subject, Derrida argues that everyone is related to an alterity that they do not control or comprehend. As Derrida's late work makes clear, this negativity in relation to knowledge opens ethical possibilities.

Time and Justice

Time is central to Derrida's deconstruction of conscious subjectivity. In "Différance" he writes, "The alterity of the 'unconscious' makes us concerned not with horizons of modified – past or future – presents, but with a 'past' that has never been present, and which never will be, whose future to come will never be a production or a reproduction in the form of presence."[29] Whereas some theories of time portray the past as that which was present and the future as that which is produced by the present, Derrida describes a temporality that is (like the unconscious) heterogeneous to presence. Because presence is the modality of consciousness and therefore of conception, Derrida concludes that the future and the past cannot be conceived. He explains, "*Différance* maintains our relationship with that which we necessarily misconstrue, and which exceeds the alternative of presence and absence."[30] On Derrida's understanding, we cannot grasp the temporality he describes, and so any attempt to speak of it is bound to fail. For him, the past and the future serve as figures for that which is radically other.

In "Force of Law (1990)," twenty years after "Différance," Derrida elaborates on the political significance of this understanding of time. Like Emmanuel Levinas, Derrida identifies justice with the relation to the other.[31] This is, Derrida writes, "an 'idea of justice' that is infinite, infinite because irreducible, irreducible because owed to the other – owed to the

---

[28] Ibid., 20. [29] Ibid., 21. [30] Ibid., 20.
[31] Jacques Derrida, "Force of Law: The 'Mystical Foundation of Authority,'" in *Acts of Religion*, ed. Gil Anidjar (New York: Routledge, 2002), 250. Levinas was a key influence on Derrida's treatment of time in "Différance" (cf. "Différance," 21; Emmanuel Levinas, *Time and the Other and Additional Essays* [Pittsburgh, PA: Duquesne University Press, 1987], 90).

other, before any contract, because it has come, the coming of the other as always other singularity."³² In Derrida's account, whereas law involves calculation concerning which framework would be best, justice is incalculable because it is directed to an alterity that makes an infinite demand. For Derrida, justice is not simply a matter of observing certain precepts; instead, he writes, "justice, as the experience of absolute alterity, is unpresentable."³³ Although it is possible to adjudicate whether a particular rule has been followed, Derrida claims that justice cannot be identified, for justice is in his understanding futural.

Just as Derrida's early work associates time and alterity, here Derrida claims that justice is not present but to come. He writes,

> It has perhaps an *avenir*, precisely, a 'to-come' [*à-venir*] that one will have to rigorously distinguish from the future [*futur*]. The future loses the openness, the coming of the other (who comes), without which there is no justice; and the future can always reproduce the present, announce itself or present itself as a future present in the modified form of the present. Justice remains to come, it remains by coming, it has to come, it is to-come, the to-come.³⁴

Here Derrida stipulates a distinction between the French terms *futur* and *avenir* that is crucial for his later work. Although both words refer to the future, Derrida associates *futur* with a futurity that extends the present (in continuous, linear time) and *avenir* with the interruptive futurity he describes in "Différance," which is radically heterogeneous to presence. Derrida plays upon the relation between the word *avenir* (for "future") and *à-venir*, which means "to come." For him, this coming names the irruptive futurity of justice as encounter with the other. In contrast to something the self-present subject can possess, a justice of this kind is constitutively to come.

Derrida's argument draws on his earlier claim that the future is radically heterogeneous to presence and therefore to consciousness. On this understanding of time, the futurity of justice entails that it is radically elusive. To identify a particular decision as just would require calculation (concerning what justice is and how the decision in question measures up), but in Derrida's view justice is incalculable. He writes, "There is an avenir for justice and there is no justice except to the degree that some event is possible which, as event, exceeds calculation, rules, programs, anticipations and so forth."³⁵ As a relation to alterity, justice belongs to the elusive

---

³² Derrida, "Force of Law," 254.   ³³ Ibid., 257.   ³⁴ Ibid., 256.   ³⁵ Ibid., 257.

temporality of *différance* and the disruptive movement of structural play. For this reason, Derrida argues that justice requires critical vigilance. He writes, "At no time can one say presently that a decision is just, purely just ... or that someone is just, and even less, 'I am just.'"[36] In his account, it is only by negating particular claims to knowledge that one holds open the possibility for a justice that attends to the other.

At the same time, in keeping with the pattern of his earlier work, Derrida acknowledges that the realm of calculative judgment is indispensable. He writes, "Not only must one calculate ... and negotiate without a rule that would not have to be reinvented there where we are 'thrown,' there where we find ourselves; but one must do so and take it as far as possible, beyond the place we find ourselves and beyond the already identifiable zones of morality, politics, or law."[37] Derrida insists that we must respond as best we can in the situations in which we find ourselves, which requires both calculation according to rules and attention to a particularity that cannot be captured in a rule. However, he continues, this dual requirement points beyond the situations in which we currently find ourselves, toward transformed circumstances that we have not yet imagined. He writes, "The order of this [it is necessary] does not properly belong either to justice or to law. It only belongs to either realm by exceeding each one in the direction of the other – which means that, in their very heterogeneity, these two orders are undissociable."[38] Although Derrida draws a sharp distinction between law and justice, calculation and the incalculable, he claims that both are indispensable.

Derrida argues that play is radically heterogeneous to structure, *différance* to identity, future to presence, and justice to law. However, in each case he insists that the two are inseparable. In his view, play only works within determinate structures, and justice remains inseparable from law. Derrida writes, "Everything would still be simple if this distinction between justice and law were a true distinction ... But it turns out that law claims to exercise itself in the name of justice and that justice demands for itself that it be established in the name of a law that must be put to work (constituted and applied) by force 'enforced.' Deconstruction always finds itself and moves itself between these two poles."[39] Although Derrida intends to maintain a strict distinction between justice and law, he notes that the division between them is blurred by the fact that laws are applied

---

[36] Ibid., 252. [37] Ibid., 257. [38] Ibid. [39] Derrida, "Force of Law," 250–51.

in pursuit of justice and that justice is pursued within particular legal systems.⁴⁰ Rather than favoring justice over and against the law, Derrida acknowledges both demands. In practice, this means that we may pursue justice as best we can while acknowledging that our efforts are provisional and uncertain.

Provisional Judgment

Because Derrida insists that justice is radically elusive, some commentators conclude that he is unable to affirm the concrete judgments on which politics depends. Mark Lilla writes, "Derrida's radical interpretations of structuralism and Heideggerianism had rendered the traditional vocabulary of politics unusable and nothing could be put in its place ... An intellectually consistent deconstruction would therefore seem to entail silence on political matters."⁴¹ Insofar as Derrida's critique risks dissolving the principles on the basis of someone could make a decision, it could seem that he precludes practical reflection on policy. Lilla continues, "Can one still distinguish rights from wrongs, justice from injustice? Or are these terms, too, so infected with logocentrism that they must be abandoned?"⁴² If, as Derrida says, we cannot know what justice is and is not, it is not obvious how one could object to particular instances of injustice.

This objection is troubling, but Derrida's discussion of judgment indicates that Lilla's reading is misguided. In "Force of Law" Derrida writes, "Each case is other, each decision is different and requires an absolutely unique interpretation, which no existing, coded rule can or ought to guarantee absolutely."⁴³ Although it might seem that laws and regulations apply mechanically to particular cases, Derrida argues that a legal decision

---

⁴⁰ Elsewhere, he writes, "The heterogeneity between justice and law does not exclude but, on the contrary, calls for their inseparability: there can be no justice without an appeal to juridical determinations and to the force of law; and there can be no becoming, no transformation, history, or perfectibility of law without an appeal to a justice that will nonetheless always exceed it" (Jacques Derrida, *Rogues: Two Essays on Reason*, Meridian [Stanford, CA: Stanford University Press, 2005], 150).

⁴¹ Mark Lilla, *The Reckless Mind: Intellectuals in Politics* (New York: New York Review of Books, 2001), 175. Lilla develops his critique of Derrida separately from his critique of religion, but I believe they are closely related (see ibid., 190).

⁴² Lilla, *The Reckless Mind*, 179.

⁴³ Derrida, "Force of Law," 251. This is the significance of Derrida's widely misunderstood statement that "there is nothing outside of the text [*il n'y a pas de hors-texte*]" (*Of Grammatology*, 158). The line has been taken to assert (absurdly) that language is all there is, but Derrida's point is that there is no way to circumvent the work of interpretation. Derrida comments: "What I call 'text' implies all the structures called 'real,' 'economic,' 'historical,' socio-institutional, in short: all possible referents. Another way of recalling once again that 'there is nothing outside the text.' That does

requires interpretation – of the rule in question, of the particulars of the case, and of the application of the one to the other. Insofar as judgment is required, the outcome is not determined by the text of the rule alone.[44] Derrida explains, "This new freshness, the initiality of this inaugural judgment can very well – better yet, must very well – conform to a preexisting law, but the reinstituting, reinventive and freely deciding interpretation of the responsible judge requires that his 'justice' not consist only in conformity, in the conservative and reproductive activity of judgment."[45] In Derrida's view, judgment should not be untethered from the law; on the contrary, it must conform to the law through responsible interpretation. However, because conformity itself is never enough to produce a judgment, every decision is doubtful.

As Derrida's earlier work suggests, the uncertainty of judgment does not render it impossible. He writes, "I believe that there is no justice without this experience, however impossible it may be, of aporia."[46] "Aporia" can refer to an irresolvable contradiction, but Derrida uses it in a broader sense. As he notes, in Greek the word signifies the state of being without a path, *a-poros*; more broadly, it refers to a situation with no way forward. Derrida continues, "Every time that something comes to pass or turns out well, every time that we placidly apply a good rule to a particular case, to a correctly subsumed example, according to a determinate judgment, law perhaps and sometimes finds itself accounted for, but one can be sure that justice does not."[47] As we have seen, Derrida argues that justice cannot consist in the application of a rule because it is incalculable and elusive. On the contrary, any decision that mechanically applied a given rule would be no decision at all, since in Derrida's view every decision exceeds the available criteria. Where Lilla worries that deconstructive doubt will make it impossible to judge political matters, Derrida argues that uncertainty is the condition under which judgment is possible.

Lilla asks, "If deconstruction throws doubt on every political principle of the Western philosophical tradition ... are judgments about political

---

not mean that all referents are suspended, denied, or enclosed in a book, as people have claimed, or have been naive enough to believe and to have accused me of believing. But it does mean that every referent, all reality has the structure of a differential trace, and that one cannot refer to this 'real' except in an interpretive experience. The latter neither yields meaning nor assumes it except in a movement of differential referring" (*Limited Inc*, 148).

[44] Paul Kahn makes a similar argument in *Political Theology: Four New Chapters on the Concept of Sovereignty* (New York: Columbia University Press, 2011). Both Kahn and Derrida are drawing upon Carl Schmitt, *Political Theology: Four Chapters on the Concept of Sovereignty* (Cambridge, MA: MIT Press, 1985).

[45] Derrida, "Force of Law," 251.   [46] Ibid., 244.   [47] Ibid.

matters still possible?"[48] This expresses a basic misunderstanding that besets many readers of Derrida: on Derrida's terms, if everything is subject to doubt, this means that every judgment is doubtful, not that judgment is precluded. According to Lilla, "there is an unresolvable paradox in using language to claim that language cannot make unambiguous claims."[49] But this is only a paradox if one assumes that all claims are unambiguous; if one acknowledges that some claims are not perfectly transparent, the contradiction disappears. Similarly, Lilla complains that "[Derrida] simply cannot find a way of specifying the nature of the justice to be sought through left-wing politics without opening himself to the very deconstruction he so gleefully applies to others."[50] Rather than constituting an objection to Derrida's approach, this describes its central aim. Derrida repeatedly insists that his own work remains subject to deconstruction and is therefore only provisional. In his account, self-critique is required to remain open to what is to come.

In keeping with his diagnosis in "Structure, Sign, and Play," Derrida believes there is a risk that the attempt to live well will congeal into self-satisfaction. In "Force of Law," he argues that the possibility of "a moment of suspense ... must remain structurally present to the exercise of all responsibility if such responsibility is never to abandon itself to dogmatic slumber, and therefore to deny itself."[51] Whereas it is tempting to assert an impossible certainty in an effort to assuage the anxiety of human life, Derrida's critique interrupts this dynamic to preserve an appropriate restlessness. He continues, "This anguishing moment of suspense also opens the interval of spacing in which transformations, even juridicopolitical revolutions, take place."[52] As with his account of differential play, this suspension aims to open rather than foreclose possibility. Insofar as it opens space (and time) for that which the subject does not foresee, Derrida's negativity encourages experimental affirmation.[53]

Negativity and Politics

Derrida's ethics of uncertainty is intrinsically political. In Derrida's view, the deconstruction of law is important because law is bound up with

---

[48] Lilla, *The Reckless Mind*, 179.   [49] Ibid., 173.   [50] Ibid., 183.
[51] Derrida, "Force of Law," 248–49.   [52] Ibid., 249.
[53] In my reading, Derrida's expansive understanding of critique is similar to the arguments offered in Tyler Roberts, *Encountering Religion: Responsibility and Criticism after Secularism* (Columbia University Press, 2013); and Constance M. Furey, "Discernment as Critique in Teresa of Avila and Erasmus of Rotterdam," *Exemplaria* 26, no. 2–3 (June 1, 2014): 254–72.

Hope in a Secular Age

violence in more than one way. On the one hand, Derrida points out that for the law to function as law it requires enforcement, which risks authorizing arbitrary violence.[54] On the other hand, he observes that every system of law comes into being through a forceful act of institution. Although it would be comforting if the law could justify itself, at the moment at which a given legal system comes into being, it cannot be judged as legal or illegal according to the system itself.[55] Much as he argues in "Structure, Sign, and Play" that structure cannot ground itself, in "Force of Law" he argues that every system of law depends on something outside itself – that is, an extralegal force. This does not invalidate law; on the contrary, Derrida suggests throughout his career that there is no way to avoid being implicated in violence.[56] The point, instead, is that a law that could not be questioned would risk enshrining hegemonic violence.

Where some assume that a commitment to justice requires unquestioning conviction, Derrida argues that the opposite is true. He writes, "The fact that law is deconstructible is not bad news. One may even find in this the political chance of all historical progress."[57] In his view, although every legal and political program is questionable, this holds open the possibility of a justice that exceeds the status quo. At the same time, Derrida recognizes that a justice that fails to engage specific injustices would be obscene. He writes, "Justice, however unpresentable it remains, does not wait. It is that which must not wait ... A just decision is always required immediately, right away, as quickly as possible."[58] Derrida insists that justice is to come, but he acknowledges that it is also urgent here and now. In the face of this urgency, one must decide what to do, and one should decide as justly as possible. Derrida's negativity underscores that one can never be sure that one has decided well, and so one should always be open to revising one's decision.

In *Rogues* (2003), thirty-four years after "Différance," he explicitly connects his early work to his later political writings. Derrida writes, "The thinking of the political has always been a thinking of *différance* and the thinking of *différance* always a thinking *of* the political, of the contour and limits of the political, especially around the enigma or the autoimmune double bind of the democratic."[59] On the face of it, this claim is startling, for many readers assumed that politics was distant from

---

[54] Derrida, "Force of Law," 234. [55] Ibid., 241.
[56] Cf. Jacques Derrida, "Violence and Metaphysics: An Essay on the Thought of Emmanuel Levinas," in *Writing and Difference*, trans. Alan Bass (Chicago: University of Chicago Press, 1978), 146–48.
[57] Ibid., 242. [58] Ibid., 255. [59] Derrida, *Rogues*, 39.

the abstraction of Derrida's early essays.[60] However, Derrida was clear from the outset that every structure is disrupted by irrepressible play, whether the structure in question is conceptual or political. Indeed, in "Différance" Derrida writes, "Not only is there no kingdom of *différance*, but *différance* instigates the subversion of every kingdom. Which makes it obviously threatening and infallibly dreaded by everything within us that desires a kingdom, the past or future presence of a kingdom."[61] Insofar as every authority asserts a presence that serves as its locus, the differential disruption of identity indicates that every regime is vulnerable to subversion.

In *Rogues* Derrida explains that democracy concerns *différance* because it is resolutely elusive. He writes, "Democracy is what it is only in the *différance* by which it defers itself and differs from itself."[62] Much as he argued in "Force of Law" that justice is constitutively to come, Derrida claims that democracy is directed toward the future. Against those who claim that democracy is already achieved, Derrida argues that democracy is unrealized both in principle and in fact. According to Derrida, it would violate the futurity of democracy to say that it is instantiated in a given political system, but it is no better to say that, even though democracy does not exist, we can conceive democracy as an ideal.[63] In his view, the futurity of democracy requires the critique both of every existing political regime and of our understanding of democracy itself. Derrida writes, "The expression 'democracy to come' does indeed translate or call for a militant and interminable political critique ... It protests against all naïveté and every political abuse, every rhetoric that would present as a present or existing democracy, as a de facto democracy, what remains inadequate to the democratic demand."[64] In his view, democracy requires continual critique to prevent it from being used to authorize a given political system.

In my reading, Derrida's negativity represents an ethical discipline with political implications.[65] Derrida worries that the aura of democracy will be appropriated by political systems that remain, in many respects,

---

[60] For helpful commentary on this dynamic, see Herman Rapaport, *The Theory Mess: Deconstruction in Eclipse* (New York: Columbia University Press, 2001), 132.
[61] Derrida, "Différance," 22.   [62] Derrida, *Rogues*, 38.
[63] Jacques Derrida, *Specters of Marx: The State of the Debt, the Work of Mourning, and the New International* (New York: Routledge, 1994), 81.
[64] Derrida, *Rogues*, 86.
[65] In relation to the cognate concept *khōra*, Derrida writes, "No politics, no ethics, and no law can be, as it were, deduced from this thought. To be sure, nothing can be done with it. And so one would have nothing to do with it. But should we then conclude that this thought leaves no trace on what is to be done – for example in the politics, the ethics, or the law to come?" (ibid., xv).

undemocratic. As he explains, some societies assert that they embody the realization of democratic ideals, but this obscures the ways in which they fall short of democratic representation (in their treatment of poverty, incarceration, immigration, and so forth). This is not the only point that needs to be made for a healthy politics, but there is good reason to think that it is important. In 2015, writing on recent events in *The New Yorker*, George Packer notes that "what seemed like clear morality two decades ago has gone completely dark. Intervention in Libya created a failed state, a base for jihadists, and more killing. Non-intervention in Syria allowed for a failed state, a base for jihadists, and massive killing. No one should be sleeping well."[66] In a different context but to similar effect, Derrida insists that the task of political reflection is never finished, for there is always more to be done. Although Derrida's negativity does not, in itself, determine what actions an individual should take, it is political insofar as it keeps policy debate in motion, struggling toward greater justice.

Critique and Transformation

Whether one finds Derrida's negativity compelling depends on whether one agrees that naïveté and complacency are a genuine danger. In recent years, a number of theorists have argued that other issues are more pressing, and other techniques are needed. Eve Kosofsky Sedgwick notes that critical readers are surprisingly credulous when it comes to the value of exposure. As she observes, whether it is helpful to unveil hidden violence depends on the context and should not be held as a universal rule.[67] Bruno Latour argues that negativity run amok makes it difficult to counter the misinformation that deforms modern politics.[68] In his view, "in these most depressing of times," we require intellectual methods whose aim "will no longer be to debunk but to protect and to care."[69] Although critique often styles itself as politically progressive, Rita Felski argues that it has no intrinsic political effects; on her account, its effects can be progressive or regressive, depending on how it is deployed.[70] She writes, "What is needed, in short, is a politics of relation rather than negation, of mediation rather than cooption, of alliance and assembly rather than alienated critique."[71] On this view, critique is not what the world needs, at least for some people, perhaps especially now.

---

[66] George Packer, "Dark Hours: Violence in the Age of Terror," *The New Yorker*, July 20, 2015, 75.
[67] Sedgwick, *Touching Feeling*.   [68] Latour, "Why Has Critique Run out of Steam?"
[69] Ibid., 226, 232.   [70] Felski, *The Limits of Critique*.   [71] Ibid., 147.

Felski identifies the following elements as key to critique: "A spirit of skeptical questioning or outright condemnation, an emphasis on its precarious position vis- à-vis overbearing and oppressive social forces, the claim to be engaged in some kind of radical intellectual and/or political work, and the assumption that whatever is not critical must therefore be uncritical."[72] This description could be applied to Derrida's work, particularly as it has been received by others. Derrida focuses on concepts such as play and *différance* that are marginal in relation to dominant structures; this suggests that he sees his own work as disrupting the status quo. Indeed, Derrida aligns deconstruction with a radical justice that is distinct from any existing system of law. He exhibits the skeptic's sensitivity to self-contradiction, sometimes to an exhausting degree. Derrida is not the only target that these theorists have in mind, but he is among them.[73]

According to Felski, "Critique is as much a matter of affect and rhetoric as of philosophy or politics."[74] In her view, although critique presents itself as dispassionate method, it depends on value judgments that are driven by a particular mood. For this reason, she writes, "It colors the texts we read, endows them with certain qualities, places them in a given light."[75] Felski worries that this distortive effect tends toward self-confirmation, excluding other ways of seeing on the grounds that they are uncritical. She writes, "Casting the work of the scholar as a never-ending labor of distancing, deflating, and diagnosing, critique rules out the possibility of a different relationship to one's object."[76] Along similar lines, Sedgwick suggests that critique (which she calls "paranoid") anticipates the negative in an attempt to neutralize the threat of pain and surprise.[77] She claims that critique overrides other affects – joy, nostalgia, and so forth – so as to foreclose anticipated danger.[78]

I think Latour, Sedgwick, and Felski are right to claim that negativity can (like everything else) become hegemonic. However, Derrida suggests that this is a sign of too little critique rather than too much. Whereas a critique that is only directed at others reinforces the critic's authority, deconstructive self-critique underscores its limitations. He writes, "This questioning of foundations ... even questions, or exceeds the very possibility, the ultimate necessity, of questioning itself, of the questioning form of thought, interrogating without confidence or prejudice the very history

---

[72] Ibid., 2.   [73] Cf. Ibid., 131.   [74] Ibid., 3.   [75] Ibid., 21.   [76] Ibid., 150.
[77] Sedgwick, *Touching Feeling*, 137–38.   [78] Ibid., 146.

of the question and of its philosophical authority."[79] When viewed from the timeless perspective of a system of propositions, a questioning that questions itself could seem contradictory, but this neglects the fact that people exist in time. Once self-critique is situated within the context of an unfolding life, its function is not to disbelieve what one believes – which would be impossible – but to hold one's beliefs loosely, available for future development.

Derrida's discussion of *différance* exemplifies his reflexive negativity. Because presence is implied by the concept of the sign, Derrida explains that *différance* is not a sign, not a concept, not even a word – "that is, what is generally represented as the calm, present, and self-referential unity of concept and phonic material."[80] Where each of these terms posits a basic unity, Derrida claims that *différance* cannot be contained in this way. He explains, "If *différance* is (and I also cross out the is) what makes possible the presentation of the being-present, it is never presented as such."[81] Because *différance* cannot be represented, Derrida denies that even the apparently innocuous "is" would apply to it. But he also crosses out this crossing out to emphasize that *différance* is not presented even negatively. This entails that *différance* eludes Derrida's work as well. After all, he admits, "*différance* remains a metaphysical name."[82]

Rather than turning the key terms of his thought into shibboleths that set him apart from others, Derrida insists that they too are provisional. In this respect, he places himself in the same position as the theorists he critiques, a gesture that is rather different from what Felski imagines. She writes: "As a style of academic reading, however, the hermeneutics of suspicion knows its vigilance to be justified. Something, somewhere – a text, an author, a reader, a genre, a discourse, a discipline – is always already guilty of some crime."[83] Derrida has no interest in accusations of this kind: rather than condemning his interlocutors, he attends to the

---

[79] Derrida, "Force of Law," 236. Derrida acknowledges that critique itself can become dogmatic: "I believe in the political necessity of taking Marxist argumentation or critique into account, to listen to it, and to never close off access to it, provided that this Marxist critique itself remain alive, open, that it not become sclerotically dogmatic" (Jacques Derrida, "Politics and Friendship," in *Negotiations: Interventions and Interviews, 1971–2001*, Cultural Memory in the Present, ed. Elizabeth Rottenberg [Stanford, CA: Stanford University Press, 2002], 188).
[80] Derrida, "Différance," 11.   [81] Ibid., 6.   [82] Ibid., 26.
[83] Felski, *The Limits of Critique*, 39.

tensions within a given text to open new horizons for thought.[84] Thus, in relation to Lévi-Strauss, Saussure, and others, although he identifies metaphysical tendencies in their work, he admits his own work is metaphysical as well.

Derrida's method resembles what Sedgwick terms "reparative" reading. Whereas paranoid critique aims to avoid pain and uncertainty through negativity, reparative reading is guided by pleasure and improvement.[85] Sedgwick writes, "To read from a reparative position is to surrender the knowing, anxious paranoid determination that no horror, however apparently unthinkable, shall ever come to the reader as new; to a reparatively positioned reader, it can seem realistic and necessary to experience surprise."[86] Derrida's project is explicitly oriented toward a futurity that cannot be assimilated in advance; in his view, such surprise opens the possibility of horrific evil but also of unpredictable development. Sedgwick suggests that reparative practices teach "the many ways selves and communities succeed in extracting sustenance from the objects of a culture – even of a culture whose avowed desire has often been not to sustain them."[87] By attending to the latent meaning of the texts he interprets, Derrida opens them for a constructive use of this kind.

Felski is perplexed by those who respond to the deficiencies of critique by recommending more critique.[88] In Derrida's case, at least, the call for more critique does not seek more of the same. On the contrary, Derrida's reflexive negativity aims to open the subject to that which is different, to pursue a justice that remains unforeseeable. As Saba Mahmood observes, the willingness to learn something from another person requires self-critical recognition of one's own limits.[89] As she describes it, the experience of being reshaped through encounter with the other is not only

---

[84] In keeping with this method, Derrida's critique is deeply traditional. He writes, "Deconstruction [in the sense of a philosophical activity] presupposes the most intensely cultivated, literate relation to the tradition. Thus, it is a matter of keeping the field of tradition open ... One must pursue the critical project of philosophy as far as possible; and one must also understand that there is no deconstruction without this critique, even if deconstruction is not simply critique" (Jacques Derrida, "Negotiations," in *Negotiations: Interventions and Interviews, 1971–2001*, Cultural Memory in the Present, ed. Elizabeth Rottenberg [Stanford, CA: Stanford University Press, 2002], 15; cf. Joan Wallach Scott, "Against Eclecticism," *Differences* 16, no. 3 [December 1, 2005]: 133). (ibid., 133). Samir Haddad has explicated this aspect of Derrida's work in *Derrida and the Inheritance of Democracy* (Bloomington: Indiana University Press, 2013).
[85] Sedgwick, *Touching Feeling*, 144. [86] Ibid., 146. [87] Ibid., 150.
[88] Felski, *The Limits of Critique*, 150.
[89] Mahmood writes: "Critique, I believe, is most powerful when it leaves open the possibility that we might also be remade in the process of engaging another's worldview, that we might come to learn things that we did not already know before we undertook the engagement. This requires that we occasionally turn the critical gaze upon ourselves, to leave open the possibility that we may be

negative, for it opens new ways of being. In similar fashion, Derrida's ethics of uncertainty opens possibilities that are unconstrained by the subject's present understanding. Rather than foreclosing affirmation, Derrida's negativity nurtures an affirmation without assurance. It is for this reason, I think, that it displays the discipline of hope.

An Ascetic Hope

In *Specters of Marx* (1993) Derrida expands upon the affirmative significance of his negativity. He writes, "A deconstructive thinking, the one that matters to me here, has always pointed out the irreducibility of affirmation and therefore of the promise, as well as the undeconstructibility of a certain idea of justice (dissociated here from law). Such a thinking cannot operate without justifying the principle of a radical and interminable, infinite ... critique."[90] Although some suppose that deconstruction is simply destructive, Derrida argues that his project juxtaposes affirmation and critique. What confuses some readers is that these two moments are intertwined, such that to think "the irreducibility of affirmation" itself entails "infinite ... critique." This tension characterizes Derrida's early work, which attends to a futurity that is (as such) indeterminate while acknowledging that it eludes Derrida's own (determinate) discourse. Derrida's reference in this passage to "the promise" refers to this account of temporality; his point (put poetically) is that there is always a promise insofar as there is still a future to come.[91] This originary affirmation signals that critique cannot have the last word, but it also entails that critique is required.

As usual, in these passages Derrida is engaged in a practice of reading. He writes, "To continue to take inspiration from a certain spirit of Marxism would be to keep faith with what has always made of Marxism in principle and first of all a radical critique, namely a procedure ready to

---

remade through an encounter with the other" (Saba Mahmood, *Politics of Piety: The Islamic Revival and the Feminist Subject* [Princeton, NJ: Princeton University Press, 2005], 36–37).

[90] Derrida, *Specters of Marx*, 112.

[91] He explains, "Whether the promise promises this or that, whether it be fulfilled or not, or whether it be unfulfillable, there is necessarily some promise and therefore some historicity as future-to-come" (ibid., 92). Derrida explains elsewhere that every act of speech, regardless of its modality, implicitly affirms a promise to tell the truth (Jacques Derrida, "How to Avoid Speaking: Denials," in *Psyche: Inventions of the Other, Volume II*, ed. Peggy Kamuf and Elizabeth Rottenberg [Stanford, CA: Stanford University Press, 2008], 82–84; cf. Jacques Derrida, "A Number of Yes," in *Psyche: Inventions of the Other, Volume II*, ed. Peggy Kamuf and Elizabeth Rottenberg [Stanford, CA: Stanford University Press, 2008], 231–40).

undertake its self-critique. This critique wants itself to be in principle and explicitly open to its own transformation, re-evaluation, self-reinterpretation."[92] Derrida argues that Marx's self-critique is at odds with dogma of any kind. (Though in his view some Marxists betray this critical spirit by insisting upon an orthodox analysis of labor, class, and so forth.) At the same time, because it is oriented toward continual improvement, this critique entails a sort of affirmation. He writes, "If there is a spirit of Marxism which I will never be ready to renounce, it is not only the critical idea or the questioning stance . . . It is even more a certain emancipatory and messianic affirmation."[93] In contrast to a Marxism that disavows eschatology altogether and against an anti-Marxism that advances an eschatology with a particular (neoconservative) content, Derrida discovers in Marx a messianic affirmation that is premised upon negativity.[94]

In describing this affirmation, Derrida draws upon messianic religious traditions, though he does not intend to affirm any one of them. He writes, "We will not claim that this messianic eschatology common both to the religions it criticizes and to the Marxist critique must be simply deconstructed. While it is common to both of them, with the exception of the content . . . it is also the case that its formal structure of promise exceeds them or precedes them."[95] Rather than endorsing a particular eschatological vision, Derrida affirms a structure that he finds in both Marxist and religious eschatologies. It is for this reason that he brackets the content of particular messianisms: whereas they issue predictions concerning what is to come, Derrida is concerned with an incalculable futurity. He continues, "It is perhaps even the formality of a structural messianism, a messianism without religion, even a messianic without messianism [*un messianique, même, sans messianisme*]."[96] Derrida distinguishes the messianic structure he has in mind from messianism; the point of this paradox is to underscore that the future to come cannot be determined in advance. As he argued in his earlier discussion of justice, any talk of what is to come calls for self-critique.

Derrida associates this self-critical affirmation with hope. He writes, "Ascesis strips the messianic hope of all biblical forms, and even all determinable figures of the wait or expectation; it thus denudes itself in view of responding to that which must be absolute hospitality, the 'yes' to

---

[92] Derrida, *Specters of Marx*, 110. [93] Ibid., 111.
[94] See, for example, Francis Fukuyama, *The End of History and the Last Man* (London: Penguin, 1992).
[95] Derrida, *Specters of Marx*, 74. [96] Ibid.

the arrivant(e), the 'come' to the future that cannot be anticipated."[97] Here Derrida uses a term – *ascèse* – that derives from the Greek word for "training" or "exercise." Applied in its broadest sense, the term refers to any disciplined practice. In the context of early Christian monastic movements, the term came to connote self-denial. Derrida suggests that hope requires a discipline of this kind, which maintains its openness to the unforeseeable through continual self-critique. He continues, "Without this latter hopelessness [*ce désespoir-là*] and if one could *count* on what is coming, hope [*l'espérance*] would be but the calculation of a program."[98] The French *espérance* refers to hope, but it also connotes a range of meanings including certitude, confidence, and conviction. Whereas confident calculation assumes that one's present understanding will hold fast in the future, Derrida describes a hope against hope that is directed toward the unforeseeable. As I will argue in Chapter 3, such a hope is the precondition of the ethics of uncertainty that animates his project.

[97] Ibid., 211.   [98] Ibid., 212. Translation modified.

CHAPTER 2

Negative Theology
Critique and Commitment

Reflection on religion is bedeviled by the widespread assumption that it is antithetical to critique. While some religious leaders do assert an unshakable authority, I aim to show that some forms of religious thought are just as critical as the deconstructive negativity I described in Chapter 1. My argument focuses on Dionysius the Areopagite, a key progenitor of the tradition of Christian negative theology. Dionysius argues that, if God transcends the world (as its creator), the categories of human thought do not properly apply to God. However, although he concludes that every name for God must be negated, Dionysius proliferates positive claims about God. This tension between unreserved negation and unrestrained affirmation is the central challenge confronting interpreters of Dionysius, and it is key to his relevance for modern debates over religion.

Because Dionysian negative theology is resolutely affirmative, scholars such as Stathis Gourgouris argue that the tradition still asserts idolatrous access to God. According to Gourgouris, no religion, however negative, can circumvent the fact that religious commitment limits critical rationality. Specialist interpreters such as Alexander Golitzin reinforce this assessment by claiming that Dionysius's Christian commitments qualify his negativity, but I think this conclusion is mistaken. In my reading, Dionysius juxtaposes affirmation and negation without giving either pole priority, and this tension – which he calls *apophasis*, Greek for "unsaying" – renders Christian faith radically uncertain.

Whereas many interpreters construe *apophasis* as a linguistic technique that responds to an epistemological problem, I will argue that it is an ethical discipline oriented toward future transformation. Although the tension between affirmation and negation could appear to be mere contradiction when evaluated from the (synchronic) perspective of logical analysis, it becomes the means of ethical transformation when plotted (diachronically) in time. Dionysian *apophasis* resists the danger of self-satisfaction by highlighting the gap between present practice and union with God, which remains yet to come. It is therefore unnecessary to resolve the Dionysian tension either in favor of negation (by making Dionysius a quasi-postmodern pluralist) or affirmation (by making him an uncritical adherent of dogmatic Christian orthodoxy). On the contrary, Dionysius demonstrates that the robust affirmation of Christian commitment requires self-critique.

My ethical reading of *apophasis* helps to address a second tension within the Dionysian corpus, which corresponds to the first. Dionysius coins the term "hierarchy," and his corpus is hierarchical through and through. Dionysius claims that people have access to God through an unbroken chain of mediation that descends from the highest ranks of angels, through the lower angels, and down through the hierarchy of the church. At the same time, he argues that no one has access to God (which places angels, bishops, and priests on the same level as everyone else). My reading of *apophasis* reframes this ambivalence: the juxtaposition of affirmation and negation entails that any institution or practice that is directed toward God can only possess provisional authority, but they may be affirmed nonetheless. In contrast to common stereotypes about religion, Dionysius affirms particular commitments while acknowledging their uncertainty, working within institutional structures while holding them open to future revision. For this reason, although he rarely uses the word, I think his project is premised upon a self-critical hope.

Affirmative and Negative Theology

Dionysius the Areopagite is the pseudonym of a mysterious figure who lived sometime around the sixth century CE.[1] The New Testament mentions a Dionysius who was converted in Athens by the Apostle Paul; by taking this name, "Dionysius" connects himself both to the apostolic tradition and to Greek philosophy.[2] Both influences are apparent: he

---

[1] Ronald Hathaway details twenty-two hypotheses concerning the Areopagite's identity, ranging from "an Alexandrian member of a secret Christian fraternity" ca. 150 (by E. Corsini) to "Damascius Diadochus or one of his pupils" ca. 544 (by A. Kojève) (*Hierarchy and the Definition of Order in the Letters of Pseudo-Dionysius: A Study in the Form and Meaning of the Pseudo-Dionysian Writings* [The Hague: Nijhoff, 1969], 31–35). None of these conjectures has been established.
[2] Acts 17:34.

quotes extensively from the Bible even as he borrows key concepts from Neoplatonism.³ In light of the biblical account of creation, Dionysius adapts the Neoplatonic idea that all reality is an emanation from God.⁴ He describes an ordered system whereby every being is arranged in a stratified hierarchy leading to the divine, while (at the same time) God is radically distinct from everything as the creator. According to Dionysius, every created thing speaks of God, but because God is beyond creation, no name for God is adequate. For this reason, Dionysius claims that the writers of scripture prefer "the way up through unsaying [*tēn dia tōn apophaseōn anodon*]" – that is, *apophasis*.⁵

In *The Mystical Theology*, Dionysius systematically negates the names for God: "It is not soul or mind ... It has no power, it is not power, nor is it light. It does not live nor is it life ... It is not wisdom. It is neither one nor oneness, divinity nor goodness ... It falls neither within the predicate of nonbeing nor of being."⁶ Dionysius dissolves the privileged categories of Christian discourse, including the notion of divinity itself. It might seem as

---

³ In 1895, Hugo Koch and Josef Stiglmayr established that, because Dionysius borrows phrases from the fifth-century philosopher Proclus, his claim to be a contemporary of the Apostle Paul could not be true (Josef Stiglmayr, "Der Neuplatoniker Proclus Als Vorlage Des Sogen: Dionysius Areopagiten in Der Lehre Vom Übel," *Historisches Jahrbuch* 16 [1895]: 721–48; Hugo Koch, "Der Pseudo-Epigraphische Character Der Dionysischen Schriften," *Theologische Qartalschrift* 77 [1895]: 353–421). The point was demonstrated conclusively by Henri Dominique Saffrey in "Un Lien Objectif Entre Le Pseudo-Denys et Proclus," in *Studia Patristica*, vol. 9, 1966, 98–105; and "Nouveaux Liens Objectifs Entre Le Pseudo-Denys et Proclus," *Revue Des Sciences Philosophiques et Théologiques* 63, no. 1 (January 1979): 3–16.

⁴ Dionysius's debt to Neoplatonism has scandalized some. Martin Luther famously claimed that Dionysius "is downright dangerous, for he is more of a Platonist than a Christian" (Martin Luther, *Luther's Works, Vol. 36: Word and Sacrament II*, ed. Abdel Ross Wentz [Philadelphia: Fortress Press, 1959], 109). Many scholars share his assumption that Platonism and Christianity are incompatible (John Aberth, "Pseudo-Dionysius as Liberator: The Influence of the Negative Tradition on Late Medieval Female Mystics," *Downside Review* 114, no. 395 [April 1996]: 96; Vladimir Lossky, *The Mystical Theology of the Eastern Church* [London: J. Clarke, 1957], 32, 38; Andrew Louth, "Pagan Theurgy and Christian Sacramentalism in Denys the Areopagite," *Journal of Theological Studies* 37, no. 2 [1986]: 434; Jan Vanneste, "Is the Mysticism of Pseudo-Dionysius Genuine?," *International Philosophical Quarterly* 3, no. 2 [1963]: 296; Filip Ivanovic, "The Ecclesiology of Dionysius the Areopagite," *International Journal for the Study of the Christian Church* 11, no. 1 [February 2011]: 28). Exceptions to this consensus include John M. Rist, "A Note on Eros and Agape in Pseudo-Dionysius," *Vigiliae Christianae* 20, no. 4 (1966): 235–43; Gregory Shaw, "Neoplatonic Theurgy and Dionysius the Areopagite," *Journal of Early Christian Studies* 7, no. 4 (Winter 1999): 573–99; Vladimir Kharlamov, *The Beauty of the Unity and the Harmony of the Whole: The Concept of Theosis in the Theology of Pseudo-Dionysius the Areopagite* (Eugene, OR: Wipf & Stock Publishers, 2008); Sarah Klitenic Wear and John M. Dillon, *Dionysius the Areopagite and the Neoplatonist Tradition: Despoiling the Hellenes*, Ashgate Studies in Philosophy & Theology in Late Antiquity (Aldershot, UK; Burlington, VT: Ashgate, 2007).

⁵ DN 981B, 130. Translation modified.

⁶ MT 1048A, 141. It is noteworthy that here Dionysius is more radical than his Middle Platonist predecessors but close to Plotinus; cf. Deirdre Carabine, *The Unknown God: Negative Theology in the*

if such negation ultimately erases affirmation, leaving people unable to say or do anything in relation to God, but Dionysius is clear that neither affirmation nor negation is adequate. He writes, "What has actually to be asserted [*tithenai*] about the Cause of everything is this ... [It is] beyond privations, beyond every denial, beyond every assertion [*thesin*]."[7] This indicates that pure negation is impossible: at the very moment at which he says that God is beyond every assertion, Dionysius is making an assertion about God (*tithenai*, which shares the same root as *thesin*, the term for assertion). For this reason, Dionysian *apophasis* does not entail that theological discourse must simply be negated, for even negative statements make a positive claim about God.

Rather than insisting that theology must cease, Dionysius claims that the structure of creation requires proliferating speech about God. He writes, "The unnamed goodness is not just the cause of cohesion or life or perfection so that it is from this or that providential gesture that it earns a name, but it actually contains everything beforehand within itself."[8] According to Dionysius, God should not be named selectively, as if some things speak of God but not others. Because Dionysius sees creation as the outpouring of God's own self, he thinks that every created thing points back to God. For this reason, he says, every name drawn from creation must be used to speak of God.[9] In his view, it would be inappropriate to select only nice names for God – God must be called by every name, however incongruous.

In Dionysius's account, just as negative statements about God constitute a form of affirmation, the logic of theological affirmation inevitably demonstrates its inadequacy. After all, "the God of infinite names"[10] is effectively nameless, for the expansiveness of theological discourse defies any attempt to arrange it within an ordered system. Dionysius writes that "as Cause of all and as transcending all, [God] is rightly nameless and yet has the names of everything that is."[11] The logic of creation sets both affirmation and negation in motion, requiring at the same time that God be called by every name and by none. Dionysius explains, "[God] is all things in all things and he is no thing among things. He is known to all

---

Platonic Tradition, Plato to Eriugena, Louvain Theological & Pastoral Monographs no. 19 (Louvain: Peeters Press, 1995), 120–21.

[7] MT 1000B, 136. Translation modified.   [8] DN 596D, 56.
[9] DN 596D, 56. This argument depends on Dionysius's claim that everything contains some measure of the Good, whereas evil is (strictly speaking) nothing (DN 716D, 85ff).
[10] DN 969A, 126.   [11] DN 596C, 56.

from all things and he is known to no one from anything."[12] Each of Dionysius's four treatises therefore proliferates speech about God that undoes itself. Dionysius leads us to expect that, if we are attentive, we will see theological discourse continually rebuilding and breaking down.

Although many commentators construe *apophasis* as the negation of theological statements, Dionysius is clear that this is not what he means. He writes,

> Since it is the Cause of all beings, we should posit and affirm [*kataphaskein*] all the affirmations we make in regard to beings, and, more appropriately, we should unsay [*apophaskein*] all these affirmations, since it surpasses all being. Now we should not conclude that unsaying [*tas apophaseis*] is simply the opposites of the affirmations [*tais kataphasesin*], but rather that the cause of all is considerably prior to this, beyond privations [*hyper tas stereseis*], beyond every denial [*aphairesin*], beyond every assertion [*thesin*].[13]

In this passage, Dionysius outlines the structure I have described: because God is the creator of everything, one must affirm (*kataphaskein*) every name for God, but it is necessary to unsay (*apophaskein*) every divine name as well. Dionysius underscores that apophatic unsaying is not the inversion of cataphatic affirmation. On the contrary, he identifies two forms of negation: privative negation (*stereseis*), by which qualities are denied that would connote some deficiency in God, and removal (*aphairesis*), which inverts a particular name for God.[14] Whereas affirmation and negation

---

[12] DN 869D, 108–9. Amy Hollywood's comment is apposite: "There is no 'apophatic theology' within Christianity, then, but only the interplay between cataphasis and apophasis. Some emphasize one movement over the other. Some bury or forget the one movement in favor of the other. Yet when this happens, the liveness of the tradition – its very capacity to signify and to be handed down – is in danger" (Amy Hollywood, *Acute Melancholia and Other Essays* [New York: Columbia University Press, 2016]). I would simply add that the phrase "apophatic theology" (or its synonym, "negative theology") exemplifies this interplay insofar as the first term ("apophatic"/"negative") denotes negativity whereas the second ("theology") names affirmative discourse.

[13] MT 1.2 1000B, 136. Translation modified.

[14] In *The Mystical Theology*, *aphairesis* takes the form of terms to which Dionysius adds the prefix "a," which has the effect of negating the term in question. Scholars disagree over the relation between these three forms of negativity (*apophasis*, *aphairesis*, and *steresis*). John N. Jones argues that *apophasis* simply denies that God is a particular being without implying that all speech about God is inadequate; on this account, *apophasis* would consist in negative language (as distinct from "denial," which Jones equates to *aphairesis*) that does, in his view, adequately represent God ("Sculpting God: The Logic of Dionysian Negative Theology," *Harvard Theological Review* 89, no. 4 [O 1996]: 355–71). Aimee Light observes in response that, where Jones quotes *The Celestial Hierarchy* to show that Dionysius identifies words that may be unproblematically applied to God, in fact these "negations" apply in context to the angels as well, which means that "negation" does not function as Jones says it does ("Sculpting God: An Exchange (1)," *The Harvard Theological Review* 91, no. 2 [1998]: 206). Timothy Knepper's view is different again; in his view, "Whereas aphairesis constitutes Dionysius' method of hymning the hyper-being God through the removal of predicate-terms, apophasis serves as Dionysius' hermeneutic for interpreting such negative terms excessively

each fail to attain the divine, *apophasis* holds the two in tension to indicate that there is no grasping God.[15]

Apophatic Ethics

Christian history offers other models of theological self-critique, but the negativity Dionysius describes is distinctive for its schematic clarity.[16] However, some Christians are reluctant to accept that their theologies revolve into incoherence, and so they assert a foundation for theological knowledge that is exempt from global critique. Some even enlist Dionysius in this effort: one well-established interpretation, stretching from Thomas Aquinas into the present, holds that *apophasis* is consistent with the claim that human language properly applies to God. According to Thomas, Dionysius claims that God's essence is beyond what we can understand, but we can nevertheless know that some statements about God are true. He writes, "Such names as these, as Dionysius shows, are denied of God for the reason that what the name signifies does not belong to Him in the ordinary sense of its signification, but in a more eminent way."[17] On this reading, Dionysian negativity functions to remind the theologian that language does not apply to God in its ordinary sense but rather supereminently, by exceeding itself.

---

rather than privatively" ("Three Misuses of Dionysius for Comparative Theology," *Religious Studies* 45, no. 2 [June 2009]: 211). The textual evidence for this view is thin, however, and Knepper's claim that "negative predicate-terms ... reveal God's mysteriously superabundant possession of some property" (ibid.) does not accord with Dionysius's claim that God is beyond negation. For this reason, I agree with Janet Williams that, whereas *steresis* and *aphairesis* negate particular names of God, *apophasis* indicates the failure of any form of speech to capture the divine ("The Apophatic Theology of Dionysius the Pseudo-Areopagite," *Downside Review* 117, no. 408 [1999]: 167–69).

[15] I use the term "negativity" to refer to *apophasis* so as to denote a general process of undoing (in contrast to the negation of a particular object). Diana Coole comments in a different context: "Negativity thus conveys a restlessness that disturbs the slumbers of the given; that undermines any reified plenitude, presence, power or position, be it representational or political. It is affirmative in its engendering (creative, although sometimes in a destructive mode), yet negating (critical, transgressive, subversive, etc.) vis-à-vis the positive. As such, the motif of negativity itself refuses definition in terms of any simple binary opposition (positive/negative)" (Diana H. Coole, *Negativity and Politics: Dionysus and Dialectics from Kant to Poststructuralism* [London; New York: Routledge, 2000], 74).

[16] Rowan Williams writes, "What the narrative of Christ's suffering does is to invite our ironic appreciation of the scale of misrecognition that is involved in human authority judging the divine: an appreciation that entails a particularly intense self-questioning" (*The Tragic Imagination* [Oxford: Oxford University Press, 2016], 133).

[17] Aquinas, *The Summa Theologica*, trans. Fathers of the English Dominican Province, Second and Revised Edition, 1920 I 13.3.

This interpretation finds some support in the Dionysian corpus. Dionysius writes that "we cannot know God in his nature, since this is unknowable and is beyond the reach of mind or of reason. But we know him from the arrangement of everything, because everything is, in a sense, projected out from him, and this order possesses certain images and semblances of his divine paradigms."[18] This passage could be taken to imply that, like Thomas, Dionysius thinks there is a sense in which we can know God. On this reading, we cannot know God in God's essence, but we can know God as God shows Godself in creation. However, even as Dionysius claims that "of God there is conception, reason, understanding, touch, perception, opinion, imagination, name, and many other things," he immediately adds that "on the other hand he cannot be understood, words cannot contain him, and no name can lay hold of him."[19] In contrast to Thomas, who claims that we can have a partial but genuine knowledge of God, Dionysius places knowledge and unknowing in unresolved tension.

Dionysius insists (contra Thomas) that Christian theology is profoundly unstable. Where Thomas claims that it is possible to refer to the attributes of God, Dionysius argues that even the best names for God instead refer to God's causal activity in the world. Thomas writes, "When we say, 'God is good,' the meaning is not, 'God is the cause of goodness,' or 'God is not evil'; but the meaning is, 'Whatever good we attribute to creatures, preexists in God,' and in a more excellent and higher way."[20] Dionysius disagrees: "When, for instance, we give the name of 'God' to that transcendent hiddenness, when we call it 'life' or 'being' or 'light' or 'Word,' what our minds lay hold of is in fact nothing other than activities apparent to us, activities which deify, cause being, bear life, and give wisdom."[21] Where Thomas says that some theological speech is adequate and that God is thereby properly known, Dionysius insists that "we fail to know [*agnooumen*] [God's] incomprehensible [*anoēton*] and ineffable [*arrēton*] transcendence and invisibility."[22] Whatever the virtues of Thomas's approach on its own merits, it resolves a tension that Dionysius leaves unqualified.[23]

---

[18] DN 869D, 108–9.   [19] DN 869D, 108–9.   [20] Aquinas, *The Summa Theologica* I 13.2.
[21] DN 645A, 63–64.   [22] CH 141A, 150. Translation modified.
[23] A great deal has been written on Thomas's relation to Dionysius. Denys Turner argues that Thomas and Dionysius are actually quite close, perhaps even here (*Faith, Reason, and the Existence of God* [Cambridge; New York: Cambridge University Press, 2004], 187–90). In contrast, Alan Darley argues convincingly that Thomas qualifies the Areopagite's insistence upon the unknowability of God ("'We Know in Part': How the Positive Apophaticism of Aquinas Transforms the Negative

In my view, the difference between Thomas and Dionysius on the level of metaphysics hinges on a difference in ethics. The ordered distinctions of Thomas's system function to help Christians navigate between apparently conflicting authorities to arrive at right belief. For his part, Dionysius is more worried about the temptation of idolatry. He writes, "We have a habit of seizing upon what is actually beyond us, clinging to the familiar categories of our sense perceptions, and then we measure the divine by our human standards."[24] Treating God as a knowable object is comforting insofar as it suggests that one's own capacities are adequate; seizing upon what is beyond is therefore a form of self-reinforcement. For this reason, Dionysius argues, relation with God requires the dispossession of the self.

To resist what he calls "our willingness to be lazily satisfied by base images,"[25] Dionysius describes an ethical discipline. He writes, "The way up through denial [*dia tōn apophaseōn anodon*] ... stands the soul outside [*existōsan*] everything that is like itself [*symphylōn*]."[26] Dionysius is clear that *apophasis* is not simply a linguistic operation – here he claims that it constitutes a discipline that changes one's relation to everything, and not only knowledge. The term Dionysius uses for this change – *existōsan* – refers most broadly to a change of position, but it also carries the sense of abandonment. As Dionysius explains in *The Mystical Theology*, the pursuit of union with God requires "an undivided and absolute abandonment [*ekstasei*] of yourself and everything."[27] The effect of *apophasis* is to abandon everything familiar in order to open oneself to unforeseeable development. For this reason, it constitutes a way – a dynamic process, not a static structure. Whereas the juxtaposition between affirmation and

---

Theology of Pseudo-Dionysius," *Heythrop Journal*, 2011). If Kevin Hector is right that, for Thomas, "we can use it ["being"] as a common term between God and creatures," the fact that Dionysius closes *The Mystical Theology* by denying "being" of God suggests that the difference between them is decisive (Kevin Hector, "Apophaticism in Thomas Aquinas: A Re-reformulation and Recommendation," *Scottish Journal of Theology* 60, no. 4 [2007]: 392). John D. Jones argues convincingly that Aquinas's reading of Dionysius is led astray by his dependence upon John Sarracen's translation of *hyparxis* by *essentia* ("The Divine Names in John Sarracen's Translation: Misconstruing Dionysius's Language about God?," *American Catholic Philosophical Quarterly* 82, no. 4 [Fall 2008]: 661–82). Fran O'Rourke notes that Thomas "reduces at every opportunity the negative or 'agnostic' character of Dionysius' thought" and adds, "Dionysius' theory undergoes, however, an even more radical metamorphosis in its adoption into Aquinas' system" with respect to Thomas's reinterpretation of the notion of being (*Pseudo-Dionysius and the Metaphysics of Aquinas*, Studien Und Texte Zur Geistesgeschichte Des Mittelalters, Bd. 32 [Leiden; New York: E. J. Brill, 1992], 55).

[24] DN 865C, 106   [25] CH 141B, 150.
[26] DN 981B, 130. I have modified Luibheid's translation of *symphylōn* (as "which is correlative with its own finite nature") in the direction of literality. The verb *existōsan* denotes displacement and separation, but also abandonment and voluntary dispossession.
[27] MT 1.1 1000A, 135.

negation appears paradoxical when considered in abstraction, within an unfolding life it becomes a means of ethical transformation.[28]

Cosmic Hierarchy

Where most commentators read *apophasis* as a linguistic operation, I have argued that it is an ethical discipline that enacts the dispossession of the self. This reading reframes the feature of Dionysius's thought that is most difficult to reconcile with the instincts of most moderns: its insistent affirmation of a rigidly stratified order. Dionysius situates Christian practice within a cosmic order that he calls "hierarchy," a term he invents to refer to "holy order" or "sacred rule." This presents a problem for my attempt (in later chapters) to draw on Dionysius as a resource for reflection on secular hope and democratic politics, but the problem is first of all internal to the Dionysian corpus. Whereas Dionysius often argues that God is radically elusive, his account of hierarchy suggests that ecclesial structures offer access to the divine. For this reason, the hierarchical dimension of the corpus could seem to contradict the apophatic discipline I have described.

Dionysius claims that created reality comprises a network of relations in which everything is organized according to the love of God. He writes, "All things must desire, must yearn for, must love, the Beautiful and the Good. Because of it and for its sake, subordinate is returned to superior, equal keeps company with equal, superior turns providentially to subordinate, each bestirs itself and all are stirred to do and to will whatever it is they do and will."[29] Dionysius goes so far as to claim that this love motivates all action, including the pursuit of evil (insofar as it represents a malformed desire for the good). He writes, "Their longing for the Good makes them what they are and confers on them their well-being."[30] The differences among creatures are thus accounted for by the degree of their love of God:

---

[28] My argument intersects with that of Susannah Ticciati, who draws on apophatic theology in a broader register: "Doctrinal articulation is itself incipiently transformative. It does not just state (indicatively) that God is ungeneralisable (as if this were a predicate like any other): it debunks generalisability (by the oxymoronic creation 'out of' 'nothing', by the jarring identification of God with God's own goodness, and by the paradoxical uniting of divine and human natures in Christ); and it instructs us not to generalise regarding faith and sin. Thus it actively propels one towards the particular transformations it has in view as its endpoint" (Susannah Ticciati, "Doctrine in a Radically Apophatic Register," *Scottish Journal of Theology* 69, no. 2 [May 2016]: 137; Susannah Ticciati, *A New Apophaticism: Augustine and the Redemption of Signs*. [Leiden: Brill, 2015], 3). See also Tamsin Jones, *A Genealogy of Marion's Philosophy of Religion: Apparent Darkness* (Bloomington: Indiana University Press, 2011), 46.

[29] DN 708A, 79. [30] DN 693C, 72.

the intelligent possess a greater capacity for such love than do the living, and the living possessing a greater capacity than do inanimate objects that merely are. For this reason, Dionysius says, "The more a thing participates in the one infinitely generous God, the closer one is to him and the more divine one is with respect to others."[31] All reality, in his view, is knit together in ordered degrees of proximity to God.[32]

This ontology has political implications, for it determines the way in which individuals should interact. Dionysius writes, "Beings of lower ranks have their share of fire, of wisdom, of knowledge, of openness to receive God, but this is so in a lesser fashion and on condition that they look upward to those intelligent beings of the first rank through whom, as the ones primarily worthy of imitating God, they will be uplifted to the possible likeness of God."[33] Those beings with a lesser capacity for God are to look to those that possess more, and it is the latter who elevate the former toward the divine. According to Dionysius, "Hierarchy causes its members to be images of God in all respects, to be clear and spotless mirrors reflecting the glow of primordial light and indeed of God himself. It ensures that when its members have received this full and divine splendor they can then pass on this light generously and in accordance with God's will to beings further down the scale."[34] Hierarchy allows the divine ray to be reflected on each level, passed from one to the next. Each being reflects the divine with the intensity appropriate to its nature, but it is only by their connection to one another that the splendor is spread.

The glow begins with the highest rank of angels, who exist in maximal proximity to God. Dionysius writes, "This first of the hierarchies … possesses the highest order as God's immediate neighbor, being grounded directly around God and receiving the primal theophanies and perfections."[35] The ordered mediation of grace extends all the way up to God.

---

[31] DN 817B, 97–98.
[32] Rosemary Arthur argues that Dionysius's account of hierarchy entails the supposedly inclusive, anti-Christocentric theology exemplified by the modern Sea of Faith Network (Rosemary A. Arthur, *Pseudo-Dionysius as Polemicist: The Development and Purpose of the Angelic Hierarchy in Sixth Century Syria*, Ashgate New Critical Thinking in Religion, Theology and Biblical Studies [Aldershot, UK; Burlington, VT: Ashgate, 2008], 191–98). In my view, Arthur's claim that "the only thing that we dare say is that God is One" (ibid., 197) falsifies the Dionysian system insofar as, first, to say that "God is One" remains for Dionysius subject to negation and, second, the extent of this negativity allows for the unimpeded proliferation of affirmative speech.
[33] CH 304A, 178. Here Dionysius is speaking of heavenly beings, but the principle applies broadly.
[34] CH 165A, 154.   [35] CH 205B, 161.

The uppermost angels (seraphim, cherubim, and thrones) receive grace directly from God, without intermediary, for they are grounded directly around the divine. Dionysius explains, "The name cherubim signifies the power to know and to see God, to receive the greatest gifts of his light, to contemplate the divine splendor in primordial power, to be filled with the gifts that bring wisdom, and to share these generously with subordinates as a part of the beneficent outpouring of wisdom."[36] The highest angels both know and see God, and this allows them to disseminate their good gifts to the next rank of angels, who pass them on to the next, eventually including the ecclesial order. Dionysius explains, "All angels bring revelations and tidings of their superiors. The first bring word of the God who is their inspiration, while the others, according to where they are, tell of those inspired by God."[37] In this way, the arrangement of hierarchy enables a process of elevation toward God.

In Dionysius's account, the heavenly hierarchies lend their authority to the ecclesial order in a chain of mediation that extends unbroken from the highest rank of angels, through the lowest, to incorporate the church. He writes, "The revealing rank of principalities, archangels, and angels presides among themselves over the human hierarchies, in order that the uplifting and return toward God, and the communion and union, might occur according to proper order, and indeed so that the procession might be benignly given by God to all hierarchies and might arrive at each one in a shared way in sacred harmony."[38] The lowest rank of heavenly beings distributes the divine gifts to the highest level of the human hierarchy, that of the clergy. In this fashion, all beings are connected to God in harmonious order. Dionysius explains, "The source of spiritual perfection ... made our own hierarchy a ministerial colleague of these divine hierarchies by an assimilation, to the extent that is humanly feasible, to their godlike priesthood."[39] By means of the connection between the order of hierarchs and the order of the angels, human hierarchy is drawn into the heavenly, and the whole is brought nearer to God.

---

[36] CH 205C, 162.
[37] CH 273B, 173. My purpose here is to describe the broad outlines of Dionysius's account of the hierarchies without unpacking the intricate structures that he describes. René Roques's account of the latter is helpful; cf. René Roques, "Introduction," in *La Hiérarchie Céleste*, by Pseudo-Dionysius, Sources Chrétiennes, no. 58, trans. Maurice de Gandillac (Paris: Éditions du Cerf, 1958), xlii–lvii.
[38] CH 260B, 171.   [39] CH 124A, 147.

Dogmatic Idolatry

According to Dionysius, because God is hidden, knowledge of God must be mediated by celestial beings.[40] Dionysius says of the highest rank of angels that "to be like God is their special gift."[41] On the one hand, because these beings are "in immediate proximity to God," they are like God to the utmost extent, and their ability to distribute divine gifts to the lower ranks depends upon this proximity.[42] On the other hand, he writes that "God is in no way like the things that have being and we have no knowledge at all of his incomprehensible and ineffable transcendence and invisibility."[43] This follows from Dionysius's argument about the order of creation, which sets God at infinite remove from every created thing. He writes, "To the extent that [God] remains inimitable and ungraspable he transcends all imitation and all grasping."[44] The difficulty is that, if unmediated knowledge and experience of God are impossible for created beings, then there is no being (however angelic) that could begin the process of mediation by knowing God directly.

Insofar as he claims that the church hierarchy offers reliable knowledge of God, it would seem that Dionysius's negativity is only apparent. This lends support to Stathis Gourgouris's claim that religious faith constitutes a form of certainty, grounded in submission to authority, that forecloses critical reason. Gourgouris writes, "*Pistis* [i.e., faith] does not stand for belief as point of view or even trust in one's own opinion, but rather for knowing the true (following the permutations of Platonism), an entirely different construction of language that essentially maps the passage from *doxa* to *dogma*, which is in effect the passage from the Greek to the Christian imaginary."[45] In contrast to *nomizein*, which denotes "believing in the sense of having a point of view," Gourgouris claims that *pistis* lays claim to dogmatic knowledge. He continues: "Dogma can never be indifferent by definition, but *doxa* is constituted precisely by the sort of belief that is attached to nothing other than the risk of opinion in the shared, but contentious, realm of the opinions of others."[46] In his view, religious dogma lays claim to obedience, whereas everyday belief is open to critical evaluation in conversation with others. The problem, according to

---

[40] CH 180B, 157.   [41] CH 208C, 163.   [42] CH 212A, 165.   [43] CH 141A, 150.
[44] Ep 1069A, 263.
[45] Stathis Gourgouris, *Lessons in Secular Criticism* (New York: Fordham University Press, 2013), 71–72.
[46] Ibid.

Gourgouris, is that religion claims divine authority for norms and institutions that are all too human.

In fact, although Dionysius says that "the sacred institution and source of perfection ... modeled [our hierarchy] on the hierarchies of heaven,"[47] there are signs that the structure he describes is a human construction.[48] Dionysius coins the term "hierarchy" from the Greek word for priest (*hiereus*) and *archē*, meaning rule or order. The Dionysian hierarchies have both cosmic and ontological dimensions, but they are construed on the model of priestly structures. Because Dionysius admits that knowledge of the heavenly orders is beyond him, the consonance he describes between angelic and ecclesial life could seem a bit too convenient. Instead of uncovering the secret order of creation, it seems that Dionysius transposes earthly order onto the celestial realm. In doing so, Dionysius appears to confirm Gourgouris's claim that every religion is idolatry.

Although monotheistic religions reject material idols, Gourgouris claims that every religion identifies something as sacred (whether material or conceptual) that is actually a human creation. Gourgouris writes, "Religion is instituted in order to counter the abyssal terrain of being, the fact ... that human existence is at the limit groundless and all established signification fails it."[49] According to Gourgouris, the purpose of religion is to hide the fact that life lacks a foundation; it provides the illusion of safety by positing a transcendent ground that people (at least some of them) can access. He continues a few pages later: "Religion is basically a social practice of encountering and concealing the abyss of existence ... Though such creations are often times concrete material objects (icons, statues, totems, sacred texts), they are equally likely and often more powerfully to be abstract and immaterial (the Word become Flesh, the Trinitarian

---

[47] CH 121C, 146.

[48] To take one example, Dionysius says that the clerical orders are distinguished from each other by the fact that "the order of hierarchs has the task of consecration and of perfection, that the illuminative order of priests brings light, and that the task of the deacons is to purify and to discern the imperfect" (EH 508C, 238). Since elsewhere he attributes these three activities to God, here they represent the affinity between church hierarchy and the divine. As he goes on to explain, in the progress toward God, the soul is first purified, then illuminated, and then perfected, and the clerical orders are sequentially arranged according to this scheme. For this reason, the hierarch is responsible for the work of initiation (EH 516A, 242); nevertheless, in the consecration of monks (who are the highest of the three lay ranks), initiation is performed by a priest. Since Dionysius is clear that this consecration is the means by which "the sacred ordinance has bestowed a perfecting grace on [the monks]" (EH 532D, 245), this contradicts his earlier account, in which perfection is the province of the hierarchs alone. See René Roques, *L'univers Dionysien; Structure Hiérarchique Du Monde Selon Le Pseudo-Denys*, Théologie 29 (Paris: Aubier, 1954), 335.

[49] Stathis Gourgouris, "Every Religion Is Idolatry," *Social Research* 80, no. 1 (2013): 109.

substance ... , and so on)."⁵⁰ Whereas the monotheistic critique of idolatry often focuses on material objects, Gourgouris claims that religious concepts serve the same function. He concludes, "In all cases, such social imaginary creations that constitute the space of the sacred are idols, reified simulacra of the abyss they represent and at the same time conceal."⁵¹

This poses a forceful challenge to my reading of Dionysius. I have argued that a key aim of the Dionysian system is to strictly distinguish the divine from everything created. Like Gourgouris, Dionysius recognizes that the problem posed by idolatry is not only about literal images: he also worries about divinizing that which is worldly. However, Gourgouris observes that idolatry persists among those who critique the use of images for God. He writes, "In a monotheistic imaginary, iconoclasm merely reorients idol worship from the utterable and representable to the unutterable and unrepresentable."⁵² On this view, Dionysius's insistence that God is beyond naming simply resituates the danger of idolatry to another level. Although Dionysius acknowledges that particular images for God are at risk of becoming idolatrous, Gourgouris argues that the invisibility of God can itself become an idol.⁵³ According to Gourgouris, to name transcendence (even as "nameless") is idolatry, for it conceals the groundlessness of existence by locating ultimate meaning.

Varieties of Mysticism

As if to confirm this complaint, some readers of Dionysius argue that his apparent negativity is circumscribed by the affirmation of Christian worship. Alexander Golitzin argues that the ascent into darkness in *The Mystical Theology* is "nothing more nor less than an image of the Church at worship."⁵⁴ Whereas I have argued that Dionysian negativity renders Christian practice radically tenuous, Golitzin claims that "the summit, veiled in cloud and darkness, corresponds to the altar within the sanctuary veils of Dionysius's neighborhood church."⁵⁵ On this reading, the Dionysian corpus is not self-critical; instead, its apparent negativity simply reinforces the affirmation of Christian worship. Although Golitzin acknowledges the gap between "the Christian's present life in the Church

---

⁵⁰ Ibid., 113.   ⁵¹ Ibid.   ⁵² Ibid., 118.   ⁵³ Ibid., 119.
⁵⁴ Alexander Golitzin, "The Mysticism of Dionysius Areopagita: Platonist or Christian?," *Mystics Quarterly* 19, no. 3 (1993): 103.
⁵⁵ Ibid.

and the advent of the Kingdom to come,"⁵⁶ he asserts that "the Areopagite's Church ... remains our single reality, the meaning of our universe and the latter's unique hope – and assurance – of stability and final salvation."⁵⁷ Against my reading, Golitzin claims that Dionysius takes the church to provide the certainty of salvation.

Golitzin's Dionysius exemplifies the idolatry that Gourgouris describes, critiquing some images of God only to install a nameless divinity as the unshakable source of security. Golitzin's argument rests on the assumption that the Dionysian corpus should be read as a unity, and I think he is right. On his reading, Dionysian unknowing actually refers to the church's worship, and so it reinforces (rather than relativizes) his ecclesial commitments. I think Golitzin helpfully corrects the tendency of earlier scholars to read the two sides of the Dionysian corpus in isolation from each other. However, he forgets that the Dionysian corpus may be read in the other direction, situating Dionysius's affirmation of the church within the apophatic tension between affirmation and negation.

At the outset of *The Mystical Theology* Dionysius writes, "By an undivided and absolute abandonment of yourself and everything, shedding all and freed from all, you will be uplifted [*anachthēsē*] to the ray of the divine shadow which is above everything that is."⁵⁸ This unmitigated abandonment enacts the askesis of any horizon that might allow union with God to be recognized. Dionysius goes on to enact the negation of every category for God, finally denying that God is soul, mind, speech, understanding, number, order, greatness, smallness, equality, inequality, similarity, dissimilarity, power, light, life, eternity, time, knowledge, truth, kingship, wisdom, oneness, divinity, goodness, spirit, sonship, fatherhood, nonbeing, being, darkness, light, error, and truth.⁵⁹ This cannot be construed as a simple affirmation of ecclesial practice; on the contrary, the darkness of unknowing calls into question every claim to grasp the divine.

Because Dionysius does not exempt Christian practice from critique, it is misleading to call him (as many do) a "mystic."⁶⁰ Dionysius writes, "Someone beholding God and understanding what he saw has not actually

---

⁵⁶ Alexander Golitzin, "Review Essay, *Pseudo-Dionysius: A Commentary on the Texts and an Introduction to Their Influence* by Paul Rorem," *Mystics Quarterly* 21, no. 1 (March 1994): 37.
⁵⁷ Alexander Golitzin, *Et Introibo Ad Altare Dei: The Mystagogy of Dionysius Areopagita with Special Reference to Its Predecessors in the Eastern Christian Tradition* (Thessaloniki: Patriarchikon Idruma Paterikōn Meleton, 1994), 165.
⁵⁸ MT 1.1 100A, 135.   ⁵⁹ MT 5 1045D, 141.
⁶⁰ Cf. Lossky, *The Mystical Theology of the Eastern Church*, 38; Robert Paul Seesengood, *Paul: A Brief History* (Chichester, UK; Malden, MA: Wiley-Blackwell, 2010), 123; F. Samuel Brainard, *Reality and Mystical Experience* (University Park: Pennsylvania State University Press, 2000), 239; Daniel

seen God himself..., for he himself solidly transcends mind and being."[61] Since God eludes every category of understanding, there is no way that an experience of God could be understood as such an experience. In this way, Dionysius calls every supposed experience of God into question.[62] Dionysian faith does not correspond to the dogmatic knowledge that Gourgouris describes, for on Dionysius's terms the belief that one encounters the divine (whether through mystical experience or liturgical practice) is fundamentally uncertain.

For Dionysius, the *mystikos* (Greek for "hidden") is insurmountably unknown. In *The Mystical Theology* [*Peri Mystikēs Theologias*] Dionysius writes, "My advice to you as you look for a sight of the mysterious things [*ta mystika theamata*], is to leave behind you everything perceived and understood, everything perceptible and understandable, all that is not and all that is."[63] Dionysius usually uses variations of *mystikos* as an adjective to modify things (as in this quotation), sometimes as an adverb to characterize actions, but never as a noun for a particular type of person (as with the modern figure of the mystic). Lest one assume that this promises an experience of God, abandoning "everything perceptible" would leave one unable to perceive the "sight of the mysterious things" that it promises. What is more, if the things in question are truly hidden, it would seem that they could not serve as the object of intentional action. Dionysian mysticism does not apply to some things but not others, as if God were hidden only from some. In his account, the divine darkness is insurmountable.

Self-Critical Faith

Where Gourgouris claims that religion is idolatrous insofar as it identifies some things as sacred, Dionysius desacralizes every claim to identify the divine. Gourgouris writes, "Encountering the cunning of the sacred is more than just unveiling or repealing the occultation of the underlying chaos because the cunning of the sacred consists not only in occulting

---

L. Migliore, *Faith Seeking Understanding: An Introduction to Christian Theology.* (Grand Rapids, MI: Eerdmans Publishing, 1991), 404.

[61] EP 1 1065A, 263.

[62] When Dionysius speaks of the mysterious experiences of others (e.g., DN 3.2 684A, 70 and Ep. 8.6, 1097C, 278), these seem to have a liturgical context as well. Dionysius describes an experience he shared with his teacher Hierotheus and the apostles James and Peter: "We and he and many of our holy brothers met together for a vision of that mortal body, that source of life, which bore God" (DN 3.2 681D, 70). This is a vision, to be sure: the literal sight of the actual body of Mary, the mother of Jesus.

[63] MT I.1 997B, 135.

chaos but simultaneously in presenting chaos and giving it form. It is this simultaneity, this duplicity, that desacralization aims to break. For there is nothing to be unveiled."[64] On this view, the affirmation that something is sacred occludes the risk of human life, and so sacrality must be opposed through secular criticism. Dionysius agrees that there is a danger that the formless will be domesticated once it is given the form of a definite meaning, and (as I discuss at length in Chapter 6) he too attempts to break this dynamic through desacralization. However, Dionysius rejects Gourgouris's final claim – that "there is nothing to be unveiled." Dionysius is clear that God "is" not, God is not a "thing," and God cannot be "unveiled," but that does not mean that one must cease to speak of God. Instead of abandoning the sacred altogether, Dionysius develops a robust sacramental theology while insisting upon its inadequacy.

On my reading, Gourgouris's critique of religion is fully consistent with Dionysius's affirmation of faith. Gourgouris describes an atheism that "would stake out a position of living without presuming a content for the void of the Real, of living by assuming the void as core with no need to justify it, explain it, or theorize it – without a need for a transcendental, metaperformative guarantee."[65] Gourgouris takes this approach to be opposed to religion, always and as such, but Dionysius insists that the mystery of God cannot be justified, explained, or theorized, nor does Christian commitment provide a transcendental guarantee. Dionysius does not presume to give content to the Real; although he thinks the world impels us to speak of that which is ultimate, he argues that the character of transcendence also requires a rigorous circumspection. Gourgouris claims that the skepticism he describes "presupposes that we learn to be comfortable (or at least unhesitant) in the face of the extraordinary openness of horizon that uncertainty fosters," adding that "to think in terms of the future means to think as if anything is possible."[66] Dionysius suggests that such openness to an undetermined future is integral to a hope inflected by negativity. Where Gourgouris claims that atheism is required in order to avoid domesticating the void, Dionysius describes a hopeful affirmation of faith without guarantees.

According to Gourgouris, religious commitment demands obedience, which obscures its character as decision. He writes, "The decisions of believers are mere reproductions of decision ... But this alleged steadfastness of the believer's decision is a delusion, not in a pathological sense, delusional, but delusionary, because it produces a misperception that you

---

[64] Gourgouris, *Lessons in Secular Criticism*, 118–19.   [65] Ibid., 69.   [66] Ibid., 83.

Hope in a Secular Age 57

are covered, that you have a transcendental safeguard, when you don't."[67] On this view, ethical life requires people to take the risk of actively deciding on a certain course of action on the basis of independent reflection, while monotheistic traditions bracket this risk by grounding their ethics in transcendent authority. Dionysius demonstrates that this picture of religious faith is an unjustified stereotype. In his account, Christian commitment is an uncertain negotiation in community with others. He writes, "Perhaps there is something incorrect or imperfect about what I have done. Perhaps I have completely or partly strayed from the truth. If so I ask you to be charitable, to correct my unwished-for ignorance ... I beg that you pass on to me whatever you have discovered by yourself or from others"[68] Rather than handing down authoritative pronouncements that are supposedly inviolable, Dionysius places himself within a discursive community that struggles toward the truth.

Dionysius repeats the formula "as best I can [*hosē dynamis*]" throughout his corpus to indicate that what he writes is an attempt at provisional speech rather than the last word. In *The Ecclesiastical Hierarchy* he writes, "I must now try as best I can [*hosē dynamis*] to describe those divine workings."[69] In this way, he admits that his understanding of the hierarchies is a provisional effort (which is therefore imperfect). He writes in *The Celestial Hierarchy*, "This, then, is what I have to say regarding the sacred representations. Perhaps it falls a good deal short of making everything clear."[70] A little later he acknowledges that "I am at a loss when it comes to understanding their transcendent reality."[71] Earlier in this work he raises a question about the angelic orders; after describing several possible answers, he adds that "it is up to your intelligence and your critical understanding to decide on one or another of the solutions to the problem referred to."[72] Where Gourgouris assumes that Christian faith entails dogmatic certainty, Dionysius admits that his description of the hierarchies is a provisional attempt to describe what is beyond his understanding, and he acknowledges that each person is responsible for discerning for themselves what to think.

Gourgouris complains that religion paralyzes people's capacity to create new meanings, but the febrile free association that characterizes Dionysius's theological method indicates otherwise.[73] Rather than remaining

---

[67] Ibid., 78.   [68] DN 13.4 981D, 130–31.   [69] EH 440C, 220.   [70] CH 340B, 190.
[71] CH 340B, 190.   [72] CH 308B, 181.
[73] Gourgouris writes, "Religion – or what we have come to identify as religion – does operate both as end and as source of all meaning, thereby emptying out the signifying field and paralyzing people's radical capacity to imagine and create wholly other meanings" (*Lessons in Secular Criticism*, 118).

within the confines of a rigid dogmatism, Dionysius releases imagination. In doing so, he echoes the expansive vision of critique described in Chapter 1. Bruno Latour asks, "What would critique do if it could be associated with more, not with less, with multiplication, not subtraction."[74] This is precisely what Dionysius offers. As I have described, Dionysius indicates the inadequacy of theological discourse both by the negation of every divine name and by the affirmation of every possible name for God; in his view, theology must proliferate to the point of incoherence, which indicates that it has no grasp on its divine object. In my reading, apophatic negativity consists not in simple negation but in the juxtaposition of a negation and an affirmation that are equally extensive. In this way, Dionysius demonstrates that critique can operate through excessive affirmation as well as negation.

However, Dionysius goes a step beyond Latour. Latour writes that "the role of the critic is then to show that what the naïve believers are doing with objects is simply a projection of their wishes onto a material entity that does nothing at all by itself"[75] but he observes that "not one of us readers would like to see our own most cherished objects treated in this way."[76] Dionysius displays the critic's sensitivity to idolatry, but he does not exempt his own commitments from critique. On the contrary, he argues that faith in a transcendent God requires unstinting self-critique, for every theological system (including his own) is necessarily imperfect. Where some claim that critical awareness is at odds with religious commitment, Dionysius describes a creed without credulity.

Time and Negativity

I have argued that, on the level of both theological language and ecclesial practice, the Dionysian corpus is riven by an unresolved tension between affirmation and negation. Dionysius subjects theological discourse to unrestrained negation on the grounds that God transcends creation, yet he proliferates positive speech about God. His richly affirmative theology folds into negativity while negation itself falls short of the unknowing required by divine transcendence. Likewise, whereas Dionysius describes the mediation of grace by the hierarchy of created beings, this order is disrupted both by internal contradictions and by the impossibility of

---

[74] Bruno Latour, "Why Has Critique Run out of Steam? From Matters of Fact to Matters of Concern," *Critical Inquiry* 30, no. 2 (January 1, 2004): 248.
[75] Ibid., 237–38.   [76] Ibid., 240.

proximity with God. Insofar as both affirmative and negative language are both inadequate, Dionysius enacts the dispossession of speech by juxtaposing the two: this tension constitutes what Dionysius calls *apophasis*. Dionysius thinks we have the tendency to grasp at what is beyond us, reducing it to the contours of what we already know; in his account, relating to God in this way reinforces the self's status quo since the god in question is the self's own projection. *Apophasis* interrupts this process by preventing the orientation toward transcendence from hardening into either a stable set of affirmations or the stability of bare negation. Instead, *apophasis* keeps the individual in motion, open to a transcendence that incites improvisational affirmation.

This negativity carries a temporal propulsion. Dionysius writes, "The God who is transcends everything by virtue of his power ... He is the beginning and measure of eternity, the reality of time, the eternity of reality [*archē kai metron aiōnōn kai chronōn ontotēs kai aiōn tōn ontōn*], the time of events [*chronos tōn ginomenōn*]. He is being for whatever is. He is coming-to-be amid whatever happens."[77] According to Dionysius, God's role as creator entails both that God lies at the center of the created realm and, at the same time, that God lies outside of creation in total distinction from it. In this passage, Dionysius draws the conclusion that God is at the heart of time as well. He attributes a series of temporal terms to God, beginning with *archē ... aiōnōn*, the beginning of eternity. In the next phrase, *kai chronōn ontotēs*, Dionysius extends the attribution, claiming that God is the reality of time. He immediately adds, "*kai aiōn tōn ontōn*" ["the eternity of reality"], which creates an overlapping of objects and adjectives among the three phrases. The effect is one of continuous intensification: while Dionysius first says that God is the "beginning of eternity," in the third phrase eternity itself is attributed to God. While in the second phrase God is said to be "the reality of time," in the fourth phrase God is said to be time itself.

After associating God with this bewildering series of temporal terms, Dionysius immediately denies that the categories of time apply to God. He writes, "God was not [past tense of *eimi*], nor will be [future tense of *eimi*], nor did he come to be [past tense of *gignomai*], nor is he in the midst of becoming [present tense of *gignomai*], nor will he come to be [future tense of *gignomai*], nor indeed is he [present tense of *eimi*]."[78] In one

---

[77] DN 5.4 817C, 98.
[78] DN 5.4 817C, 98. "...*kai oute ēn oute estai oute egeneto oute ginetai oute genēsetai, mallon de oute estin.*" Translation modified.

continuous clause, he poetically repeats two verbs in three forms each: *eimi*, "to be," and *gignomai*, "to become." In this way, Dionysius denies both being and becoming of God, but he saves the negation of present being for last, emphasizing that God is entirely beyond the temporal categories he had earlier affirmed. Dionysius is clear that "the categories of eternity and of time do not apply to [God], since he transcends both and transcends whatever lies within them."[79] Just as theological speech and hierarchical mediation must be both affirmed and negated, God can be adequately described neither with temporal categories nor as timeless. The effect of this folded series of claims is to underscore that linear time does not pertain to God.

Dionysius argues that God is associated neither with an idealized past, nor with present experience, nor with a future that can be anticipated. On the contrary, because God is neither temporal nor timeless, God's actions take the form of an unforeseeable event. Dionysius writes,

> We now learn these things in the best way we can [*analogōs hēmin*], and as they come to us, wrapped in the hallowed veils of that love toward humanity with which scripture and hierarchical traditions cover [*perikalyptousēs*] intelligible things [*ta noēta*] with perceptible things [*aisthētois*] and what is beyond being [*ta hyperousia*] in beings ... But in time to come [*Tote de*], when we have become incorruptible and immortal, ... we shall have a conceptual gift of light from him and, somehow, in a way we cannot know [*agnōstois*], we shall be united with him beyond understanding [*hyper noun*] and, blessedly happy, we shall be struck by his blazing light.[80]

Here Dionysius describes ecclesial hierarchy as a provisional attempt to approach the divine in the present, one that is radically qualified by the fact that union with God remains yet to come. In keeping with his sacramental theology, Dionysius affirms that the perceptible symbols of Christian discourse and practice guide Christians to God, but he insists that they also veil the divine.[81] Dionysius refers to these veils as sacred, but at the same time he underscores that they are inadequate to represent what is invisible. In this way, affirmation of the sacred enacts a disciplined critique that keeps both discourse and practice in motion. For Dionysius, divine transcendence functions as a critical principle that renders hierarchical order subject to revision.[82]

---

[79] DN 5.10 825B, 103.   [80] DN 592B, 52–53. Translation modified.   [81] Cf. CH 121B, 146.
[82] My eschatological reading of Dionysius is unusual. René Roques claims that the Dionysius corpus is devoid of eschatology (René Roques, "Pierre l'Ibérien et Le 'Corpus' Dionysien," *Revue de l'histoire Des Religions* 145, no. 1 [1954]: 96), and this represents the consensus. Some commentators point to Dionysius's brief discussion of the fate of the individual soul in *The Ecclesiastical Hierarchy* (e.g.,

Dionysius writes that "we may aspire to a godlike and unblemished condition,"[83] but such beatitude remains a matter of hope rather than a present achievement. In this light, Dionysius's treatment of the hierarchies is (on his own account) inevitably inadequate. Hierarchy pertains to our present practice while God, according to Dionysius, remains inviolate. Although his understanding of the hierarchies suggests that some beings are closer to God than others, from another perspective (because God is circumscribed neither by space nor by time) God is equally distant – which is to say equally close – to everything.[84] By the same token, Dionysius argues that it is better to say some things of God than others, but he also insists that every divine name is radically incongruous. The former represents Dionysius's best attempt to speak in the present while the latter acknowledges that present practice falls immeasurably short of what is to come.

Crucially, Dionysius does not claim to have achieved union with God. On the contrary, he portrays ascent toward God as a process without end. In his view, we are "forever being raised up toward his divine enlightenments"[85] (not once and for all). Thus, although the Dionysian system can seem static, it is characterized by a progressive dynamism. He writes that "one must ceaselessly and prayerfully be raised up as much as one can [*hosē dynamis*] toward [the divine],"[86] and he repeats this qualification – "as much as one can" – in various forms across the corpus. This acknowledgment that each individual's capacity is limited entails that everyone remains open to future development, including the angels.[87] Dionysius writes in *The Divine Names*, "These, then, are the divine names . . . , and I have explained them as well as I can [*hōs ephikton*]. But of course I have

---

Josef Stiglmayr, "Die Eschatologie Des Pseudo-Dionysius," *Zeitschrift Für Katholische Theologie* 23 [1899]: 1–21). Alexander Golitzin's treatment of Dionysian eschatology centers upon death, resurrection, and final judgment – themes that receive little attention in the Dionysian corpus (Alexander Golitzin, "'On the Other Hand' (A Response to Fr Paul Wesche's Recent Article on Dionysius)," *St. Vladimir's Theological Quarterly* 34, no. 4 [1990]: 315; Golitzin, "The Mysticism of Dionysius Areopagita," 110; Alexander Golitzin, "Hierarchy versus Anarchy? Dionysius Areopagita, Symeon the New Theologian, Nicetas Stethatos, and Their Common Roots in Ascetical Tradition," *St. Vladimir's Theological Quarterly* 38 [1994]: 144). As far as I know, I am the only commentator to interpret *apophasis* itself as eschatological.

[83] EH 443B, 222.
[84] Dionysius writes, "The Trinity is not in any one location in such a manner as to be 'away from' one place. Even to speak of it as 'present in everything' is inaccurate since this does not convey the fact that it infinitely transcends everything and yet gathers everything within it" (DN 680B, 68).
[85] CH 293B, 176.   [86] EH 401C, 207.   [87] DN 4.2 696B, 72. Cf. CH 261D, 173.

fallen well short [*apoleipomenoi*] of what they actually mean."[88] Insofar as Dionysius's own corpus represents his best attempt to speak of the ineffable, it remains provisional and therefore subject to future revision. For this reason, as I will explain in Chapter 3, it is premised upon an uncertain hope.

---

[88] DN 981C, 130. Lest it seem extreme to refer to falling short as a failure, these two possibilities lie within the word *apoleipō*, which Dionysius uses here to refer to the failure of human and angelic speech and elsewhere to refer to the fact that God's activity never fails (Ep. 9.1, 281).

CHAPTER 3

The Discipline of Hope

Over the last two chapters I have argued that Derrida and Dionysius independently develop a form of critique that is not corrosive. Both authors believe that people are tempted to project themselves onto that which is different, and they both worry that this forecloses the unexpected. To resist this tendency, they both insist upon practices that open the individual to that which is beyond themselves. In my reading, Derrida's deconstruction and Dionysian *apophasis* are not primarily discursive techniques; instead, they enact an ethical discipline of openness to the unexpected. Crucially, however, both authors indicate that negation is not enough. Rather than concluding that one should cease speaking about the unknowable, they continue to affirm particular claims about justice (for Derrida) and God (for Dionysius). Because such affirmation exceeds the limits of reason, it is radically uncertain, but they demonstrate that it may persist through the discipline of hope.

Since hope sometimes functions as a pacifying fantasy, some conclude that it is best avoided. From Aristotle to Albert Camus, philosophers have argued that hope distracts from sober reflection on the world as it exists. Others claim that, although some attitudes toward the future are unjustified, hope is constrained by criteria of rational evaluation, which ensures that it remains tethered to reality. In my view, both sides in this debate are wrong. Where some claim that hope is always naïve, I argue that it can incorporate a lucid negativity. Rather than distracting from life here and now, a self-critical hope intensifies attention by acknowledging the distance between desire and its realization. Insofar as hope holds desires that may remain unfulfilled, it energizes the struggle for a future that has not yet come into view.

In my view, Derrida and Dionysius affirm hopes that differ in content but not in kind. Where Derrida hopes for the advent of a democracy to come, Dionysius looks toward the coming kingdom of God. They suggest, however, that religious and secular hopes must both must reckon with a future that transcends present understanding, which leaves them vulnerable to disappointment. On my account, in contrast to complacency and despair, hope constitutes a resolute persistence in the face of uncertainty, and for this reason it incorporates both affirmation and negativity. In response to Camus's critique of hope, Derrida and Dionysius suggest that maintaining this tension allows one to acknowledge that the world offers no assurance while continuing undeterred.

Hope means different things in different contexts, but in any case it concerns what is to come. To say "I hope ..." is already to admit that the outcome is uncertain; however, hope doesn't take uncertainty as a cause to quit. In response to those who claim that hope is (or ought to be) rational, I argue that it is disengaged from the calculation of probabilities. Prudence has its place, but hope is not limited to what one believes will (or can) occur. On the contrary, hope is sometimes directed toward outcomes that appear to be impossible. For this reason, hope is unavoidably perilous: as I will argue, it is detached from rational criteria, oriented toward the unknown, and subject to disappointment. However, this does not mean that it must be abandoned. Hope acknowledges that vulnerability is indelible, but it demonstrates that the loss of security is not necessarily crushing. On the contrary, hope names the possibility of enduring danger undaunted.

Camus's Critique of Hope

In everyday life, the way that people talk about hope can make it seem suspiciously easy – as if it were unambiguously good but ultimately banal, the moral of movies made for children and the mantra of the self-help industry. Faced with this relentless positivity, Albert Camus argues that hope is a projection that divorces us from the world as it is. He writes, "The typical act of eluding ... is hope. Hope of another life one must 'deserve' or trickery of those who live not for life itself but for some great idea that will transcend it, refine it, give it a meaning, and betray it."[1] Camus's concern is that the promise of future fulfillment invests life with a meaning that is illusory. In his view, hope displaces attention from the present to the future, thereby distracting from the absurdity of existence.

In *The Myth of Sisyphus*, Camus argues that daily life is on the whole habitual: "Rising, streetcar, four hours in the office or the factory, meal, streetcar, four hours of work, meal, sleep, and Monday Tuesday

---

[1] Camus, *The Myth of Sisyphus*, 8.

Wednesday Thursday Friday and Saturday according to the same rhythm – this path is easily followed most of the time."[2] When one is swept along by the rhythm of regularity, whether the world has meaning does not emerge as an issue. However, Camus continues, "One day the 'why' arises and everything begins in that weariness tinged with amazement."[3] Exhaustion born of monotonous rhythm leads some people to the beginning of consciousness, and as a result they discover that the universe has a denseness that defies understanding. According to Camus, although we desire the depth of meaning, the intellect cannot reach beyond appearances, leaving us alienated from a world that is strange to us.[4] It is this confrontation between the individual's desire for meaning and the obscurity of the world that Camus calls the absurd.

Camus claims that hope denies the absurdity of existence by claiming false comfort. He writes, "I understand then why the doctrines that explain everything to me also debilitate me at the same time. They relieve me of the weight of my own life, and yet I must carry it alone."[5] Camus criticizes religious doctrines that promise resolution in the afterlife and political doctrines that point to fulfillment in some future state. He argues that such theories distract from the difficulty of existing here and now; in his view, to look to the future is to look away from the present, covering over things as they are with a fantasy of what may be. Camus rejects suicide, but he argues that hope is no better – on his account, both hope and suicide constitute an escape from the absurd.

Because Camus believes that we inhabit "a universe suddenly divested of illusions and lights," he argues that hope is unsustainable.[6] He writes, "So long as the mind keeps silent in the motionless world of its hopes, everything is reflected and arranged in the unity of its nostalgia. With its first move this world cracks and tumbles: an infinite number of shimmering fragments is offered to the understanding."[7] Camus admits that hope provides some reassurance, but he claims that it relies upon the artificial coherence imposed by an isolated mind. In contrast to hope, Camus commends a stubborn resolve that he calls revolt. He writes, "[Revolt] is an insistence upon an impossible transparency. It challenges the world anew every second … It is not aspiration, for it is devoid of hope. That revolt is the certainty of a crushing fate, without the resignation that ought to accompany it."[8] On Camus's account, whereas hope is a pacifying fantasy, revolt demands lucid attention to things as they are. According

---

[2] Ibid., 12–13. [3] Ibid., 13. [4] Ibid., 14. [5] Ibid., 55. [6] Ibid., 6. [7] Ibid., 18.
[8] Ibid., 54.

to Camus, the absurd person focuses on what is before them rather than what is beyond, and so they refuse to invest the world with warmth.

Although Camus does not use the term "secularization," he describes what some theorists mean by that word. According to Charles Taylor, in some times and in some places, people have experienced the world as porous to mysterious forces, but many people today experience the world as silent and self-sufficient.[9] In Taylor's account, this new understanding of the world was linked to a distinctively modern understanding of the self as a self-contained individual with a firm boundary between self and other. Camus vividly describes what it is like to be such a self: "The absurd man thus catches sight of a burning and frigid, transparent and limited universe in which nothing is possible but everything is given, and beyond which all is collapse and nothingness. He can then decide to accept such a universe and draw from it his strength, his refusal to hope, and the unyielding evidence of a life without consolation."[10] As Camus observes, once the world is disenchanted, hope can seem like a phantasm. When one experiences the world as full of meaning – guaranteed, perhaps, by a benevolent God – then hope can seem entirely natural, but once this assurance shatters, hope may evaporate as well. In this way, Camus poses the problem of hope in a secular age.

I think Camus is right that hope often functions as a form of false comfort, but I think he is wrong to suppose that it is always an evasion. Camus worries that hope aims to neutralize the absurd by explaining the world; in response, I will argue that, on its own terms, Christian hope ought to acknowledge that it is groundless and therefore explains nothing. Where Camus opposes religious hope to a lucidity that refuses illusions, Dionysius and Derrida suggest that religious and secular hopes can both incorporate a rigorous negativity. In my view, a hope of this kind reinforces the resolute lucidity that Camus describes.

Dionysius's Hope against Hope

Camus's critique responds to a common conception of Christian hope. David Elliot claims that "theological hope ... sustains us from the demoralisation and despair that threaten us in this life, it gives a transcendent meaning and dignity to our lives, it assures us that we were created by love

---

[9] See Taylor, *A Secular Age*, 27–39. It is notable that Taylor returns to Camus throughout *A Secular Age*, e.g. on 699–703.
[10] Camus, *The Myth of Sisyphus*, 60.

and for love, and it encourages us with the anticipation of perfect beatitude."[11] In this passage, Elliot's "us" does not include his non-Christian readers: in his view, theological hope provides Christians with a security that unbelievers necessarily lack. Elliot explains, "The hopeful see their existence differently from those without hope, believing there is an ultimate meaning and transcendent point to their lives and world."[12] On this view, Christian hope consists in a confident expectation of ultimate blessedness that is justified by the promises of God. This confirms Camus's claim that Christian hope imposes meaning on the world that it does not, in his view, possess.

Gabriel Marcel shares Elliot's conviction that Christian hope constitutes a form of confidence. He describes Christian hope as "the inner disposition of one who, setting no condition or limit and abandoning himself in absolute confidence ... would experience a security of his being."[13] Marcel emphasizes that this security is a gift, not a possession, but this gesture of humility only intensifies the believer's security. He continues, "From the moment I abase myself in some sense before the absolute Thou ... it seems as though I forbid myself ever again to despair."[14] According to Marcel, because this confidence rests upon divine grace rather than human will, it is entirely secure. In contrast, he claims that existential revolt of the kind Camus affirms inevitably falls into despair since it lacks the counterweight of authentic transcendence.[15] This suggests that Camus is correct to claim that religious hope is incompatible with the disillusionment he describes.

Marcel claims that "outside of a positive or real religion announcing the resurrection of the body, there is only room for absolute pessimism."[16] Camus agrees, though he thinks pessimism is the only honest response to the absurdity of existence. Camus writes of Christian existentialists such as Kierkegaard, "Through an odd reasoning, starting out from the absurd over the ruins of reason ... they deify what crushes them and find reason to hope in what impoverishes them. That forced hope is religious in all of them."[17] Although Camus acknowledges his affinity with these authors, he

---

[11] Elliot, *Hope and Christian Ethics*, 41.   [12] Ibid., 99.
[13] Ibid.; Gabriel Marcel, *Homo Viator: Introduction to the Metaphysic of Hope* (South Bend, IN: St. Augustine's Press, 2010), 40. See also A. Phillips Griffiths, "Certain Hope," *Religious Studies* 26, no. 4 (1990): 453–61.
[14] Marcel, *Homo Viator*, 41.
[15] Ibid., 277. Marcel writes, "Has Mr. Camus any suspicion that the spiritual attitude he advocates is at bottom only a more subtly destructive equivalent of the suicide against which he has taken up his position?" (211).
[16] Ibid., 281.   [17] Camus, *The Myth of Sisyphus*, 32.

argues that they deny the absurd by inventing reasons to hope where there are none. Like Marcel, these thinkers present their leap as an act of humility, but Camus claims that this gesture is disingenuous because it asserts a firm assurance. According to Camus, "In all religions, man is freed of the weight of his own life" insofar as religious commitment claims certainty through submission to God.[18]

In my reading, Dionysius presents an alternative understanding of Christian hope – one that is fully consistent with Camus's pessimism. In contrast to Marcel, Dionysius does not derive reassurance from the promise of an afterlife. His only clear reference to the general resurrection comes in the context of a discussion of the rites for the dead. Dionysius writes that "sacred souls which in this life can tumble into sin will acquire in their rebirth an unshakable conformity to God. And the purified bodies yoked to and traveling with these sacred souls … themselves will enjoy the reward of the resurrection."[19] This reference to future blessedness comes as a brief aside before he develops a lengthy treatment of the apparent paradox of praying for the dead.[20] Dionysius affirms the promise of the resurrection, but he does not describe what is to come, and he does not suppose that it solves anything in the present. Instead, his central concern is how to live here and now.

Since Dionysius displays little interest in the traditional themes of Christian eschatology – heaven, hell, and so forth – the consensus among specialist interpreters is that the Dionysian corpus is devoid of eschatology.[21] I think this supposition is mistaken. As I argued in Chapter 2, the Dionysian corpus situates Christian life within the tension between the present (in which, he says, "we now learn these things in the best way we can") and the future (when "somehow, in a way we cannot know, we shall be united with [God] beyond understanding").[22] Dionysius argues that, because God transcends the world, every name for God must be negated, but at the same time (and for the same reason) he proliferates positive claims about God. I have argued that this tension – which Dionysius calls *apophasis* – is an ethical practice oriented toward future transformation. For Dionysius, Christian life is a provisional

---

[18] Ibid., 136. [19] EH 7.1 553A, 249–50.
[20] See Eric Perl's comment that "Dionysius characteristically transposes the eschatological future into the metaphysical present" (Eric David Perl, *Theophany: The Neoplatonic Philosophy of Dionysius the Areopagite* [Albany: State University of New York Press, 2007], 122).
[21] For instance, Paul Rorem, *Pseudo-Dionysius: A Commentary on the Texts and an Introduction to Their Influence* (New York: Oxford University Press, 1993), 122.
[22] DN 1.4 592B, 52–53. Translation modified.

attempt that is relativized by the unforeseeable future. Because the entirety of Dionysius's project is marked by this gap between the present and the future, it is eschatological through and through.

In my reading, rather than abandoning eschatology, Dionysius shifts its focus from claims concerning future events to the present practice of hope. He writes, "We should be taken wholly out of ourselves and become wholly of God, since it is better to belong to God rather than to ourselves. Only when we are with God will the divine gifts be poured out onto us."[23] Dionysius insists that "the divine gifts" cannot be grasped, for they remain yet to come. In the meantime, he suggests, to maintain an appropriate comportment toward this future requires an ethical discipline of dispossession. This provides an alternative to the confidence claimed by some theologians. According to Elliot, "If we cannot affirm the full coming and final victory of the kingdom, hope loses its certainty and confidence, turning into a theological maybe with nothing to prevent an agnostic eschatology."[24] In contrast, Dionysius suggests that Christian eschatology is necessarily agnostic. In his view, union with God is a hope oriented toward a future that is unknowable, but this does not mean that it cannot be affirmed. Where Elliot assumes that hope requires certainty and confidence, Dionysius demonstrates that Christian eschatology requires a disciplined unknowing."

Dionysius's uncertain hope finds support in Christian scripture. One of the canonical sources for Christian reflection on hope is Hebrews 11:1, which reads: "Faith is the substance [*hypostasis*] of things hoped for [*elpizomenōn*], the conviction [*elenchos*] of things not seen [*pragmatōn . . . ou blepomenon*]." English translations of this text are divided between those that construe the central Greek terms – *hypostasis* and *elenchos* – as assurance and evidence, on the one hand, or as substance and conviction on the other. Whereas the former suggests that the hiddenness of the invisible offers enough evidence to sustain a justified assurance, the latter suggests that faith and hope entail a conviction that does not depend upon justification. Because *blepomenon* can refer to bodily sight, to perception in general, to contemplation, and to understanding as such, this suggests that faith is directed at that which can neither be seen, perceived, understood, nor contemplated. It does not follow that faith must therefore be relinquished: on the contrary, in keeping with the disciplined negativity that Dionysius describes, this text indicates that faith is sustained through a resolute hope.

---

[23] DN 865C, 106. [24] Elliot, *Hope and Christian Ethics*, 54.

Hope, Secular and Religious

By describing a hope robust enough to acknowledge its uncertainty, Dionysius suggests that secular and religious hopes require the same resilience. His third epistle reads in full:

> What comes into view, contrary to hope [*par' elpida*], from previous obscurity [*ek tou teōs aphanous*], is described as sudden [*exaiphnēs*]. As for the love of Christ for humanity, the Word of God, I believe, uses this term to hint that the transcendent has put aside its own hiddenness and has revealed itself to us by becoming a human being. But he is hidden even after this revelation, or, if I may speak in a more divine fashion, is hidden even amid the revelation. For this mystery [*mystērion*] of Jesus remains hidden [*kekryptai*] and can be drawn out by no word or mind [*oudeni logō oute nō*]. What is to be said of it [*legomenon*] remains unsayable [*arrhēton*]; what is to be understood of it [*nooumenon*] remains unknowable [*agnōston*].[25]

Rather than relieving the weight of human life, as Camus fears, Dionysius argues that Christian hope cannot circumscribe present uncertainty. Where some theologians claim that belief in Jesus Christ transmutes Christian hope into certain assurance, Dionysius insists that it is here that *apophasis* is most urgently required. In typical fashion, he claims that anything said about the incarnation of Jesus Christ must also be unsaid; in his view, whatever is revealed in Jesus cannot be known. According to Dionysius, the incarnation constitutes a sudden event, which is (in a phrase drawn from Paul's letter to the Romans) "*par' elpida*," contrary to hope. In Greek, *elpis* signifies both hope and expectation. In my reading, Dionysius denies hope as confident expectation in order to preserve a hope that is premised upon uncertainty.[26]

By using the Greek term *exaiphnēs* (i.e., "sudden") to refer to the incarnation, Dionysius places himself within a tradition that portrays

---

[25] Ep. 3 1069B, 264. Translation modified. Elsewhere Dionysius writes, "It was the most divine Gabriel who guided Zechariah the hierarch into the mystery that, contrary to all expectation [*par' elpida*] and by God's favor, he would have a son who would be a prophet of the divine and human work of Jesus, who was beneficently about to appear for the salvation of the world" (CH 4.4 181B, 158. Translation modified).

[26] Cf. Romans 4:18. John Webster contrasts Christian confidence with a "hopeless a-moral and a-political" postmodernism (John Webster, "Eschatology, Anthropology and Postmodernity," *International Journal of Systematic Theology* 2, no. 1 [2000]: 25). He writes, "If this suggests that Christian eschatology is more modest than postmodernism allows, it is not because the Christian shares postmodernism's extreme apophaticism, but because the object of Christian eschatological certainty is Jesus Christ himself" (22). Apart from the fact that Webster's understanding of "postmodernism" has a loose relationship with the texts he has in mind, Dionysius suggests that "eschatological certainty" is an oxymoron that shatters upon the incomprehensible Christ.

Hope in a Secular Age 71

God's actions as unpredictable even for the faithful.[27] The Gospel of Luke reports that at the birth of Jesus "an angel of the Lord suddenly [*exaiphnēs*] stood before [some shepherds] ... and they were terribly frightened."[28] This event caught these witnesses unprepared, and so too the scholar known as Saul: the book of Acts says that "as he was going along and approaching Damascus, suddenly [*exaiphnēs*] a light from heaven flashed around him. He fell to the ground and heard a voice saying to him, 'Saul, Saul, why do you persecute me?'"[29] Bedazzled and befuddled, Saul responds, "Who are you?" – evidently he did not know in advance.[30] In the Gospel of Mark, Jesus warns that the end times will arrive like a master who "suddenly [*exaiphnēs*]" returns;[31] this suggests that whatever he reveals remains mysterious, beyond the grasp of his closest followers. In each case, the appearance in question comes as a surprise to those who experience it, which means that they had to revise the hopes they previously held. By situating his own account of the incarnation within this context, Dionysius suggests that Christians should not claim to possess privileged knowledge concerning what is to come.[32]

Because Derrida does not share Dionysius's Christian commitments, he does not hold the same hopes. However, the two authors relate to the commitments they hold in a similar way. As I argued in Chapter 1, Derrida's early work responds to the challenge of uncertainty. In "Structure, Sign, and Play" (1966), he argues that the assertion of

---

[27] It is worth noting that Dionysius is also alluding to Plato: his third Epistle echoes the third hypothesis of Plato's Parmenides, where *exaiphnēs* refers to "something interposed between motion and rest, not existing in any time" (Plato, *Plato 4: Cratylus, Parmenides, Greater Hippias, Lesser Hippias*, trans. Harold North Fowler [Cambridge, MA; London: Harvard University Press, 1939], 289, 156e). For Plato, *exaiphnēs* enables temporal change while remaining irreducible to it. For Damascius, a fifth-century commentator on the Parmenides, the moment is transposed onto the human soul, which lives at the border of the temporal and eternal (Sara Ahbel-Rappe, "Damascius on the Third Hypothesis of the Parmenides," in *Plato's Parmenides and Its Heritage, Vol. 2*, ed. John Douglas Turner and Kevin Corrigan [Atlanta: Society of Biblical Literature, 2010], 153). Raoul Mortley comments, "Clearly Dionysius is attempting to reconcile the Christian incarnation with the Neoplatonic moment of transformation" (Raoul Mortley, *From Word to Silence*, Theophaneia 30 [Bonn: Hanstein, 1986], 237). Carlo Mazzucchi goes so far as to identify Damascius as the author of the Corpus Dionysiacum, but this seems far-fetched (Carlo Maria Mazzucchi, "Damascio, Autore Del Corpus Dionysiacum, e Il Dialogo 'Peri Politikes Epistemes,'" *Aevum: Rassegna Di Scienze Storiche Linguistiche e Filologiche* 80, no. 2 [2006]: 299–334).
[28] Luke 2:9, NASB.   [29] Acts 9:3–4, NRSV. Cf. Acts 22:6.   [30] Acts 9:5, NRSV.
[31] Mark 13:32–36, NRSV.
[32] For this reason, I think Alan Mittleman is wrong to claim that "waiting for a future event or state in a universe ruled by a providential God is different from waiting in an absurd, contingent universe, as pictured by Samuel Beckett, Bertrand Russell, or Albert Camus" (Alan Mittleman, *Hope in a Democratic Age: Philosophy, Religion, and Political Theory* [Oxford: Oxford University Press, 2009], 116).

metaphysical certainty is motivated by an understandable desire for safety. In response, Derrida models an alternative response to instability, acknowledging that everything remains unpredictably in motion. In "Différance" (1968), Derrida construes this irrepressible play in terms of the future, which is incalculable. In "Force of Law" (1990) and *Rogues* (2003), he argues that justice and democracy are futural in this sense; in his view, they can never be fully instantiated but are always to come. In each case, Derrida emphasizes the impossibility of knowledge, but he does not conclude that we must cease speaking about such things. Instead, as I have argued, Derrida models an affirmation that presses forward without the assurance of safety. In my reading, this persistence exemplifies the discipline of hope.[33]

Like Dionysius, Derrida suggests that a hope inflected by negativity may sustain an uncertain faith. He refers to "a hypercritical faith, one without dogma and without religion, irreducible to any and all religious or implicitly theocratic institutions."[34] This does not entail that the faith he has in mind is opposed to the religious; on the contrary, Derrida's point is that this faith is not exhausted by any particular religious tradition. He immediately adds, "It is what I have called elsewhere the awaiting without horizon of a messianicity without messianism."[35] In this passage, Derrida does not specify the link between faith and this messianic hope, but I take it that on his terms faith constitutes a commitment that goes beyond the available evidence, while hope is the discipline that enables affirmation to persist in the face of uncertainty.

Although Derrida rarely names hope explicitly, I argued in Chapter 1 that hope is implicit throughout his work insofar as he describes (in a variety of registers) a commitment that persists in the face of uncertainty. Occasionally, however, the link becomes explicit. In an interview published in 2003, Derrida was asked, "So you see an important role for Europe?" He responded:

---

[33] Derrida writes elsewhere, "Unfortunately, I do not feel inspired by any sort of hope which would permit me to presume that my work of deconstruction has a prophetic function ... The fact that I declare it 'unfortunate' that I do not personally feel inspired may be a signal that deep down I still hope. It means that I am in fact still looking for something. So perhaps it is no mere accident of rhetoric that the search itself, the search without hope for hope, assumes a certain prophetic allure." (Jacques Derrida, "Deconstruction and the Other," in *Debates in Continental Philosophy: Conversations with Contemporary Thinkers*, by Richard Kearney [London: Fordham University Press, 2004], 150).

[34] Derrida, *Rogues*, 153.   [35] Ibid.

> I hope for it, but I do not see it. I have not seen anything in the facts that would give rise to any certainty or knowledge. Only a few signs to interpret. If there are responsibilities to be taken and decisions to be made, responsibilities and decisions worthy of these names, they belong to the time of a risk and of an act of faith. Beyond knowledge ... As for what I have just risked on the subject of "Europe," let's say that I am raising a few questions, in the midst of a certain night and on the basis of a certain number of signs. I decipher, I wager, I hope.[36]

In this passage, Derrida affirms his faith in the European project, but because faith is (as such) uncertain, he acknowledges that it is a wager that must be sustained by hope. Derrida underscores that each person must take responsibility for pursuing particular aims, but (as I have argued) the uncertainty of such a decision does not render it impossible. Instead, Derrida indicates that hope allows commitment to continue in the absence of knowledge, and it enables affirmation to endure self-critique.

Derrida and Dionysius are different in many respects. Where Derrida places his faith in multinational institutions, Dionysius affirms Christian commitment. They hold different beliefs about God and the world, they undertake different practices, and they are formed by different communities. These differences are real, but they throw the two authors' similarity into sharper relief. Dionysius and Derrida demonstrate that it is neither necessary to avoid negativity in order to preserve the possibility of affirmation nor to avoid religious commitment in order to preserve the possibility of critique. Although Derrida's affect tends melancholic while Dionysius seems more sanguine, the two authors share an uncertain hope.[37] In this way, they suggest that religious and secular hopes should not be opposed.

Where Camus claims that hope is a form of false comfort, Derrida and Dionysius suggest that it is predicated upon uncertainty. Both authors worry that confident expectation forecloses the future by projecting the subject's present understanding onto that which is different. For this reason, they both insist upon practices of dispossession that undercut the presumption of security. They both argue that the future is unforeseeable,

---

[36] Habermas and Derrida, *Philosophy in a Time of Terror*, 118. For similar professions of faith, see Jacques Derrida, *Paper Machine*, Cultural Memory in the Present (Stanford, CA: Stanford University Press, 2005), 116; Derrida, *Rogues*, xiv; Jacques Derrida, *Without Alibi*, trans. Peggy Kamuf, Meridian (Stanford, CA: Stanford University Press, 2002), 202.

[37] My argument is consistent with Kevin Hart's claim that the relation between deconstruction and negative theology is structural rather than thematic, but I locate the affinity differently than he does (Hart, *The Trespass of the Sign*, 64).

but neither of them concludes that we must simply fall silent. Rather than negating the absurdity of existence by asserting the certainty of final satisfaction, such hope is a risk that remains vulnerable to disappointment. Because this hope is unknowing, it depends upon an act of will, and so it is consistent with a thoroughgoing pessimism concerning its prospects for success. Where Camus assumes that lucid confrontation with the absurd entails despair, Derrida and Dionysius demonstrate that hope can endure darkness.

Hope's Content

My argument indicates that, despite their differences, Derrida and Dionysius share a hope that is identical in kind though not in content. However, many readers assume that the two authors disagree over whether hope ought to have any content at all. John Caputo writes, "Derrida is dreaming of what is not and never will be present, what is structurally to come (*a-venir*) ... The prayers and tears of Jacques Derrida are not a matter of wishing, willing, or wanting some determinable, foreseeable object."[38] According to Caputo, Derrida affirms an indeterminate openness that stands opposed to the specific hopes of particular messianic traditions, and many commentators agree.[39] Following Caputo, Kevin Hughes argues that Derrida's messianism is ultimately empty. Hughes writes, "One is left crying endlessly '*Viens, oui, oui*' to one knows not what *for* one knows not what. One is called to hope in nothing at all."[40] According to Hughes, Christian eschatology offers a hope that is confident and contentful, while Derrida's indeterminacy is actually hopeless.

It is true that Derrida does express some anxiety about determinate hopes. In *A Taste for the Secret* (1996) he writes, "Why do I claim that justice is eschatological and messianic ...? Perhaps because the appeal of

---

[38] Caputo, *Prayers and Tears*, 118. Caputo sometimes acknowledges that messianism always takes a determinate form (142). However, I believe this contradicts his repeated claim that Derrida's hope is indeterminate. Also see John D. Caputo, *Hoping against Hope: Confessions of a Postmodern Pilgrim* (Minneapolis: Fortress Press, 2015), 10–21, 96–102.

[39] James K. A. Smith comments that "it is precisely the determination of Christian (and Marxist) hope which implicates it in violence," whereas "Derrida's hope lacks determination" (James K. A. Smith, "Determined Hope: A Phenomenology of Christian Expectation," in *The Future of Hope: Christian Tradition amid Modernity and Postmodernity*, ed. Miroslav Volf and William Katerberg [Grand Rapids, MI: William B. Eerdmans Pub. Co., 2004], 204–5).

[40] Kevin Hughes, "The Crossing of Hope, or Apophatic Eschatology," in *The Future of Hope: Christian Tradition amid Modernity and Postmodernity*, ed. Miroslav Volf and William Katerberg (Grand Rapids, MI: William B. Eerdmans Pub. Co., 2004), 104.

the future ... – which overflows any sort of ontological determination, which overflows everything that is and that is present ... – is committed to a promise or an appeal that goes beyond being and history."[41] As we have seen, Derrida argues that justice is characterized by a futurity that is heterogeneous to presence. In this passage he explains that the promise of justice is not determined by what is, by what is present, or by being itself. He continues, "This is an extremity that is beyond any determinable end of being or of history, and this eschatology ... has necessarily to be the only absolute opening towards the non-determinability of the future."[42] Thus, Derrida distinguishes the eschatology he has in mind from those visions of the future that specify a particular end.

According to Derrida, because justice is radically elusive, we cannot know what the realization of justice would look like, and so we must not confuse the future with our expectations. This does not mean, however, that Derrida's hope is purely indeterminate. He continues a few paragraphs later:

> The question of the political, ethical, juridical, consists in finding, as the occasion demands, the schemata required to articulate justice and law, justice and politics, justice and history, justice and ontology. But ... I think that the instant one loses sight of the excess of justice, or of the future, in that very moment the conditions of totalization would, undoubtedly, be fulfilled – but so would the conditions of the totalitarianism of a right without justice, of a good moral conscience and a good juridical conscience, which all adds up to a present without a future.[43]

In this passage Derrida repeats the pattern that I traced in Chapter 1. On the one hand, he recognizes that political action requires people to make concrete judgments concerning how best to pursue justice; on the other hand, the incalculable character of justice requires that every conception of justice remains subject to critique. In this context, Derrida's emphasis upon indeterminacy serves a specific function: it aims to disrupt the assurance that justice is already realized. At the same time, although the future is undecidable, Derrida acknowledges that undetermined openness is not a state that people can achieve. On his account, comportment toward the future exists in the tension between

---

[41] Jacques Derrida, "'I Have a Taste for the Secret,'" in *A Taste for the Secret*, by Maurizio Ferraris and Jacques Derrida, ed. Giacomo Donis and David Webb, trans. Giacomo Donis (Cambridge: Polity, 2001), 20.
[42] Ibid.   [43] Ibid., 22.

determinate forms (which are unavoidable) and self-critique (which keeps discernment in motion).

In *Specters of Marx* (1993), Derrida explains, "The idea, if that is still what it is, of democracy to come ... is the opening of this gap between an infinite promise ... and the determined, necessary, but also necessarily inadequate forms of what has to be measured against this promise."[44] As I described in Chapter 1, Derrida argues that democracy (like justice) is constitutively to come. This entails that it cannot be identified, even as an ideal, but that does not mean that we must cease to speak of it. On the contrary, Derrida holds the indeterminate futurity of democracy to come in tension with determinate attempts to promote democracy in particular contexts. He continues, "The effectivity or actuality of the democratic promise ... will always keep within it, and it must do so, this absolutely undetermined messianic hope at its heart."[45] In his view, particular attempts to pursue democracy carry within them a hope for democracy that is undetermined. Rather than opposing indeterminate openness and determinate commitments, as Caputo claims, Derrida suggests that they are inseparable.

In similar fashion, although Dionysius affirms particular (Christian) hopes, he insists upon an equally radical negativity. Hughes claims that "what is proleptically *present* to the mystic, and expressed rhetorically in mystical traditions, is *anticipated* in eschatology, and expressed in images of the fullness of the kingdom of God that is yet to come."[46] Hughes takes Dionysius to be an exemplar of this tradition, but Dionysius precludes any confidence concerning the presence of God. Where Hughes takes mystical theology to concern the consciousness of divine presence, I argued in Chapter 2 that such awareness is impossible according to Dionysius. Instead, Dionysius claims that, because union with God remains yet to come, our present situation is radically uncertain. Hughes claims that the only defense against emptiness is "a theology confident in its

---

[44] Derrida, *Specters of Marx*, 81. Derrida writes elsewhere, "When I try to think the most rigorous relation with the other I must be ready to give up the hope for a return to salvation, the hope for resurrection, or even reconciliation" ("Terror, Religion, and the New Politics," in *Debates in Continental Philosophy: Conversations with Contemporary Thinkers*, by Richard Kearney [London: Fordham University Press, 2004], 5). Derrida does not say that one must actually give up these hopes; on the contrary, he has just said to his interlocutor, "You ... would not give up the hope of redemption, resurrection, and so forth, and I would not either." Derrida's point is that in order to respect alterity one must be ready to suspend the hopes that one does, in fact, hold.
[45] Derrida, *Specters of Marx*, 81.
[46] Hughes, "The Crossing of Hope, or Apophatic Eschatology," 113.

predications."⁴⁷ However, Dionysius demonstrates that an uncertain hope can sustain affirmations that acknowledge their uncertainty.

Although Caputo claims that Derrida does not wish, will, or want "some determinable, foreseeable object," Derrida frequently affirms particular hopes.⁴⁸ As Derrida acknowledges, even the ostensibly indeterminate "democracy to come" is itself a determinate figure that draws upon a particular history: "Did we not have some idea of democracy, we would never worry about its indetermination. We would never seek to elucidate its meaning or, indeed, call for its advent."⁴⁹ Similarly, although Dionysius insists that the future is unforeseeable, he fills out his hope for union with God with imagery drawn from Christian scripture. Dionysius and Derrida draw upon different sources, but the gesture is the same. They both affirm particular hopes that are informed by the traditions that have formed them while also insisting that every affirmation remains subject to revision. In contrast to the stereotyped expectations that commentators such as Caputo and Hughes bring to their work, Derrida and Dionysius recognize that hope is directed toward the future, nourished by the past, and sustained in the present.

Hope's Reasons

Where Camus claims that hope is a fantasy that evaporates once the world is disenchanted, I have argued that hope can incorporate a disciplined

---

⁴⁷ Ibid., 121. Along similar lines, Paul Fiddes complains that Derrida "abandons us to wandering in a world of traces with little sense of self-identity and without any possibility of arrival" (Paul Fiddes, *The Promised End: Eschatology in Theology and Literature* [Oxford; Malden, MA: Blackwell Publishers, 2000], 40). Fiddes remarks that "we can, I believe, learn a good deal [from Derrida] about the openness of meaning of texts," yet he judges that "the inability to make an end also means a loss of confidence in any value and meaning at all" (38). I disagree with Fiddes concerning both the interpretation of Derrida (who does not exclude arrival) and the importance of closure (which is not, in my view, a requirement for meaning).

⁴⁸ See Jacques Derrida, "Not Utopia, the Im-Possible," in *Paper Machine* (Cultural Memory in the Present) (Stanford, CA: Stanford University Press, 2005), 122; Jacques Derrida, "Events? What Events?," in *Negotiations: Interventions and Interviews, 1971–2001*, Cultural Memory in the Present, ed. Elizabeth Rottenberg (Stanford, CA: Stanford University Press, 2002), 75; Jacques Derrida, "The Deconstruction of Actuality," in *Negotiations: Interventions and Interviews, 1971–2001*, Cultural Memory in the Present, ed. Elizabeth Rottenberg (Stanford, CA: Stanford University Press, 2002), 112; Jacques Derrida, "Taking Sides for Algeria," in *Negotiations: Interventions and Interviews, 1971–2001*, Cultural Memory in the Present, ed. Elizabeth Rottenberg (Stanford, CA: Stanford University Press, 2002), 122–23.

⁴⁹ *Rogues*, 18. Elsewhere he elaborates, "If nonetheless I still cling to this old noun democracy and speak so often of the 'democracy to come,' it is because I see in it the only word for a political regime that, because it carries conceptually the dimension of inadequation and the to-come, declares both its historicity and its perfectibility" (Derrida, "Not Utopia, the Im-Possible," 130).

negativity. Some theologians claim that religious hope provides a security that unbelievers lack, but Dionysius and Derrida suggest that secular and religious commitments are sustained by an uncertain hope. In my reading, this disciplined resilience can incorporate the pessimistic lucidity on which Camus insists. Rather than resolving the pain of the present, hope holds desires that are vulnerable to disappointment, affirming particular aims while acknowledging that every affirmation is only provisional. For this reason, I think Derrida and Dionysius offer a compelling response to the problem of hope in a secular age.

However, some could conclude that a hope of this kind is not worth having. Philosophers have often worried that hope is at odds with careful reflection. Aristotle observes that hopeful investment in the future can impair calm judgment; in his view, the effervescence of hope provides a jolt of pleasure, which interrupts reason. He writes, "For the young the future is long, the past short; ... which makes them easy to deceive, for they readily hope."[50] On this account, hope is the opposite of sober judgment; because its investment in the future forgets the past, hope makes a person susceptible to deception. Aristotle goes on to explain that, where young people are characteristically hopeful, the old are fearful.[51] In contrast, people in the prime of life virtuously avoid both hope and fear, "neither trusting nor distrusting all, but judging rather in accordance with actual facts."[52] According to Aristotle, hope is an enthusiasm that is at odds with wisdom.

In similar fashion, Baruch Spinoza argues that hope is an irrational passion that is at odds with reason. He writes, "Hope is an inconstant pleasure, arising from the idea of something past or future, whereof we to a certain extent doubt the issue."[53] According to Spinoza, hope is an emotion, the enjoyment one gets when imagining something desired but doubtful. Since Spinoza defines emotion as "a confused idea," this suggests that hope is fleeting and unreliable.[54] He elaborates, "Emotions of hope and fear ... show defective knowledge and an absence of power in the mind ... Wherefore the more we endeavour to be guided by reason, the less do we depend on hope."[55] In his view, the relation between hope and reason is a zero-sum game: the more one reasons, the less one hopes.

---

[50] Aristotle, *The "Art" of Rhetoric*, trans. John Henry Freese (London: Heinemann, 1926), 249.
[51] Ibid., 251.   [52] Ibid., 255.
[53] Benedict de Spinoza, *Ethics*, trans. E. M. Curley (London; New York: Penguin Books, 1996), 106, III.
[54] Spinoza, *Ethics* III.   [55] Ibid., 141, IV.47.

Some philosophers respond to criticisms of this kind by arguing that hope incorporates rational deliberation. Adrienne Martin offers the most extensive recent treatment of hope from the perspective of analytic philosophy. In her view, hope is rational insofar as it depends upon two judgments: first, that its object is possible but not certain and, second, that the act of hoping serves the hoper's practical ends.[56] She explains, "Although hope is beholden to considerations of truth-approximation via its constituent probability estimate, what determines whether it is correct for a hopeful person to then see that probability in the licensing way is whether it promotes her rational ends to do so."[57] In Martin's view, hope is not a passion that floats free of rational evaluation. On the contrary, she thinks every hope depends on the belief that the object of hope is possible and that the act of hoping advances one's aims.

I think Martin is right that hope is not simply a passive emotion, but I think she is wrong to locate its active dimension in reason. Martin writes, "It is just crazy, clearly, to be hopeful in the ways described about an outcome one believes has literally no chance of occurring or that one believes is certain to occur."[58] This is the consensus position among analytic philosophers, but it is not convincing. Because every judgment concerning possibility is fallible, one's judgment may always be misguided. Even if one holds the strongest possible conviction that the outcome in question has no chance of occurring, that conviction remains doubtful. It follows that, even if one believes that the object of hope is impossible, the uncertainty of this belief means that it cannot exclude the possibility of hope. This is particularly clear in the case of those who believe that God intervenes directly in worldly affairs: even if they have every reason to think an outcome has no chance of occurring in its own right, they think that God may bring otherwise unpredictable events into being. However, one needn't believe in miracles to acknowledge that events can take one by surprise. For this reason, people often find themselves hoping for outcomes that are (as far as they can tell) impossible.

In contrast to the philosophical consensus, Derrida and Dionysius suggest that aims which outstrip the subject's understanding of what is possible are the paradigm of hope. As I have described, Dionysius looks to a union with God that is unforeseeable. Because the object of this desire is beyond understanding, the individual cannot evaluate whether it is possible – to do so would be beyond their capacity. Similarly, Derrida's messianic hope is directed toward a democracy that is constitutively to

---

[56] Martin, *How We Hope*, 7–8.   [57] Ibid., 37.   [58] Ibid., 51.

come. Since Derrida associates presence with consciousness, an event that could be anticipated would not be futural in Derrida's sense, and so he claims that the futurity he has in mind is impossible – that is, entirely foreign to evaluation on the basis of the subject's present understanding of possibility.[59] Derrida and Dionysius agree that hope is not constrained by considerations of this kind.[60]

Many commentators share Martin's view that hope must have an object that the hoper judges to be possible. To take a canonical example, Dante's *Inferno* describes an inscription above the gate to Hell: "'Surrender as you enter every hope you have.'"[61] Alan Mittleman comments, "When one passes through the gates of Hell, one loses all reason to hope ... The damned can wish for, desire, or dream of release, but ... they cannot hope for it. They cannot hope for it because there is no realistic means by which they can fulfill their hope."[62] On this view, there is no hope in Hell because escape is impossible. However, the Italian phrase in question – "Lasciate ogne speranza, voi ch'intrate" – can be read either as imperative or indicative.[63] Like Mittleman, many readers assume that there can be no hope in Hell because God precludes it, but it may be that giving up hope is instead what makes one damned. Mittleman claims that "Dante's damned souls have certainty: the dreadful certainty of eternal punishment,"[64] but there is reason to think that perfect certainty is never available, least of all when it comes to God. After all, Dante says that the gates of Hell are open: this suggests that the damned are only certain of their fate if they have already chosen to despair. Against Mittleman, my

---

[59] Derrida, *Rogues*, 144. He refers to the impossible as "what must remain (in a nonnegative fashion) foreign to the order of my possibilities, to the order of the 'I can,' ipseity, the theoretical, the descriptive, the constative, and the performative" (84). Derrida writes, commenting on Plato, "All this is of the order of the possible, of the nonimpossible. This each in turn of the one and only, this inalterable alternation, is not negatively impossible. It is necessary to insist on this in thinking of the future, of a to-come that would be neither a chimera nor a regulative Idea nor a negative and simply impossible impossibility" (77). Derrida explains, "The possibility of the impossible, of the 'more impossible' that as such is also possible ('more impossible than the impossible'), marks an absolute interruption in the regime of the possible that nonetheless remains, if this can be said, in place" (Jacques Derrida, "Sauf Le Nom (Post Scriptum)," in *On the Name* (Meridian: Crossing Aesthetics), ed. Thomas Dutoit [Stanford, CA: Stanford University Press, 1995], 43).

[60] Derrida, *Rogues*, 84. This seems close to what Martin calls "unimaginable hope," in which the hoped-for outcome exceeds the ability of the hopeful person to conceive it (*How We Hope*, 66, 98–108). However, where Martin claims that unimaginable hopes possess an unshakeable confidence, Dionysius and Derrida suggest that they function as a critical principle that destabilizes every vision of the future (*How We Hope*, 108).

[61] Dante Alighieri, *The Divine Comedy. 1, Inferno*, trans. Robin Kirkpatrick (London; New York: Penguin Books, 2010), l. 3.9.

[62] Mittleman, *Hope in a Democratic Age*, 2.   [63] I owe this insight to Vittorio Montemaggi.

[64] Ibid., 3.

argument indicates that hopelessness stems from failure of will, not from the evaluation of probabilities. As a discipline of resilience, hope may persist even when one has lost every reason to hope.

Terry Eagleton claims that "you can act positively even when you regard the situation as hopeless, but you cannot act hopefully if you regard it as hopeless."[65] Experience suggests that this is false – it is possible to maintain hope even when one judges that the situation is hopeless, and in fact people often do. This indicates that a situation is neither hopeful or hopeless in itself, for hope is an act of the will, not a fact about the world. Martin may be right that it is unreasonable to hope when a situation seems hopeless, but people are sometimes unreasonable in precisely this way.[66] To be sure, even if hope is sometimes directed toward things that appear to be impossible (such as a hope for the end of patriarchy), it may be that some hopes are best relinquished (such as a hope for the ability to levitate). In my account, however, such discernment is extrinsic to hope: the problem with unhealthy hopes is that they are unhealthy, not that they aren't genuine hopes.

Although Dionysius and Derrida suggest that hope does not depend upon rational evaluation, they both acknowledge that discernment is indispensable. As I argued in Chapter 1, Derrida claims that justice and democracy are incalculable, but he recognizes that calculation must continue. In particular cases we must decide how to pursue justice as best we can. However, because the future is unforeseeable, Derrida insists that the hope for justice is not limited by present understanding.[67] In similar fashion, Dionysius develops a theological system that is rationally ordered, but he claims that the divine shatters the structure of reason.[68] He thinks people ought to pursue God, but he insists that any such attempt remains subject to future revision. For both authors, people are responsible to reason as well as they can, but hope lies on another level.

---

[65] Terry Eagleton, *Hope without Optimism* (New Haven, CT; London: Yale University Press, 2017), 61.

[66] Martin argues that one may hope for improbable things (*How We Hope*, 141). Nevertheless, by excluding a hope for the impossible, I think she overstates the importance of reason relative to will in the practice of hoping.

[67] Derrida writes, "It is necessary to know, to be sure, to know that knowledge is indispensable; we need to have knowledge, the best and most comprehensive available, in order to make a decision or take responsibility. But the moment and structure of the 'il faut,' of the 'it is necessary,' just like the responsible decision, are and must remain heterogeneous to knowledge. An absolute interruption must separate them, one that can always be judged 'mad.' ... That is why what I say here, I'm well aware, involves a serious risk" (Derrida, *Rogues*, 145).

[68] In MT 1000B, 136 Dionysius contradicts Aristotle's commonsensical claim that negations are the opposite of affirmations.

Hope's Vulnerability

On my account, hope is a resolute desire that persists in the face of uncertainty. For this reason, contra Martin, I think the active dimension of hope is located within the will rather than reason. Martin argues that hope takes the desire for an outcome and the assessment of its probability as justification for hopeful activities; in her view, this practical judgment ties together the various features of hope. However, the hope I have described encourages a critical distance from one's theoretical and practical judgments. For this reason, hope can persist even when one is unsure whether doing so serves one's ends. It is possible to ask whether a particular hope serves one's well-being, but concluding that it does not is sometimes insufficient to banish the hope. This widespread experience indicates that hope does not depend upon theoretical or practical justification. No process of reasoning is enough to determine whether a certain set of considerations justifies maintaining a particular hope. Hope is decision added to desire: a discipline of the will, not the conclusion of a proof.

In my reading, Derrida and Dionysius suggest that hope is distinct from despair (which gives up the desire) and from complacency (which assumes that its realization is certain). Derrida and Dionysius suggest that hope and hopes, verb and noun, relate dialectically: the discipline of hope settles upon particular objects while simultaneously unsettling particular hopes, setting them in motion once more. While hope requires an object in order to work in the world, a disciplined persistence is necessary to sustain particular hopes in the face of disappointment. It is for this reason, as I have described, that Dionysius and Derrida hold determinate affirmations in tension with a negativity that opens future development.

However, hope is associated with darkness in more than one way: in my account, it depends upon a disciplined unknowing, but it is also dangerous. Although some speak of hope as if it were a cheerful thing, maintaining the desire for a distant outcome is sometimes the source of suffering.[69] Since hope accentuates the distance of the desired future, the dullness of despair can feel like a relief. Cicero writes, "Senseless people live in hope for the future, and since this cannot be certain, they are consumed by fear

---

[69] The modality of my argument differs from that of most analytic philosophers, including Adrienne Martin. Her intention is to describe what people *in fact* mean when they talk about hope. I think people mean many things; rather than insisting that everyone does (or should) mean a certain thing when they talk about hope, I seek to describe one understanding of hope that might help us think about trenchant problems, particularly concerning religion and public life.

and anxiety."⁷⁰ Because hope is vulnerable to disappointment, it can be easier to rest content with what one already has. Spinoza writes that "hope and fear cannot exist without pain," and I believe he is correct: imagining hope's realization can be a source of pleasure, but confronting its uncertainty is often a source of pain.⁷¹ As Lauren Berlant observes, the thing one desires sometimes serves as an obstacle to one's flourishing; in her view, this dynamic is especially cruel when it is directed toward an object that is perpetually out of reach.⁷² Insofar as it is detached from rational calculation, hope is a risk.

Where some philosophers mitigate this danger by arguing that hope is rational, I have argued that it is an act of will that outstrips what the hoper understands. (Because I believe rationality is extrinsic to hope, I am reluctant to call hope a virtue: whether hope is good or bad depends upon its content, but hope itself lacks the criteria required to adjudicate such questions.⁷³) Martin may be right that a hope for the impossible is crazy, but that does not entail that it must be abandoned. Although reason promises an appealing safety, it is not necessary to limit our hopes, our loves, and our commitments to that which we are able to justify. Because we are sometimes drawn to what we do not understand, no one lives within the limits of reason. Instead, human life inhabits the tension that I have described, stretching into a future that holds the promise (and threat) of surprise.

I think Derrida and Dionysius are right that people are often tempted to make things seem more certain than they are. This is understandable: since instability is unsettling, it is natural to seek security. However, both complacency and despair make it harder to live responsibly, for they foreclose the complexity of things. To take one example, as Joseph Winters argues, the confidence of many Americans in their country's exceptional greatness has made it harder to acknowledge the racial violence that runs

---

⁷⁰ Cicero, De finibus, I, 18, 60, quoted in Pierre Hadot, *Philosophy as a Way of Life: Spiritual Exercises from Socrates to Foucault*, ed. Arnold Davidson (Malden, MA: Blackwell, 1995), 223.
⁷¹ Spinoza, *Ethics*, 141, IV.47.
⁷² Lauren Berlant, *Cruel Optimism* (Durham, NC: Duke University Press, 2011), 1–2, 14, 20–21. I find Berlant's argument compelling, but I do not think it counts as an objection to my account of hope. Although Dionysius and Derrida describe a hope that incorporates a sort of indeterminacy, they do not claim that the object of their hope can never arrive – the point is simply that any such arrival would remain in excess of our ability to identify it. I think the prudential considerations that Berlant raises concerning the danger of desire are enormously important; I simply think they operate on a different level than that of hope.
⁷³ For similar reasons, Josef Pieper argues that hope is not a virtue as such; however, he claims that hope is a theological virtue insofar as it is directed toward God (*On Hope*, 26). In my view, Pieper is overly sanguine about theological hope, which is at least as dangerous as its secular counterpart.

through the country's history.[74] Winters shows that such optimism sustains itself by denying the pain and disappointment that exists, in the past and in the present. For this reason, the oscillation between complacency and despair undermines the work of building responsible lives and responsive communities.

In response to this danger, I have argued that hope can incorporate a self-critical vigilance that opens the possibility of unpredictable development. Although (as Camus observes) some hopes are stultifying, it may motivate attempts to improve the present in the recognition that the future is fragile. Through the discipline of hope, it is possible to admit that even the most extensive rationality is inadequate to protect against the fragility of human existence. Rather than explaining away the pain of the present, a self-critical hope enables us to face the indelible vulnerability of human life. The danger of hope ought to be unsettling, but hope names the possibility of persisting in the face of uncertainty.

---

[74] Joseph Richard Winters, *Hope Draped in Black: Race, Melancholy, and the Agony of Progress*, 2016.

CHAPTER 4

Beyond Indeterminacy and Dogma

Over the course of the last three chapters, I have argued that deconstruction and negative theology both construe critique as an ethical discipline that opens future development. In Chapter 1 I argued that negativity is needed to hold open the possibility of transformation beyond what the self can foresee. Although critique can become hegemonic, Derrida develops a form of critique that encourages unpredictable affirmation. In Chapter 2 I argued that religious commitment can incorporate self-critique. Where some assume that religion requires unquestioning submission to authority, Dionysius demonstrates that Christian commitment requires a disciplined negativity. In Chapter 3 I argued that this conjunction of affirmation and critique clarifies the character of hope. It is true that hope sometimes functions as a pacifying fantasy, but Derrida and Dionysius show that it can incorporate a frank attention to fragility.

My reading of Dionysius and Derrida has a performative dimension. As I have described, the two authors differ in many ways. Whereas Derrida is a modern atheist prone to melancholy, Dionysius is a medieval monk with a sanguine bent. It is due to their differences in content and tone that their structural affinity is so striking. If I am right that Derrida and Dionysius share a hope that is identical in kind (though not in content), this indicates that the boundary between religion and its other is unstable.

Because Derrida engaged with negative theology (and Dionysius in particular) throughout his career, the relation between deconstruction and negative theology has become a key site for reflection on the relation between religion and modernity. Unfortunately, this literature tends to reinforce oppositions that bedevil debates over religion and public life. On the one hand, John Caputo argues that Derrida develops a "religion without religion," which exhibits a religious spirit without the concrete dogmas of particular religious traditions. On the other hand, commentators such as Jean-Luc Marion appeal to Dionysius to defend Christian faith against Derrida's supposed hostility to religion. Both Caputo and Marion have been enormously influential, but in my view they misunderstand both the texts in question and the issues at stake. Where Caputo's "religion without religion" insists upon an indeterminacy that no one can actually sustain, Marion's affirmation of Christian worship claims a confidence that is unjustified. The trouble is that both approaches risk collapsing under the complexity of embodied life.

Caputo and Marion both claim that Derrida rejects negative theology as insufficiently negative. Because negative theology is as negative as Christian thought can get, they both conclude that Derrida rejects theology altogether. In response, drawing upon the reading of Derrida I developed in Chapter 1, I will show that Derrida's engagement with negative theology is more subtle and extensive than this reading allows. Although Derrida worries that Dionysius preserves an affirmation that violates the circumspection of negative theology, he recognizes that such affirmation is unavoidable. Rather than opting for indeterminacy over and against determinate affirmation, Derrida and Dionysius both hold affirmation and negation in tension in order to resist the danger of complacency and despair. For this reason, where the literature on deconstruction and negative theology tends to focus on the status of predicative statements, I argue that the key point of contact between Derrida and Dionysius concerns ethics rather than epistemology.

Caputo and Marion address deconstruction and negative theology to clarify the possibilities for faith in secular modernity. In light of their reading, they suggest that those who wish to maintain some connection to religion must choose between the secure assertion of traditional dogma and an attenuated religiosity abstracted from any determinate content. Where Marion and Caputo map this dichotomy onto deconstruction and negative theology, I will argue that Dionysius and Derrida offer an alternative that is urgently needed. In the context of pluralistic societies, the claim that a particular tradition possesses unquestionable authority rings false, but decontextualized gestures toward higher meaning are vague and unsatisfying. My account of hope responds to this need by demonstrating that it is possible to affirm religious commitments in all their particularity while holding those commitments open to transformation.

Caputo's Complaint

John Caputo's interpretation of Derrida has been enormously influential, but in my view it has led to a widespread misunderstanding of Derrida's relation to religion. Caputo's interpretation hinges upon the relation between deconstruction and negative theology: his *Prayers and Tears of Jacques Derrida* begins with a lengthy chapter titled "The Apophatic," and it progressively develops the complaint that negative theology is overly determinate. Caputo writes:

> The story of Derrida's religion without religion begins with Derrida's first encounter of a close kind with theology, with the claim (charge/congratulation) made early on that deconstruction is a negative theology ... But the story is, on my telling, always slightly out of focus if you do not move on. For it is necessary to get past his dialogues with Christian Neoplatonism to his more biblical, prophetic, Jewish side, past the apophatic to the messianic that shows up in his most recent work.[1]

Although Caputo acknowledges some connection between deconstruction and negative theology, he claims that their apparent similarity is ultimately misleading. In his view, Derrida is Hebraic rather than Hellenic, biblical rather than Neoplatonic, messianic rather than apophatic. On this basis, Caputo concludes that "the point of view of Derrida's work as an author is religious – but without religion and without religion's God."[2]

According to Caputo, both deconstruction and negative theology are moved by desire for the wholly other, but Derrida requires a more resolute negativity. He writes, "The difference is that in negative theology the *tout autre* [wholly other] always goes under the name of God, and that which calls forth speech is called 'God,' whereas for Derrida every other is wholly other."[3] Caputo argues that, where negative theology specifies otherness by calling it "God," Derrida is concerned with an otherness that is entirely indeterminate. Caputo explains, "Deconstruction differs from the Christian mystical theology of Pseudo-Dionysius or of Meister Eckhart as an indeterminate differs from a determinate affirmation of the impossible."[4] According to Caputo, by giving alterity a determinate name, theologians (however negative) narrow the scope of the otherness they have in view. Caputo claims that "way down deep, negative theologians know what they are talking about," whereas Derrida (apparently to his credit) does not.[5]

Caputo's characterization of negative theology hinges upon a Greek term, *hyperousios*, that occurs more than 100 times in the Dionysian corpus. As used by Dionysius, the word signifies the state of being beyond or above (*hyper*) being or substance (*ousia*). Caputo claims that Dionysius surreptitiously predicates that God exists, albeit on a higher level than ordinary existence. He writes, "If Derrida admires the discursive resources

---

[1] Caputo, *Prayers and Tears*, xvii. [2] Ibid., xviii. [3] Ibid., 3–4.
[4] John D. Caputo, "Apostles of the Impossible," in *God, the Gift, and Postmodernism*, ed. John D. Caputo and Michael J. Scanlon (Bloomington: Indiana University Press, 1999), 198.
[5] Caputo, *Prayers and Tears*, 11.

of negative theology, he begs to differ with it insofar as negative theology turns out, upon analysis, to be actually a higher way to trump language and representation ... by means of a hyper-being which exceeds our powers to speak or name it."[6] In Caputo's view, Derrida recognizes that deconstruction is formally similar to negative theology in its use of language, but Derrida concludes that negative theology is ultimately an attempt to circumvent the play of *différance* by appealing to a being beyond being. Caputo continues, "Thus conceived, the God of negative theology is a transcendental signified, the dream of being without *différance*, of being outside the text, outside the general text, outside the play of traces."[7] In Caputo's reading, the prefix *hyper-* secures a superessential reference to that which is supposedly unspeakable, allowing God to function as the stable point around which a system of knowledge is organized. Caputo repeatedly claims that "negative theology is worlds removed from deconstruction" because it "is always a higher, more refined way of affirming that God exists."[8]

Derrida's early discussion of negative theology in "Différance" could seem to confirm Caputo's complaint. On the one hand, Derrida notes that "the detours, locutions, and syntax in which I will often have to take recourse will resemble those of negative theology, occasionally even to the point of being indistinguishable from negative theology."[9] As we saw in Chapter 1, Derrida argues that *différance* eludes discourse altogether, and so his discussion of *différance* resorts to acrobatic self-critique. Derrida continues: "Already we have had to delineate that *différance* is not, does not exist, is not a present-being in any form; and we will be led to delineate also everything that it is not, that is, everything."[10] Derrida recognizes that *différance* resembles the God of negative theology insofar as it requires the denial of everything, including denial itself. However, Derrida immediately adds:

> And yet those aspects of *différance* which are thereby delineated are not theological, not even in the order of the most negative of negative theologies, which are always concerned with disengaging a superessentiality

---

[6] Ibid., 10. [7] Ibid., 11.

[8] Ibid., 2, 7. Caputo repeats a few sentences later, "Derrida has consistently maintained this view, and I think has been consistently right" (8). See also John D. Caputo, *Philosophy and Theology*, Horizons in Theology (Nashville, TN: Abingdon Press, 2006), 66; John D. Caputo, *More Radical Hermeneutics: On Not Knowing Who We Are*, Studies in Continental Thought (Bloomington: Indiana University Press, 2000), 253; Caputo, "Apostles of the Impossible," 188; John D. Caputo, "On the Power of the Powerless: Dialogue with John D. Caputo," in *After the Death of God*, ed. Jeffrey W. Robbins (New York: Columbia University Press, 2007), 117.

[9] Derrida, "Différance," 6. [10] Ibid.

beyond the finite categories of essence and existence, that is, of presence, and always hastening to recall that God is refused the predicate of existence, only in order to acknowledge his superior, inconceivable, and ineffable mode of being.[11]

In light of this passage, many readers conclude, following Caputo, that Derrida thinks the negativity of even the most negative negative theology gives way to a superessentialist affirmation that is incompatible with deconstruction. As we shall see, however, this reading is premised upon a fundamental misunderstanding.

Revisiting Deconstruction and Negative Theology

Derrida's discussion of negative theology in "Différance" is cursory, and he does not elaborate at length until "How to Avoid Speaking," eighteen years later. Many commentators conclude that this essay reiterates Derrida's view that negative theology is always superessentialist.[12] Following Caputo, Mary-Jane Rubenstein notes that Derrida admits the analogy between deconstruction and negative theology, but she claims that "Derrida goes on to say – without footnote, qualification, or parenthetical remark – 'No, what I write is not negative theology.'"[13] Although this claim corresponds to Caputo's reading, it is not supported by the passage in question. Derrida writes:

> No, what I write is not "negative theology." First of all, *in the measure* to which this belongs to the predicative or judicative space of discourse, to its strictly propositional form ... Next, in the measure to which "negative theology" seems to reserve, beyond all positive predication, beyond all negation, even beyond Being, some hyperessentiality, a being beyond Being.[14]

---

[11] Ibid.
[12] For instance, James K. A. Smith's essay "Determined Hope" presents itself as a critique of Derrida's account of hope, but it quotes Caputo as often as Derrida, and it treats Caputo's comments as if he spoke for Derrida (James K. A. Smith, "Determined Hope: A Phenomenology of Christian Expectation," in *The Future of Hope: Christian Tradition amid Modernity and Postmodernity*, ed. Miroslav Volf and William Katerberg [Grand Rapids, MI: William B. Eerdmans Pub. Co., 2004], 200–27). In the most extreme example of the widespread elision between Caputo and Derrida, Michael Horton goes so far as to attribute to Derrida words that were actually written by Caputo ("Eschatology after Nietzsche: Apollonian, Dionysian or Pauline?," *International Journal of Systematic Theology* 2, no. 1 [March 1, 2000]: nn. 35–38, 40).
[13] Mary-Jane Rubenstein, "Dionysius, Derrida, and the Critique of 'Ontotheology,'" *Modern Theology* 24, no. 4 (2008): 727. Rubenstein cites Caputo at important points in the body of her text (e.g., 727, 732), and she acknowledges that "this project is deeply indebted to his insight" (740).
[14] Jacques Derrida, "How to Avoid Speaking: Denials," in *Derrida and Negative Theology*, ed. Harold G. Coward and Toby A. Foshay (Albany: State University of New York Press, 1991), 77; emphasis

As few readers acknowledge, Derrida's claim that "what I write is not 'negative theology'" is qualified by the decisive phrase (italicized in the original) "*in the measure* to which." Rather than denying negative theology altogether, Derrida distances himself from it only to the extent that negative theology (first) remains propositional and (second) attempts to refer to a being beyond Being. This entails that Derrida and Dionysius might be very close "*in the measure* to which" another reading of Dionysius is possible.

In fact, Derrida repeatedly acknowledges the possibility of such a reading. Directly before this passage Derrida writes, "Until now, confronted by the question or by the objection [concerning the affinity between deconstruction and negative theology], my response has always been brief, elliptical, and dilatory. Yet it seems to me already articulated in two stages."[15] As he goes on to describe, his qualified disavowal of negative theology corresponds to the first of these stages, in which (he says) "I thought I had to forbid myself to write in the register of 'negative theology,' because I was aware of this movement toward hyperessentiality."[16] So he thought, but his reading evolved over the course of his career. Derrida continues, "Turning to what was often the second stage of my improvised responses: the general name of 'negative theology' may conceal the confusions it causes and sometimes gives rise to simplistic interpretations."[17] Derrida undermines the assumption that the name "negative theology" corresponds to a univocal movement. Instead, he argues that the tradition can be read in more than one way.

Throughout "How to Avoid Speaking" Derrida's discussion of the tradition attends to its complexity. He generally places the phrase "negative theology" in quotation marks, which indicates that it is a shorthand that may be misleading. In his earlier work, this caution is already evident. In the decisive passage of "Différance," he adds a phrase in French that is omitted in the English translation: *comme on sait*, "as one knows."[18] This

---

original. He immediately adds, "This is the word that Dionysius so often uses in the *Divine Names*: *hyperousios, -ôs, hyperousiotes*. God as being beyond Being or also God as *without* Being."

[15] Ibid. [16] Ibid., 79. [17] Ibid., 82.

[18] "Et pourtant ce qui se marque ainsi de la différance n'est pas théologique, pas même de l'ordre le plus négatif de la théologie négative, celle-ci s'étant toujours affairée à dégager, comme on sait, une supra-essentialité par-delà les catégories finies de l'essence et de l'existence, c'est-à-dire de la présence, et s'empressant toujours de rappeler que si le prédicat de l'existence est refusé à Dieu, c'est pour lui reconnaître un mode d'être supérieur, inconcevable, ineffable" (Jacques Derrida, *Marges De La Philosophie*, in *Collection "Critique"* [Paris: Éditions de Minuit, 1972], 6). Five years earlier, Derrida had reflected on the theme of superessentiality in Dionysius in connection with Philo, Plotinus, John Scot Eriugena, and Nicholas of Cusa (Jacques Derrida, "L'argument Ontologique et Autres Preuves de l'existence de Dieu," March 1962, 23–24, 219DRR/220/6, Fonds Jacques Derrida, IMEC, Saint-Germain-la-blanche herbe, Normandie.).

highlights the conventional character of an opinion he comes to complicate. Derrida's early worry concerning superessentialism was never intended to serve as a blanket evaluation of the texts in question. Instead, he describes this stage in his reading of negative theology as a hesitation rather than a developed objection, and he refers to "my uneasiness" in the past tense.[19]

Derrida's unpublished papers demonstrate that his preoccupation with negative theology began much earlier than most commentators recognize. In 1949, while a student at Lycée Louis-le-Grand, Derrida mentions Dionysius in a paper written for a course with Etienne Borne, "Recherches sur L'Hellenisme."[20] Here Dionysius serves as a link between Platonism and Christianity. A few years later, at the outset of Derrida's teaching career, Dionysius reappears in a pair of courses Derrida taught at the Sorbonne. In "Le sense du transcendental" (1961–62), Derrida discusses Dionysius in the context of an examination of medieval theology that stretches over much of the semester.[21] In the next year, Derrida's course on "L'argument Ontologique et autres preuves de l'existence de Dieu" reflects upon on the theme of superessentiality in Dionysius in connection with Philo, Plotinus, John Scotus Eriugena, and Nicholas of Cusa.[22] Derrida's treatment of negative theology in "Différance" and "How to Avoid Speaking" thus occurs in the context of a longstanding engagement with medieval Christian thought and with Dionysius in particular.

Derrida's first published reference to negative theology comes in one of his earliest publications, "Edmond Jabès and the Question of the Book" (1964). Here his worry about superessentialism does not appear at all.[23] When Derrida does mention superessentialism later that year in "Violence and Metaphysics" (1964), he comments that it is "in its literality" that negative theology concerns itself with an infinite existent. This suggests

---

[19] Derrida, "How to Avoid Speaking: Denials," 78–79.
[20] Jacques Derrida, "Recherches Sur L'Hellenisme (Khâgne, Lycée Louis-le-Grand, première année)," 1949, 37, 219DRR/336/7, Fonds Jacques Derrida, IMEC, Saint-Germain-la-blanche herbe, Normandie.
[21] Jacques Derrida, "Le Sens Du Transcendental (Enseignement à la Sorbonne)," 1961, 219DRR/219/13, Fonds Jacques Derrida, IMEC, Saint-Germain-la-blanche herbe, Normandie.
[22] Derrida, "L'argument Ontologique." Some years later (1986–87), Dionysius appears again in one of Derrida's unpublished lectures: Jacques Derrida, "Théologico-Politique: Nationalité et Nationalisme Philosophique," 1986, 219DRR/175/1, Fonds Jacques Derrida, IMEC, Saint-Germain-la-blanche herbe, Normandie. Cf. Edward Baring, *The Young Derrida and French Philosophy, 1945–1968* (Cambridge: Cambridge University Press, 2011), 67.
[23] Jacques Derrida, "Edmond Jabès and the Question of the Book," in *Writing and Difference*, trans. Alan Bass (Chicago: University of Chicago Press, 1978), 71.

92   Beyond Indeterminacy and Dogma

once again that other readings remain possible.[24] A few years later, in "From a Restricted to a General Economy" (1967), Derrida again qualifies the suggestion that negative theology reserves a predication beyond being: "Perhaps: for here we are touching upon the limits and the greatest audacities of discourse in Western thought."[25] In "Ellipsis" (1967), "Qual Quelle" (1971), *Dissemination* (1972), *The Truth in Painting* (1978), and "What Remains by Force of Music" (1978) Derrida's references to negative theology are all neutral, and none raises the specter of superessentialism.[26] In Derrida's later texts, his discussion of negative theology becomes more overtly positive, and his early worry about superessentialism rarely appears.[27]

Since Derrida refers to "negative theology" repeatedly throughout his career, usually without mentioning superessentialism, and since Derrida's concern regarding superessentialism is qualified each time it appears, Caputo is wrong to claim that Derrida consistently complains that negative theology is superessentialist.[28] In an essay written in 1981, five years before

---

[24] Derrida, "Violence and Metaphysics," 146.
[25] Jacques Derrida, "From a Restricted to a General Economy," in *Writing and Difference*, trans. Alan Bass (Chicago: University of Chicago Press, 1978), 271.
[26] Jacques Derrida, "Ellipsis," in *Writing and Difference*, trans. Alan Bass (Chicago: University of Chicago Press, 1978), 297; Jacques Derrida, "Qual Quelle," in *Margins of Philosophy*, trans. Alan Bass (Chicago: University of Chicago Press, 1982), 282; Jacques Derrida, *Dissemination* (Chicago: University Press, 1981), 5; Jacques Derrida, *The Truth in Painting* (Chicago: University of Chicago Press, 1987), 176; Jacques Derrida, "What Remains by Force of Music," in *Psyche: Inventions of the Other, Volume I*, Meridian: Crossing Aesthetics (Stanford, CA: Stanford University Press, 2007), 87–88.
[27] See Derrida, "A Number of Yes," 237; Jacques Derrida, "A Madness Must Watch over Thinking," in *Points . . .: Interviews, 1974–1994*, Meridian: Crossing Aesthetics (Stanford, CA: Stanford University Press, 1995), 353; Jacques Derrida, "Circumfession," in *Jacques Derrida*, Religion and Postmodernism, by Geoffrey Bennington and Jacques Derrida (Chicago: University of Chicago Press, 1993), 44; Derrida, "Sauf Le Nom (Post Scriptum)," 35ff; Jacques Derrida, *Aporias*, Meridian: Crossing Aesthetics (Stanford, CA: Stanford University Press, 1993), 19, 80; Jacques Derrida, *Monolingualism of the Other, or, The Prosthesis of Origin*, Cultural Memory in the Present (Stanford, CA: Stanford University Press, 1998), 71; Derrida, *Rogues*, 8, 82; Jacques Derrida, "Abraham, the Other," in *Judeities: Questions for Jacques Derrida*, ed. Bettina Bergo, Joseph D Cohen, and Raphael Zagury-Orly (New York: Fordham University Press, 2007), 25.
[28] Derrida warned against just this sort of reading at a conference convened by Caputo himself: "My texts on the subject [negative theology] are written texts, by which I mean that they are not a thesis on a theme. They have a pragmatic aspect, a performative aspect that would require another kind of analysis . . . Each time I address the question of negative theology, I very cautiously put these words in quotation marks, in the plural" (Jacques Derrida, "Derrida's Response to Jean-Luc Marion," in *God, the Gift, and Postmodernism*, ed. John D. Caputo and Michael J. Scanlon [Bloomington: Indiana University Press, 1999], 43). In one of the earliest interventions in the debate over Derrida and negative theology, Kevin Hart writes, "While [Derrida's remarks upon negative theology] are often dogmatic, they also show signs of a certain unease. The dogmatism is explained by Derrida's perfectly legitimate desire to establish that his discourse is not a negative theology . . . Writing of Pseudo-Dionysius, Meister Eckhart or even Georges Bataille, Derrida has the one theme: 'The

"How to Avoid Speaking," Derrida explains that "I am ... quite convinced of the need for a rigorous and differentiated reading of everything advanced under this title (negative theology)."[29] In contrast to his interpreters, Derrida claims that negative theology must be read on more than one level rather than simply rejected. He continues, "What is called 'negative theology' (a rich and very diverse corpus) does not let itself be easily assembled under the general category of 'onto-theology-to-be-deconstructed.'"[30] Caputo claims that, according to Derrida, "negative theology is caught up in a higher moralization of onto-theo-logy."[31] In contrast, the range of Derrida's engagement with the tradition indicates that, for him, the question concerning the status of predicative discourse is secondary. In keeping with his commitment to an ethics of uncertainty, Derrida's primary interest in negative theology is ethical.[32]

From Predication to Praise

Jean-Luc Marion's treatment of deconstruction and negative theology shifts focus from the narrow issue regarding the status of predication by interpreting Dionysius through the lens of liturgical praise. In *The Idol and Distance* (1977), Marion argues that Dionysius describes "a nonpredicative theory of discourse ... a discourse in the modality of praise."[33] According to Marion, predication is inappropriate to the divine because it collapses the distance between God and everything else. Marion writes, "When it predicates categorically, language produces objects and, whatever they might be, eliminates distance through that very appropriation."[34] Marion concludes that any attempt to appropriate God through a category of thought is inevitably idolatrous. In his reading, however, "[Dionysius] tends to substitute for the *to say* of predicative language another verb,

---

negative movement of the discourse on God is only a phase of positive ontotheology'" (*The Trespass of the Sign*, 188–89). Although I generally agree with Hart's argument in this book, I think Derrida's engagement with negative theology is more complex than he allows.

[29] Jacques Derrida, "Letter to John P. Leavey," *Semeia* 23 (1982): 61. [30] Ibid.
[31] Caputo, *Prayers and Tears*, 7.
[32] In my view, Mary-Jane Rubenstein is right that most commentators focus on the discursive analogy between deconstruction and negative theology, to the neglect of the ethico-political dimension ("Dionysius, Derrida, and the Critique of 'Ontotheology,'" 728). In seeking to correct this lacuna, my argument is close to Thomas Carlson's *Indiscretion: Finitude and the Naming of God* (Chicago: University of Chicago Press, 1999).
[33] Jean-Luc Marion, *The Idol and Distance: Five Studies*, Perspectives in Continental Philosophy no. 17 (New York: Fordham University Press, 2001), 138.
[34] Ibid., 184.

hymnein, to praise," which indicates "the passage from discourse to prayer."³⁵ On this view, praise no longer attempts to establish the correspondence of predicate to subject, opting instead for a "praise as" that is no longer categorical.³⁶ In contrast to the idolatrous violation of distance that occurs in predication, here language is iconically comprehended by distance.³⁷ "Thus," Marion says, "distance . . . can be endlessly traversed."³⁸

Twenty years later, in "In the Name" (1997), Marion argues that Dionysius's third way – besides (predicative) affirmation and negation – is the source of his superiority. Marion writes, "Negative theology does not furnish deconstruction with new material or an unconscious forerunner, but with its first serious rival, perhaps the only one possible. In short, for deconstruction what is at issue in 'negative theology' is not first of all 'negative theology,' but deconstruction itself, its originality and its final pre-eminence."³⁹ In Marion's view, Derrida stops too soon, whereas Dionysius goes further, giving us a God who is nevertheless deconstructed.

Marion claims that negative theology threatens Derrida with irrelevance insofar as it "claims to put us in the presence of God in the very degree to which it denies all presence."⁴⁰ For this reason, he concludes that negative theology undermines deconstruction's supposed superiority. Marion claims that "for Derrida . . . the task is to stigmatize 'negative theology's' persistence in making affirmations about God."⁴¹ In his view, Derrida misses the central aim of the Dionysian corpus, which is to place one in the presence of God through nonpredicative praise. To this end, Marion argues that Derrida attempts to "disqualify the latter (*hymnein*) as a disguised form of predication."⁴² However, a close reading reveals that Derrida is more concerned with pragmatics than predication. Derrida writes that "an experience must yet guide the apophasis toward excellence . . . This experience is that of prayer."⁴³ Derrida's concern is not that this constitutes a contraband predication; instead, his point is that (on the level of practice) a prayer of this kind identifies an object in a way that circumscribes the negativity of *apophasis*. "It adjusts discursive asceticism," Derrida says, mitigating apophatic critique by directing language toward a specified end.⁴⁴ He writes that "prayer in itself . . . implies nothing other than the supplicating address to the other," whereas "the encomium [i.e., praise], although it is not a simple attributive speech,

---

³⁵ Ibid. For the definitive treatment of Marion's reading of Dionysius, see Jones, *A Genealogy of Marion's Philosophy of Religion: Apparent Darkness*.
³⁶ Marion, *The Idol and Distance*, 186.   ³⁷ Ibid., 187.   ³⁸ Ibid., 186.
³⁹ Marion, "In the Name," 22.   ⁴⁰ Ibid.   ⁴¹ Ibid., 23.   ⁴² Ibid.
⁴³ Derrida, "How to Avoid Speaking: Denials," 110.   ⁴⁴ Ibid.

Hope in a Secular Age 95

nevertheless preserves an irreducible relationship to the attribution."[45] On this view, insofar as a prayer praises God for particular things, it attributes qualities to its object. Even if this does not take the form of a straightforward predication (such as "God is good"), to praise God for God's goodness indirectly attributes goodness to God.[46] Thus, when Dionysius writes that "one of the inspired prophets lifts a hymn of praise to the 'good' spirit," the address *to* is separable from the praise *as* "good."[47] Derrida's primary concern is not whether praise is secretly predicative, but rather the way in which (pragmatically) it determines the object of prayer.[48]

Derrida's reading highlights the tension I described in Chapter 2 between Dionysius's apophatic negativity and his affirmation of Christian practice. Marion writes, quoting Dionysius, "At the very moment of recognizing the superiority of the negations over the affirmations – 'and still more radically should we deny all affirmations [*kyriōteron apophaskein*]' – Dionysius still and always aims at what remains 'above every negation and affirmation [*hyper pasan kai aphairesin kai thesin*]' and therefore 'considerably above every privation [*hyper tas stereseis*].'"[49] According to Marion, Dionysian *apophasis* is finally surpassed by the discourse of praise. For this reason, he claims that "[*apophasis*] does not contend face-to-face with the affirmative way ... for both must in the end yield to a third way."[50] Marion's translation of this passage could seem to confirm this reading, but close attention to the Greek text undermines his reading. As I argued in Chapter 2, when Dionysius gestures "above every

---

[45] Ibid., 111. In response to Marion, Derrida points out that "when I read Pseudo-Dionysius, I paid a lot of attention, precisely to the liturgical, to prayer, to the non-predicative form of discourse" (Derrida, "Derrida's Response to Jean-Luc Marion," 43).

[46] Compare Derrida's comment that "since the verb *to be* and the predicative act are implied in every other verb, and in every common noun, nonviolent language, in the last analysis, would be a language of pure invocation, pure adoration, proffering only proper nouns in order to call to the other from afar ... Would such a language still deserve its name?" ("Violence and Metaphysics," 147).

[47] DN 2.1 637A, 59.

[48] Derrida, "How to Avoid Speaking: Denials," 137–38, fn. 16. Denys Turner complains that "Derrida's Denys amounted to little more than a dismembered torso; in Derrida's hands Denys' theology is cut down to fragments of a nearly, but for Derrida not quite, radical enough apophaticism snipped in gobbets out of a few pages of the *Divine Names* but mainly from the *Mystical Theology* ... in wanton neglect of the liturgical books, the *Angelic* and *Ecclesiastical Hierarchies*" (Denys Turner, "How to Read the Pseudo-Denys Today?," *International Journal of Systematic Theology* 7, no. 4 [2005]: 428–29). In fact, Derrida does cite *The Ecclesiastical Hierarchy* and the Letters multiple times (Derrida, "How to Avoid Speaking: Denials," 92–94, 118). Moreover, Derrida's concern is to discern the character of the Dionysian apophaticism, not to argue that it doesn't go far enough. In addition, his reading is not limited to Dionysius's account of theological language; as I have argued throughout this book, his primary concern is ethical.

[49] Marion, "In the Name," 26.   [50] Ibid., 24.

negation and affirmation," the word he uses for negation is *aphairesis*; in contrast, *apophasis* consists in the juxtaposition of affirmation and negation to indicate that neither mode of speech is adequate to the divine.[51] For this reason, rather than yielding to the discourse of praise, the negativity of *apophasis* remains unqualified: it subjects all discourse to critique by juxtaposing an affirmation and a negation that are equal in extent.

Where Marion appeals to praise as an alternative to *apophasis*, Dionysius situates praise within the apophatic tension. Dionysius writes:

> The purpose of what I have to say is not to reveal [*ekphainein*] that being in its transcendence [*ou tēn hyperousion ousian*], for this is something unspeakable [*arrhēton*], something unknown [*agnōston*] and wholly unrevealed [*pantelōs anekphanton*], something above unity itself. What I wish to do is to sing a hymn of praise [*hymnēsai*] for the being-making procession of the absolute divine Source of being into the total domain of being.[52]

Here *hymnein* is opposed not to predication in particular but to disclosure (*ekphainein*) as such. Since divine transcendence is "unspeakable" (*arrhēton*), according to Dionysius, the language of praise remains subject to negation. This rules out any assurance that the discourse of praise reaches its object, and it precludes any confidence concerning whether it places one in God's presence. Where Marion's appeal to praise attempts to circumscribe negativity, Dionysian *apophasis* leaves no room for reassurance. Instead, as I argued in Chapter 3, Dionysian negative theology is sustained by an uncertain hope.

Hypercritique

Whereas Derrida identifies Dionysius's superessentialism as a point of tension within the Dionysian corpus, Marion does not see it as a problem. Marion argues that the Dionysian prefix *hyper-* allows him to refer to God beyond the antinomy between affirmation and negation. According to this view, to say that God is "beyond [*hyper*] speech, mind, or being itself" would mean that God can be praised using those terms without qualification.[53] On this point, Marion assimilates Dionysius to Thomas Aquinas. Marion writes that, for Aquinas, "Affirmation finally yields to eminence because God can be named as the cause of the perfections stated by the names – though with a causality surpassing their significations 'in a more

---

[51] MT 1.2 1000B, 136.   [52] DN 5.1 816B, 96.   [53] DN 1.1 588A, 49.

excellent and higher way.'"⁵⁴ Thus, according to Marion, *hyperousios* indicates that the category of being applies to God, albeit in a higher fashion.

This reading finds some support in the Dionysian corpus. He writes, "Since the unknowing of what is beyond being [*hyperousiotētos agnōsia*] is something above and beyond [*hyper*] speech, mind, or being itself, one should ascribe [*anatheteon*] to it an understanding [*epistēmēn*] beyond being [*hyperousion*]."⁵⁵ If *hyper* is read straightforwardly as "beyond," this passage could seem to confirm that the terms it modifies (being, speech, and mind) apply to God in a supereminent sense. However, in addition to signifying "exceeding," "over," "above," and "better than," the prefix *hyper-* also means "in violation of" and "earlier than."⁵⁶ Where the first reading secures a language that remains stable, the second indicates that no created category properly applies to God. On the latter reading, Dionysius's use of the term *hyper* insists upon a radical unknowing.

Derrida's qualified reservation concerning negative theology applies to the first of these readings, but he recognizes that the other is also possible. In "How to Avoid Speaking" Derrida explains that he chose to refer to Maurice de Gandillac's canonical French translation, "which is easily accessible and was very valuable to me as a first reading of Dionysius."⁵⁷ Gandillac's influence upon Derrida was early and extensive: he taught Derrida at l'École Normale Supérieure and directed his thesis, *La Problème de la Genèse dans la Philosophie de Husserl*.⁵⁸ In Gandillac's translation of the quoted passage, the second meaning of the Dionysian *hyper* recedes under the force of several shifts in semantic range.⁵⁹ Gandillac renders Dionysius's term *hyperousiotētos* ("beyond being") as *Suressentialité*. Where the Greek prefix *hyper-* sometimes carries a contrastive sense, the French *sur-* suggests spatial superiority. Whereas *hyperousiotētos* includes the root term *ousia*, which refers broadly to being or substance, Gandillac uses the Latinate *essence*, which suggests internal quiddity. Where Dionysius's term *anatheteon* ("one should ascribe to it") suggests an act of judgment that

---

⁵⁴ Marion, "In the Name," 24. ⁵⁵ DN 1.1 588A, 49.
⁵⁶ Henry George Liddell, *A Greek–English Lexicon*, Rev. and augm. throughout (Oxford: Clarendon Press, 1996).
⁵⁷ Derrida, "How to Avoid Speaking," 307, n. 5.
⁵⁸ Jacques Derrida, *Le Problème De La Genèse Dans La Philosophie De Husserl*, 1re éd, Epiméthée (Paris: Presses Universitaires de France, 1990).
⁵⁹ "L'inconnaissance de cette Suressentialité même qui dépasse raison, pensée et essence, tel droit être l'objet de la science suressentielle" (Pseudo-Dionysius l'Aréopagite, *Œuvres Complètes Du Pseudo-Denys l'Aréopagite*, trans. Maurice de Gandillac, Bibliothèque Philosophique [Paris: Aubier, Editions Montaigne, 1943], 68).

may fall short, Gandillac opts for a phrase – "droit être l'objet de la science suressentielle" – that makes God the object of superessential knowledge.

Gandillac was unable to attend Derrida's initial presentation of "Différance" – his apologies were noted at the start of the session – but his shadow hangs over the discussion.[60] The first response from the floor was from Brice Parain, who complained, "[*Différance*] is the source of everything and one cannot know it: it is the God of negative theology."[61] Derrida's initial reply – "It is and it is not ... It is above all not ..."[62] – encapsulates his ambivalence. On the one hand, at this point in his career Derrida's inclination is to emphasize the difference between his work and negative theology. At the same time, this very "is and is not" repeats the form of Dionysian *apophasis*. Parain retorts, "It is and it is not. Thus let us not speak of it," but Derrida is not content with this conclusion.[63] He responds, "*Différance* is not, it is not a being and it is not God (if, that is, this name is given to a being, even a supreme being)."[64] Even at this early stage, Derrida's distance from negative theology is subject to a decisive qualification. If God is a being (beyond being), then *différance* is not God – but what if God is not a being after all? Derrida implies that such a God might be identified with the indeterminate play he describes.

The form of negative theology from which Derrida distances himself in "Différance" is the Thomistic interpretation offered by Gandillac's translation of Dionysius, which reads the term *hyper* as establishing a stable reference beyond the ordinary use of language.[65] However, as Derrida appreciates, another reading is possible. Dionysius writes, "Nothing that is or is known can proclaim that hiddenness [*kryphiotēta*] beyond both thought and expression [*hyper panta kai logon kai noun*] of the beyond-beingly beyond being beyond-divinity, beyond all [*tēs hyper panta hyperousiōs hyperousēs hypertheotētos*]."[66] Here Dionysius indicates that the beyondness of God entails impenetrable hiddenness, which requires an intensifying concatenation of excess. Because the strange term

---

[60] Derrida, "The Original Discussion of 'Différance,'" 83.   [61] Ibid., 84.   [62] Ibid.   [63] Ibid.
[64] Ibid., 85.
[65] Kevin Hart argues that "Derrida assumes the *Thomist* reading of Pseudo-Dionysius" (Hart, *The Trespass of the Sign*, 193). Insofar as Derrida acknowledges from the outset that other readings of Dionysius are possible, I think this statement is half true.
[66] DN 13.3 981A, 129. Translation modified. This concatenation of "beyonds" is admittedly brutal, but the Greek phrase confounds the translator insofar as "beyond-divinity" is not an immediately recognizable (grammatical) object, while the English phrase "transcendent divinity" substantializes a reference that the Greek *hypertheotētos* keeps in motion.

hypertheotētos ("beyond divinity") still refers to the divine, it remains subject to a reading in terms of supereminence, but (as I have argued) it can also be seen as radically contrastive. In this way, the ambivalence of the *hyper* encapsulates the apophatic juxtaposition of affirmation and negation that enacts the dispossession of speech.

Persistent Secrets

Insofar as the Thomistic reading of the *hyperousios* asserts that Christians have a genuine (though qualified) knowledge of God, it is at odds with central features of the Dionysian corpus. Dionysius insists that "we must not dare to apply words or conceptions [*ou tolmēteon eipein oute mēn ennoēsai*] to this secret God beyond being [*tēs hyperousiou kai kryphias theotētos*]," only to add that "we can use only what scripture has disclosed."[67] For Dionysius, the superessentiality of God forbids us from applying words to God, yet speech is nevertheless permitted. Derrida comments, "This hyperessential goodness is not entirely incommunicable; it can manifest *itself*, but it remains separated by its hyperessentiality."[68] As I argued in Chapter 2, Dionysius's account of hierarchy exhibits the paradoxical tension of *apophasis*, for his resolute negativity stands beside the affirmation that some ecclesial authorities mediate the divine. The danger is that the denial of speech serves to cement the privilege of those who claim access to secret knowledge.

Derrida notes that Dionysius's "quasi-pedagogical and mystagogical speech" is directed to Timothy – "*pros Timotheon*: the dedication of the Mystical Theology."[69] Whereas it might be tempting to pass over this address without comment, as indeed many do, Derrida asks, "What happens here?"[70] As he recognizes, *The Mystical Theology* is framed as attempt to teach Timothy how to approach the divine, and this inflects its significance. Dionysius writes, "Timothy, my friend, my advice to you as you look for a sight of hidden things [*ta mystika theamata*], is to leave behind you everything perceived and understood."[71] The suggestion that abandoning perception will allow one to see what is hidden is strange as such, and it seems stranger still in light of Dionysius's frequent insistence that God is beyond knowledge and speech. A little later Dionysius refers to "the truly hidden darkness of unknowing [*ton gnophon tēs agnōsias eisdynei*

---

[67] DN I.2 588C, 50. Translation modified.   [68] Derrida, "How to Avoid Speaking: Denials," 118.
[69] Ibid., 91.   [70] Ibid., 116.   [71] MT 1.1 997B, 135. Translation modified.

ton ontōs mystikon],"⁷² which confirms what we might suspect – if the darkness in question is truly hidden, it cannot be penetrated by knowledge. The question remains: does this denial of knowledge jeopardize the treatise's pedagogical function, or does the pedagogical frame delimit its apparent negativity?

As Derrida observes, this ambivalence has political ramifications. He writes, "Since the promise is also an order, the allegorical veil becomes a political shield, the solid barrier of a social division."⁷³ Dionysius's "advice" to Timothy is stated in the imperative; it asserts both Dionysius's authority and Timothy's privilege over others. The command that opens *The Mystical Theology* is quickly followed by another: "See to it that none of this comes to the hearing of the uninitiated [*amyētōn*]."⁷⁴ Since, Dionysius says, "initiation into the divine [*mystagōgiai*] is beyond such people [*hyper toutous*],"⁷⁵ it seems that the pedagogy he provides is to be permanently withheld from some. Dionysius writes, "Let us not suppose that the outward face of these contrived symbols [*synthēmatōn*] exists for its own sake. Rather, it is the shield [*probeblēsthai*] of the understanding of what is ineffable [*aporrētou*] and invisible to the common multitude [*tois pollois*]."⁷⁶ Whereas Dionysius elsewhere suggests that oblique modes of discourse are required by the transcendence of God, here symbolism functions as a means to separate privileged initiates from the *polloi*.⁷⁷ As we saw in Chapter 2, Dionysius insists that God is equally close to (and equally distant from) everything and everyone. For this reason, authoritarian secrecy is at odds with key features of his overall project.

This ambivalence provides *prima facie* evidence on behalf of Caputo's efforts to separate Derrida and Dionysius. Caputo writes, "Negative or mystical theology is very strong theology indeed, its deferrals serving to strengthen an absolutely central and powerful transcendence accompanied by a strong sense of who is in and who is out of the secret."⁷⁸ However, Derrida himself argues that this secrecy is not unique to Dionysius. In "Of an Apocalyptic Tone" (1980), Derrida expresses his unease with a secrecy linked to elitism. He writes, "The mystagogues claim to possess as if in private the privilege of a mysterious secret ... The revelation or unveiling

---

⁷² MT 1.3 1001A, 137. Translation modified.
⁷³ Derrida, "How to Avoid Speaking: Denials," 93.
⁷⁴ MT I.2 1000A, 136. Translation modified.   ⁷⁵ MT 1.2 100A, 136.
⁷⁶ Ep. 9.1 1105C, 283. Translation modified.   ⁷⁷ E.g. CH 2.3 141B, 150.
⁷⁸ John D. Caputo, *The Weakness of God: A Theology of the Event* (Bloomington: Indiana University Press, 2006), 302, n. 16.

of the secret is reserved to them; they jealously protect it."[79] Using the same term (*mystagōgiai*) that Dionysius employs to refer to initiation into the divine mysteries, Derrida describes the sort of secret that may be considered a secure possession. This strategic secrecy asserts the presence of a revelatory unveiling (*apocalypsis* in Greek). Derrida explains that "they say they are in immediate and intuitive relation with a mystery. And they wish to attract, seduce, lead toward the mystery and by the mystery."[80] As Derrida notes, a secrecy of this kind is dangerous. Nevertheless, he suggests that it is impossible to avoid.

Derrida argues that even the most enlightened critique "keeps within itself some apocalyptic desire, this time as desire for clarity and revelation, in order to demystify or, if you prefer, to deconstruct apocalyptic discourse itself."[81] Because mystagogic secrecy could be opposed only by appealing to a superior unveiling, Derrida concludes that every judgment must appeal to a privileged knowledge. Indeed, he goes so far as to say that every predicative statement is apocalyptic insofar as it claims access to the truth. He comments on the Apocalypse of John, "Truth is the end and the instance of the last judgment. The structure of truth here would be apocalyptic."[82] Since every claim excludes other possibilities by asserting the presence of truth, Derrida suggests that the assertion of apocalyptic privilege is unavoidable. For this reason, although the Dionysian *hyperousios* problematically implies that some possess a privileged secrecy, Derrida himself exhibits this ambivalence.

Marion concludes that the Dionysian gesture "beyond" asserts secure access to God, and Caputo agrees. Both of them argue that this decisively divides Derrida and Dionysius, but I believe they are wrong on both counts. First, as I have described, the Dionysian *hyperousios* carries a contrastive as well as an excessive sense. On Dionysius's terms, the gesture beyond cannot secure access to God, for it also subjects any reference to God to apophatic critique. Second, rather than rejecting Dionysius as insufficiently negative, Derrida indicates that pure indeterminacy is impossible. As I argued in Chapter 1, Derrida insists that the key terms of his work – *différance*, justice, and so on – elude his own work, yet he does not take that as reason to stop speaking about them. Even as he deconstructs metaphysics with reference to *différance*, he admits that "*différance* remains

---

[79] Jacques Derrida, "Of an Apocalyptic Tone Newly Adopted in Philosophy," in *Derrida and Negative Theology*, ed. Harold G. Coward and Toby A. Foshay (Albany: State University of New York Press, 1991), 33.
[80] Ibid.   [81] Ibid., 51.   [82] Ibid., 53.

a metaphysical name."[83] Similarly, while critiquing apocalyptic mystagogy, Derrida admits that he himself is implicated within it. Derrida and Dionysius are therefore in the same situation: both insist upon a negativity that they cannot achieve, and both persist in an affirmation that is necessarily uncertain.[84] It is for this reason, as I argued in Chapter 3, they describe the discipline of hope.

Keeping a Bad Conscience

Although the scholarly literature on deconstruction and negative theology has generally focused on the status of predicative discourse, my argument indicates that the deepest affinity between Dionysius and Derrida lies on the level of ethics. As I argued in Chapter 1, Derrida's insistence upon self-critique serves an ethical function. In my reading, Derrida claims that every structure is subject to play and that identity is inevitably disrupted by *différance*. He makes this argument not to oppose metaphysics (which cannot be dispatched) but rather to resist the temptation to assert a false security. Derrida finds the same dynamic at work in apophatic negativity. He writes, "Why this language, which does not fortuitously resemble that of negative theology? How to justify the choice of negative form (aporia) to designate a duty that, through the impossible or the impracticable, nonetheless announces itself in an affirmative fashion? Because one must avoid good conscience at all costs."[85] The goal of Derrida's stringent self-critique

---

[83] Derrida, "Différance," 26.
[84] Although my emphasis on temporality is in some ways close to Richard Kearney's argument in Richard Kearney, *The God Who May Be: A Hermeneutics of Religion* (Bloomington: Indiana University Press, 2001), I read both deconstruction and negative theology differently than he does. Kearney writes, "For if the apophatic tradition – from negative theologians like Clement of Alexandria and Dionysius to Levinas, Derrida, and Marion – stresses the impossibility of saying anything meaningful about God, the opposing cataphatic tradition runs the risk of embracing overly 'positive' and foundationalist propositions. If the former, in short, tends to place God too far beyond being ... the latter is sometimes tempted to reduce God to being" (8; cf. Richard Kearney and Jens Zimmermann, eds., *Reimagining the Sacred: Richard Kearney Debates God with James Wood, Catherine Keller, Charles Taylor, Julia Kristeva, Gianni Vattimo, Simon Critchley, Jean-Luc Marion, John Caputo, David Tracey, Jens Zimmermann, and Merold Westphal* [New York: Columbia University Press, 2016], 58). As I argued in Chapter 2, for Dionysius apophatic negativity does not constitute a distinct tradition that is opposed to affirmation; instead, *apophasis* consists in the juxtaposition of affirmation and negation. In similar fashion, Derrida's critique does not preclude the possibility of saying anything meaningful about the transcendent; on the contrary, he continues to affirm particular judgments concerning justice (for instance) while holding those claims subject to revision. For this reason, I think deconstruction and negative theology inhabit the middle space that Kearney intends to affirm, but they do so without denying the need for negativity.
[85] Jacques Derrida, *Aporias*, Meridian: Crossing Aesthetics (Stanford, CA: Stanford University Press, 1993), 19.

is to resist complacency by maintaining an ethics of uncertainty, which opens an alternative to complacency and despair. In my reading, Derrida is drawn to negative theology because it, too, describes an affirmation without assurance.

As I argued in Chapter 2, Dionysius also sees intellectual complacency as a danger, and he too insists upon a self-critique that is oriented toward the future. He writes, "I myself might not have been stirred from this aporia [*ex aporias*] to my current search [*eis zētēsin*] ... had I not been confounded [*exetaraxe*] by the deformed imagery used by scripture in regard to the angels."[86] Dionysius notes that Christian scripture uses incongruous images for angels, and this is (for him) genuinely troubling. He explains, "We cannot, as mad people do, profanely visualize these heavenly and godlike intelligences as actually having numerous feet and faces. They are not shaped to resemble the brutishness of oxen or to display the wildness of lions. They do not have the curved beak of the eagle or the wings and feathers of birds."[87] Dionysius insists that these images cannot be taken at face value, for such spiritual beings surpass material symbols. But neither is an adequate interpretation available: "These pictures have to do with beings so simple that we can neither know nor contemplate them."[88] Unable either to rest content with the images as given or to see through to a higher understanding, angelic imagery presents Dionysius with no way forward. He does not take this as a cause for despair, however, but instead persists in an affirmation that he recognizes is uncertain.

Some Christians act as if theological authorities offer a certainty that absolves them of responsibility for the beliefs that they affirm, but Dionysius forecloses this maneuver. He says both that "it is not possible [*adynaton*] to know [*eidenai*] the mystery of these celestial minds" and that "I am content merely to set down, as well as I can, what it was that the sacred theologians perceived [*etheōrēthē*] of the angelic sights and what they shared with us about it."[89] Whereas this might suggest that one can circumvent the impossibility of knowledge by repeating authoritative statements, on Dionysius's terms even the most authoritative theology remains subject to negation. As I have described, the distinction Dionysius draws between present and future entails that Christian thought and practice is only provisional. On Dionysius's terms, any appeal to authority is a judgment for which one bears responsibility.

---

[86] CH 2.5 145B, 153. Translation modified.   [87] CH 2.1 137A, 147.   [88] CH 2.1 137B, 148.
[89] CH 6.1 200C, 160. Translation modified.

Derrida and Dionysius agree that complacency is a danger, and so both insist upon a strenuous negativity in order to maintain an ethical posture of openness to the future. Derrida writes, "You cannot prevent me from having a bad conscience, and that is the main motivation of my ethics and my politics."[90] Dionysius does not share Derrida's melancholic affect, but he is committed to the principle at stake. In "Sauf le nom" (1991), Derrida writes that "I trust no text that is not in some way contaminated with negative theology, and even among those texts that apparently do not have, want, or believe they have any relation with theology in general."[91] My reading suggests that he takes this view because negative theology opens the future by resisting complacency.

A few years later, in 1997, Derrida makes clear that his affinity with negative theology is politically significant. In the transcript of a conversation with Marion, Derrida explains, "Why do I insist on this, on this perplexity? Why, for instance, in *Sauf le nom*, do I try to articulate this with the problem of negative theology and phenomenology? ... I use the problematic of deconstruction and negative theology as a threshold to the definition of a new politics."[92] Here Derrida suggests that both deconstruction and negative theology exhibit a negativity that opens the possibility of political transformation. He immediately explains, "I am not saying this against Europe, against Judaism, Christianity, or Islam" – his aim is not to say that what currently obtains is bad, simply that it is not everything.[93] In his view, negative theology and *khora* provide a critical distance from the received understanding of particular traditions that form our world. By insisting upon a rigorous negativity, they relativize the status quo in favor of the unforeseeable future.

Mystical and Prophetic

Many commentators assume that mysticism is private and apolitical, but my argument indicates that mystical negativity complements the prophetic

---

[90] Jacques Derrida, "On Forgiveness: A Roundtable Discussion with Jacques Derrida," in *Questioning God*, ed. John D. Caputo, Mark Dooley, and Michael J. Scanlon (Bloomington: Indiana University Press, 2001), 69.
[91] Derrida, "Sauf Le Nom (Post Scriptum)," 69.
[92] Jacques Derrida and Jean-Luc Marion, "On the Gift: A Discussion between Jacques Derrida and Jean-Luc Marion," in *God, the Gift, and Postmodernism*, ed. John D. Caputo and Michael J. Scanlon (Bloomington: Indiana University Press, 1999), 76.
[93] Ibid.

pursuit of justice.⁹⁴ Caputo writes, "Derrida's discourse about the name of God has to do with prophetic justice, not Christian Neoplatonism. The name of God for Derrida has a prophetic not an apophatic force, and is more Jewish than Christian, more religious than theological, more concerned with the ethico-politics of hospitality than with mystical or negative theology."⁹⁵ Where Caputo divides the prophetic (which he associates with Judaism) from the mystical (which he blames upon Greek philosophy), Derrida links mystical negativity to a politics oriented toward a justice to come.⁹⁶ Similarly, in defiance of the simplistic oppositions on which Caputo relies, Dionysius draws on Greek philosophy and biblical symbolism to describe an ethical practice of openness to transformation. In my view, Dionysius and Derrida describe a disciplined hope that is politically potent.

Marion and Dionysius share certain first-order political instincts insofar as both exhibit a predilection for hierarchy. However, as I argued in Chapter 2, Dionysius subjects the hierarchical system as a whole to apophatic critique. Where Marion claims that the bishop is the only true theologian, Dionysian *apophasis* relativizes every authority in the recognition that there is no grasping God.⁹⁷ Marion's defense of Dionysius against Derrida implies that Christians require the assurance that they are directed toward God, but this is a security that Dionysius precludes. Where Marion and Caputo suggest that we must choose between a confident traditionalism and an indeterminate spirituality, Dionysius demonstrates that a robustly doctrinal Christian faith can admit that it is profoundly uncertain.

Caputo claims that for Derrida "the secret has an apophatic quality, *not* in the sense of negative theology, which is a hyperousiological high to

---

⁹⁴ Mysticism is often seen as solitary because it is associated with an extraordinary form of experience. (See William James, *Varieties of Religious Experience: A Study in Human Nature* [London: Routledge, 2002], 314, 328, 333). As I argued in Chapter 2, Dionysius undermines claims to such experience, and as I show at length in Chapter 6, his project is profoundly political.
⁹⁵ Caputo, "Apostles of the Impossible," 220–21; see Caputo, *Prayers and Tears*, xxiv, 11, 28, 30.
⁹⁶ I think Arthur Bradley is right: "[Caputo's] argument that deconstruction is a 'religion without religion' has a tendency to fall into a series of simple and potentially essentialist distinctions between specificity and generality, content and form, and so on, which concepts like the 'without', translation, secrecy, and so on, help to problematize" ("Without Negative Theology: Deconstruction and the Politics of Negative Theology," *Heythrop Journal* 42, no. 2 [2001]: 146). Caputo partially retracts his nervousness about theology in *The Weakness of God*, 301, but it nevertheless shapes his reading of Derrida.
⁹⁷ Jean-Luc Marion, *God without Being: Hors-Texte*, Religion and Postmodernism (Chicago: University of Chicago Press, 1991), 153.

which certain select initiates may be introduced ... Rather the 'absolute secret' is apophaticism itself, the stuff of ... a 'general apophatics.'"[98] This is, strictly speaking, nonsense. As I argued in Chapter 2, insofar as apophatic negativity consists in the dispossession of speech, it is inseparable from the affirmative discourse to which it responds. In my reading, this is why Dionysius uses both positive and negative modes of speech; on his account, the juxtaposition of affirmation and negation destabilizes discourse more effectively than either alone.[99] Whereas no one can live in the generalized indeterminacy that Caputo envisions, Dionysius offers a way to hold particular commitments while resisting the danger of dogmatic complacency.

As I have argued, this ethical discipline is what Dionysius and Derrida share most deeply. Where Caputo assumes that Derrida can accommodate apophatic negativity but not the affirmation of a determinate tradition, in Chapter 1 I showed that Derrida's critique allows the affirmation of particular commitments. In contrast to Caputo's insistence that Derrida's messianism is entirely indeterminate, I argued in Chapter 3 that Derrida and Dionysius both affirm particular hopes while holding them open to revision. In my account, Derrida and Dionysius hold different first-order political commitments, but they maintain a similar relation to the commitments that they hold. This is possible because they share a hope that is identical in kind though not in content – a disciplined persistence in the face of uncertainty. Insofar as hope holds desires that are vulnerable to disappointment, it is necessary neither to pretend that things are more certain than they are nor to stigmatize concrete commitment.

Against indeterminacy and dogma, Derrida and Dionysius maintain particular commitments while simultaneously acknowledging they may be misguided. In Chapter 5 I will argue that, rather than valorizing the "religious" over and against the "theological," as Caputo suggests, Derrida's hope offers a way to acknowledge the volatility of religious commitment while allowing religious communities to contribute to the public sphere of secular politics. Following this suggestion, in Chapter 6 I argue that, although Dionysius did not directly address modern politics,

---

[98] Caputo, *Prayers and Tears*, 106.
[99] I learned this from Denys Turner, *The Darkness of God: Negativity in Christian Mysticism* (Cambridge: Cambridge University Press, 1995), 34; also see Denys Turner, *Julian of Norwich, Theologian* (New Haven, CT: Yale University Press, 2011), 24–27.

he points to a politics of hope that can enrich political reflection. Where others appropriate divine authority in an effort to sacralize earthly power, Dionysius articulates a sacramental theology that desacralizes everything, including Christian worship. In this way, he models a negative political theology, which affirms particular policies while holding them open to future development.

CHAPTER 5

Atheism and the Future of Faith

The account of hope that I have developed over the previous four chapters is implicitly political. Where some theorists worry that deconstructive critique precludes constructive political reflection, I have argued that Derrida's negativity functions instead to keep political commitments in motion. Similarly, although mysticism is often seen as an extraordinary experience of union with God, I read Dionysian mystical theology as an ethical discipline that renders Christian thought and practice radically provisional. Insofar as both authors describe an affirmation without assurance, they clarify the character of hope. On my account, hope acknowledges its vulnerability to disappointment but presses forward nonetheless; in this way, it models a circumspect commitment that is essential for the health of individuals and communities. Over the next two chapters, I will make the political significance of this argument explicit.

In this chapter I will argue that my account of hope clarifies the relation between religion and secular politics. In medieval Europe most people were Christian as if by inertia. Although it was possible to disavow Christian faith, many people did not experience their religious identity as a deliberate choice – Christianity was part of the social fabric, and individuals were woven within it. This is now no longer the case. Religion has not disappeared, but people are aware that their religiosity (or lack thereof) is one option among others.[1] In some communities it is hard not to be Christian, just as in others it is hard not to be atheistic, but both are subcultures (however much they might like to claim hegemony). Because religion is no longer a source of consensus, some theorists conclude that it is not appropriate to appeal to religious reasons in political debate.[2]

---

[1] I have some differences with Charles Taylor's account of secularization in *A Secular Age*, but I think he is right on this point. See the Introduction, above, and the discussion of Taylor, Talal Asad, and José Casanova below.

[2] See John Rawls, *Political Liberalism* (New York: Columbia University Press, 1993); Robert Audi, *Religious Commitment and Secular Reason* (Cambridge; New York: Cambridge University Press,

I will argue that it is both impossible and unnecessary to exclude religion from public life, but I think the impulse is understandable. Mark Lilla claims that religion is dangerous because it disrupts rational reflection on political order. Following Thomas Hobbes, Lilla acknowledges that religion offers comfort in the face of a threatening world, but he observes that it introduces a deeper source of anxiety – since divine judgment is a threat worse than death, religious belief carries a terrifying authority. In Lilla's view, religion sets in motion a vicious cycle: fear breeds religious fanaticism, fanaticism inspires violence, and this violence in turn amplifies the insecurity that encouraged fanaticism in the first place. For this reason, according to Lilla, religion and politics should be strictly separated.

Although Derrida is rarely considered in the Anglophone debate over religion and politics, his ethics of uncertainty offers a compelling rebuttal to a programmatic secularism of this kind.[3] Like Lilla, Derrida believes that religious traditions are sometimes the source of violence, and he agrees that politics should not be dominated by theocratic authority. However, where Lilla focuses on the effects of religious authority, Derrida argues that the influence of religious traditions is subtle, subterranean, and surprisingly persistent. In parallel with recent scholarship on secularization, Derrida observes that religious patterns of thought and practice remain operative within disenchanted modernity, which suggests that the secular and the religious cannot be separated.

Derrida is an atheist of a certain sort, but his work undermines the antagonism toward religion that some interpreters attribute to him. On his account, it is impossible to exclude religion altogether, for the play of *différance* disrupts every attempt at purity. Thus, although Derrida is uneasy about religion, he draws upon religious traditions for the purpose of political reflection. Because religious traditions open imagination to a justice that transcends the status quo, Derrida suggests that politics would be impoverished without them. Where some aim to contain the disruptive

---

2000). Rawls later moderated his view in John Rawls, "The Idea of Public Reason Revisited," *University of Chicago Law Review* 64, no. 3 (1997): 756–807.

[3] The term "secularism" is used in various ways. The secularism I take Derrida to oppose is a programmatic secularism that forbids overt religiosity in the public sphere; this is distinct from a procedural secularism that prohibits the state from preferring one religious group other others. Whereas programmatic secularism seeks to exclude religion from the public sphere, procedural secularism preserves the neutrality of the state so as to allow all parties (religious and otherwise) to intervene politically. As I argue in this chapter, Derrida affirms secularism in this second, restricted sense. For more on this distinction, see Craig J. Calhoun, Mark Juergensmeyer, and Jonathan VanAntwerpen, "Introduction," in *Rethinking Secularism*, ed. Craig J. Calhoun, Mark Juergensmeyer, and Jonathan VanAntwerpen (New York: Oxford University Press, 2011), 8–9; Rowan Williams, *Faith in the Public Square* (London; New York: Bloomsbury, 2012), 2–3.

force of religion by excluding it from the public sphere, Derrida demonstrates that it is possible (through hope) to endure instability for the sake of something more important than safety.

The Great Separation

Lilla presents a compelling account of the danger religion poses to political order. Although he acknowledges that some believers patiently wait for God's kingdom to come, he claims that the faithful are inevitably tempted to bring the kingdom into being by force. In his view, eschatological desire is volatile: "Heresies, false prophecies, peasant revolts, massacres, genocides, self-immolations – the history of messianic movements bulges with them."[4] This problem is compounded by the fact that, insofar as the demands of revelation are inaccessible to unaided reason, they are not subject to the prudent evaluation that might satisfy a neutral observer. Lilla observes, "If God has commands regarding activity in the world, they will be inscrutable to outsiders and impervious to reason. In such a mindset the theological imagination becomes free to ponder extreme possibilities."[5] For this reason, Lilla concludes, religion is a danger that cannot be mitigated.

Lilla argues that the sixteenth-century wars of religion demonstrated that religion is politically corrosive. He writes, "Christian fanaticism and intolerance incited violence; violence set secular and religious leaders against one another; and the more violent and fearful political life became, the more fanatical and intolerant Christians became."[6] According to Lilla, modern political philosophers concluded in response to this pattern that it was necessary to set politics upon a different foundation. In their view, he says, "A decent political life could not be realized within the terms set by Christian political theology, which bred violent eschatological passions and stifled human development."[7] Rather than entering the tortuous debate about God's nature and intentions for the world, these philosophers decided that political reflection should be separated from theological considerations.

---

[4] Mark Lilla, *The Stillborn God: Religion, Politics, and the Modern West* (New York: Knopf, 2007), 243; see Mark Lilla, "Extremism's Theological Roots," *The Jerusalem Post*, October 8, 2001.
[5] Lilla, *The Stillborn God*, 2007, 252.
[6] Ibid., 57, cf. 83. There is reason to think that Lilla's account of the wars of religion is overly simplistic: see William T. Cavanaugh, *The Myth of Religious Violence: Secular Ideology and the Roots of Modern Conflict* (Oxford; New York: Oxford University Press, 2009).
[7] Lilla, *The Stillborn God*, 2007, 217–18.

This is what Lilla calls "the Great Separation," which he traces to Hobbes.[8] Hobbes argues that, whereas the sum of animal happiness consists in everyday pleasures, this is only because animals lack the ability to look forward (to the future) and back (to discover the cause of their pleasure and pain). Unfortunately for us, humans have the capacity to predict what is likely to happen on the basis of causal relations that we have observed in the past. For this reason, Hobbes says, "It is impossible for a man, who continually endeavoureth to secure himself against the evil he fears, and procure the good he desireth, not to be in a perpetual solicitude of the time to come."[9] In contrast to the absorption of animals in present experiences, humans are aware of their extension in time, which means that they recognize that momentary happiness is inevitably fragile. Thus, Hobbes says, "Man, which looks too far before him, in the care of future time, hath his heart all the day long, gnawed on by fear of death, poverty, or other calamity; and has no repose, nor pause of his anxiety, but in sleep."[10] In his view, because humans are conscious of time, they are consumed by the future.

According to Hobbes, people attempt to constrain their anxiety by understanding causal relationships. He writes, "Anxiety for the future time, disposeth men to inquire into the causes of things: because the knowledge of them, maketh men the better able to order the present to their best advantage."[11] Knowledge of causes is important because it allows us to protect ourselves against the dangers posed by the future. However, we cannot know what will be, and the limited knowledge we can attain is not enough. Hobbes explains, "No man can know by discourse, that this, or that, is, has been, or will be; which is to know absolutely: but only, that if this be, that is; if this has been, that has been; if this shall be, that shall be."[12] In his view, discursive reason cannot yield knowledge of what is necessary; all it can show is that one state entails another, and even these causal relationships are uncertain. For this reason, people are constantly aware that their present happiness may suddenly change.

Hobbes thinks this anxiety is what drives people to religion. He writes,

> This perpetual fear, always accompanying mankind in the ignorance of causes ... must needs have for object something. And therefore when there

---

[8] In my view, Lilla exaggerates Hobbes's hostility toward religion. For an alternative reading, see Aloysius Martinich, *The Two Gods of Leviathan: Thomas Hobbes on Religion and Politics* (Cambridge; New York: Cambridge University Press, 1992), 13–15.
[9] Thomas Hobbes, *Leviathan*, ed. Richard Tuck (Cambridge; New York: Cambridge University Press, 1991), 76.
[10] Ibid.   [11] Ibid., 74.   [12] Ibid., 46.

is nothing to be seen, there is nothing to accuse, either of their good, or evil fortune, but some power, or agent invisible: in which sense perhaps it was, that some of the old poets said, that the gods were at first created by human fear.[13]

Hobbes does not explain why it is necessary for fear to have an object, but it is not hard to imagine that fear becomes easier to bear when it is localized. In his view, people invent gods when they are unable to identify a cause for their fear. He explains, "This fear of things invisible, is the natural seed of that, which every one in himself calleth religion; and in them that worship, or fear that power otherwise than they do, superstition."[14] The point is subtle enough that one might miss it: whereas "superstition" implies an irrational credulity, Hobbes claims that its only difference from the more neutral category "religion" concerns whether the speaker worships the gods in question. Both, he believes, are born from frantic anxiety.

Hobbes concludes that religious hopes are unreliable. He writes, "There is no natural knowledge of man's estate after death ... but only a belief grounded upon other men's saying that they know it supernaturally, or that they know those, that knew them, that knew others, that knew it supernaturally."[15] Hobbes observes that, because no one knows what comes after death through normal means, religious beliefs concerning the future are based on human authority, even if they claim greater weight. For this reason, he says, religious belief is not faith in God but "Faith in men onely."[16] Hobbes concludes that religion is dangerous because it ascribes divine authority to leaders who remain all too human.

Late in *Leviathan*, Hobbes imagines a reader who wonders why he dwells so long on religion in a work devoted to politics. He explains that the mystifications of Aristotelian philosophy, mediated by scholastic theology, pose a threat to political order: "For who will endeavour to obey the Laws, if he expect Obedience to be Powred or Blown into him? ... Or who, that is in fear of Ghosts, will not bear great respect to those that can make the Holy Water, that drives them from him?"[17] According to Hobbes, religion introduces a source of authority that could compete with the state: if someone thinks that a priest possesses supernatural powers and divine authority, this may lead them to rebel against political authority.

---

[13] Ibid., 76. [14] Ibid., 75. [15] Ibid., 103. [16] Ibid., 49.
[17] Ibid., 465; cf. 260; cf. Thomas Hobbes, "Behemoth: The History of the Causes of the Civil Wars of England," in *The English Works of Thomas Hobbes, Vol. 6 (Dialogue, Behemoth, Rhetoric)*, ed. William Molesworth (Aalen: Scientia-Verl., 1839), 167, 171.

Because he believes the authority of the sovereign is absolute, Hobbes concludes that this would be disastrous.

Lilla writes, glossing Hobbes, "The reason human beings in war commit acts no animal would commit is, paradoxically, because they believe in God. Animals fight only to eat or reproduce; men fight to get into heaven."[18] Although religion is not the only source of violence, Lilla argues that it is particularly problematic insofar as it places one's ultimate fate at stake. Because religion provides a focal point for the generalized anxiety of temporal existence, it offers some comfort in the face of vulnerability. But because this comfort is unreliable, anxiety may bubble up unpredictably, thereby destabilizing political order. For this reason, Lilla concludes, religion and politics should be strictly separated.

The Persistence of Religion

Like Lilla, Derrida believes that religion is dangerous. Although Derrida frequently engages religious texts, he often does so with a palpable unease. Derrida's early work associates religion with metaphysics, and his later work worries about its political implications. He interprets ongoing conflict in the Middle East as a "war of messianic eschatologies," lamenting that "these three monotheisms fight over [Jerusalem] ... they make war with fire and blood ... , each claiming its particular perspective on this place and claiming an original historical and political interpretation of Messianism."[19] Because the conviction (on all sides) that the Messiah is on their side intensifies the conflict among them, Derrida shares Lilla's anxiety about the destabilizing effects of eschatology. What is more, in relation to particular cases, it could seem that Derrida endorses the programmatic secularism of the French state, which limits religious expression in the public sphere. In 1994, writing during the Algerian civil war, Derrida insists upon "the real dissociation of the theological and the political," explaining that "our idea of democracy implies a separation of state and religious power; that is, a radical secularism [laïcité] and a flawless tolerance."[20] This implies that Derrida agrees that religion and politics should be separated.

---

[18] Lilla, *The Stillborn God*, 2007, 84–85.
[19] Jacques Derrida, *The Gift of Death and Literature in Secret*, 2nd ed., Religion and Postmodernism (Chicago: University of Chicago Press, 2008), 73, 70.
[20] Derrida, "Taking Sides for Algeria," 122.

However, this impression is misleading. In relation to Algeria, Derrida immediately adds that the tolerance he has in mind "protect[s] the exercise of faith and, in this case, the freedom of discussion and interpretation within every religion. For example, and in the first place here: in Islam, the different readings of which, both exegetical and political, must be allowed to develop freely."[21] In Derrida's account, one function of the religious neutrality of the state is to allow religious communities to reflect in freedom upon how to intervene politically. Two years later, in 1996, Derrida reiterates his hope for a secular government in Algeria, but once again he emphasizes that such a government would not be opposed to Islam but rather "*laïc* and open to social, cultural, and religious (etc.) pluralism."[22] When he returns to the case of Algeria in 2002, his complaint against Islamist politicians is not that they brought religion into politics, but rather that they threatened to suspend democratic elections.[23] In my reading, Derrida affirms a procedural secularity that prohibits the state from preferring one religious group over others, but this does not entail that he endorses a programmatic secularism that would exclude religion from the public sphere.

Derrida often suggests that it is impossible to separate religion and politics in the way that Lilla describes. To take one example, Derrida argues that both sides in the debate over the death penalty rely on the legacy of Christianity. On the one hand, Albert Camus claims that the Christian belief in an afterlife is necessary to sustain the death penalty, and so he blames Christianity for its continued existence. On the other hand, Derrida notes that Victor Hugo opposed the death penalty by appealing to the crucifixion of Jesus Christ; according to Hugo, Christianity is the antidote rather than the disease. This indicates that Christianity has the capacity to inspire both support for and opposition to the death penalty. Derrida goes even further: "If one reflects that ... Christian monotheism is also a humanist immanentism, a belief in the mediation of God made man ... Camus's discourse ... would be more Christian, more Christlike, than he thought."[24] Although Camus's opposition to the death penalty aimed to reject Christianity in favor of humanism, Derrida suggests that this humanism is already implicit in the Christian understanding of

---

[21] Ibid.
[22] Jacques Derrida, "L'Une des pires oppressions: L'Interdiction d'une langue, interview by Aïssa Khelladi," *Algérie Littérature Action* 9 (March 1997): 105–16.
[23] Derrida, *Rogues*, 31–34.
[24] Jacques Derrida, *The Death Penalty, Vol. 1*, ed. Geoffrey Bennington, M. Crépon, and Thomas Dutoit, trans. Peggy Kamuf (Chicago: University of Chicago Press, 2014), 209.

Jesus Christ. In Derrida's reading, Camus's anti-Christian critique of the death penalty repeats a Christian gesture.[25]

Derrida observes that many of the central concepts of modern politics – tolerance, globalization, forgiveness, and secularization itself – have a theological genealogy.[26] As he observes, even the ostensibly neutral category of "religion" is often used to superimpose Christian assumptions onto other traditions; for this reason he generally prefers to focus on particular traditions.[27] He writes, "The opposition between sacred and secular is naïve; it entails a lot of de-constructive questions. Contrary to what we think we know, we have never entered into a secular era. The very idea of the secular is religious through and through – Christian really."[28] Although modernity is often portrayed as the gradual fading of religious particularity in favor of universal reason, Derrida claims that "the Enlightenment remains a Christian phenomenon."[29] In his view, the fading of Christian hegemony in the modern period expresses an impetus

---

[25] Camus's critique of hope (which I discussed in Chapter 3) also exhibits the ambivalence that Derrida identifies. Camus writes, "Henceforth man enters in with his revolt and his lucidity. He has forgotten how to hope. This hell of the present is his Kingdom at last ... Spiritual conflicts become embodied and return to the abject and magnificent shelter of man's heart. None of them is settled. But all are transfigured ... The body, affection, creation, action, human nobility will then resume their places in this mad world. At last man will again find there the wine of the absurd and the bread of indifference on which he feeds his greatness" (*The Myth of Sisyphus*, 52). On the one hand, this passage exemplifies the immanence of secularity. Alone in a universe that is itself isolated and self-sufficient, Camus's absurd person forgets hope in favor of a lucid attention to a demystified world. On the other hand, Camus describes this irreligious rapture in terms derived from Christian tradition – echoing not only the language of hell and the Kingdom of God but also the transfiguration of Christ and bread and wine of Christian worship.

[26] I think Paul Kahn is correct: "That political concepts have their origin in theological concepts is, to most contemporary theorists, about as interesting and important as learning that English words have their origin in old Norse" (Kahn, *Political Theology*, 3). I take it that Derrida's point is not simply that political concepts have a theological origin; instead, he suggests that they continue to operate theologically. For this reason, as Kahn himself argues, to understand modern politics it is necessary to draw upon theological modes of analysis.

[27] Derrida, "Above All, No Journalists!," 74; Jacques Derrida, "Faith and Knowledge: The Two Sources of 'Religion' at the Limits of Reason Alone," in *Acts of Religion*, ed. Gil Anidjar (New York: Routledge, 2002), 44–45. Like Derrida, I think "religion" is a slippery generalization that should be used with care. I use the term in this chapter because it frames the debate I am engaging, but I attempt to focus the conversation on particular texts and traditions.

[28] Derrida, "Others Are Secret Because They Are Other," 142; cf. Derrida, "On Forgiveness," 67; Derrida, *Rogues*, 28. Elsewhere he writes, "Nothing seems therefore more uncertain, more difficult to sustain, nothing seems here or there more imprudent than a self-assured discourse on the age of disenchantment, the era of secularization, the time of laicization, etc." (Derrida, "Faith and Knowledge," 100).

[29] Derrida, "Above All, No Journalists!," 66.

toward universality that originates with the biblical writer Paul.[30] Derrida suggests that "dechristianization will be a Christian victory" insofar as the death of God (in the crucifixion of Jesus Christ) is a central motif of Christian thought.[31]

Derrida finds the same dynamic at work in Hobbes. He writes, "Many expert commentators on Hobbes ... believe it necessary to insist on the modernity of their concept of sovereignty, insofar as it is supposed to be, precisely, emancipated from theology and religion and would supposedly have finally landed on purely human soil, as a political and not a theological concept, as a non-theologico-political concept. But things seem much more complex to me."[32] Derrida goes on to explain that, although Hobbes claims that the state has an anthropological origin, he nevertheless portrays the sovereign as standing in God's place. Since Hobbes calls God "the Soveraign of all Soveraigns," there is reason to think that human and divine sovereignty form a pair, each modeled upon the other.[33] For this reason, Derrida suggests, "This humanistic or anthropologistic modernity of the institution of sovereignty and the state retains a profound and fundamental theological and religious basis."[34] In Derrida's view, humanism and religion are not opposed. On the contrary, if he is right, Hobbes does not separate religion and politics as strictly as Lilla says.[35]

Like Hobbes, Lilla worries about religion because he takes it to assert an authority that could compete with political authority. Lilla writes, "If we

---

[30] See Derrida, "Autoimmunity," 130; Jacques Derrida, "Globalization, Peace, and Cosmopolitanism," in *Negotiations: Interventions and Interviews, 1971–2001*, Cultural Memory in the Present, ed. Elizabeth Rottenberg (Stanford, CA: Stanford University Press, 2002), 374–75. In similar fashion, Charles Taylor argues that Christian reform movements contributed to the disenchantment of the world by seeking to submit all of life to an exceptionless code (Taylor, *A Secular Age*, 51, 87).

[31] Jacques Derrida, *On Touching, Jean-Luc Nancy*, Meridian: Crossing Aesthetics (Stanford, CA: Stanford University Press, 2005), 54; cf. Derrida, "Above All, No Journalists!," 66–70; Derrida, *The Death Penalty, Vol. 1*, 244–45; Derrida, "Faith and Knowledge," 78–79.

[32] Jacques Derrida, *The Beast and the Sovereign, Vol. 1*, trans. Geoffrey Bennington (Chicago: University of Chicago Press, 2009), 53. On this point, Derrida agrees with Carl Schmitt (cf. Jacques Derrida, *For What Tomorrow: A Dialogue*, Cultural Memory in the Present [Stanford, CA: Stanford University Press, 2004], 91–91; Schmitt, *Political Theology*, 36). For a helpful analysis of Derrida's late work on sovereignty, see Vincent B. Leitch, "Late Derrida: The Politics of Sovereignty," *Critical Inquiry* 33, no. 2 (2007): 229–47.

[33] Hobbes, *Leviathan*, 260.   [34] Derrida, *The Beast and the Sovereign, Vol. 1*, 54.

[35] Lilla writes, "As for Hobbes, though, I don't take his theology seriously as theology. Whether he believes all the biblical citations and theological arguments he presents or not, his own argument stands alone. That's all I'm concerned with" (José Casanova et al., "A Conversation: José Casanova, Michael Jon Kessler, John Milbank, and Mark Lilla," in *Political Theology for a Plural Age*, by Michael Kessler [New York: Oxford University Press, 2013], 28). Although this gesture is convenient insofar as it enlists Hobbes in support of Lilla's project, my argument indicates that it is irresponsible.

take seriously the thought that God is a person with intentions ... then a great deal can follow. The intentions of such a God are not mute facts. They express an active will. They are authoritative. And that is where politics comes in."[36] According to Lilla, if a person believes in God, they will feel themselves constrained to submit to God's will, and it is in this way (he thinks) that religion is relevant to politics. Lilla suggests that divine sovereignty will inevitably displace political sovereignty, but this is only possible if they are the same kind of thing. Lilla recognizes that modern political philosophy was formed in conversation with Christianity, but he characterizes this process as "a backward-looking struggle."[37] If Derrida is right that sovereignty is a theological concept, it is misleading to portray the relation between Christianity and modernity as purely oppositional.

Because Lilla is a subtle reader, he recognizes that a religious heritage remains influential. He writes, "Though the principles of modern liberal democracy are not conceptually dependent on the truth of Christianity, they are genetically dependent on the problems Christianity posed and failed to solve."[38] In the story that Lilla tells, modern political thought emerged in response to conflicts caused by the ambiguity of Christian theology, so there is a sense in which modern political systems owe their origin to Christianity. However, in Lilla's view these political systems emerged by rejecting the theological heritage to which they responded; he explains, "modern liberal democracy, with its distinctive ideas and institutions, is a *post-Christian phenomenon.*"[39] This is the claim that Derrida contests. Even if we grant that Hobbes (et al.) intended to reject theological reflection on politics – which is doubtful – we need not assume that they succeeded. Where Lilla treats religion primarily as a source of overt authority, Derrida claims that religious traditions remain unconsciously influential.

Deconstructing the Secular

In my reading, Derrida's analysis of the relation between religion and politics intersects with recent scholarship on secularization. José Casanova notes that "any discussion of the secular has to begin with the recognition

---

[36] Lilla, *The Stillborn God*, 2007, 22. [37] Ibid., 18. [38] Ibid.
[39] Lilla, "Coping with Political Theology," emphasis original.

that it emerged first as a theological category of Western Christendom."[40] As Casanova goes on to explain, in medieval Europe "secular" referred to clergy who lived in the world among lay Christians, whereas "religious" referred to clergy who withdrew to cloistered life. In this context, to "secularize" meant to relocate someone or something from the monastery to the wider world. Casanova argues that the modern process of secularization responds to this medieval dualism between the secular and the religious.[41] This gave rise to a distinctively Christian form of secularization, as various reform movements (from the Middle Ages to the Reformation) demanded that all Christians should pursue holiness, not only the "religious" elite.[42] Casanova concludes that "the religious and the secular are mutually constituted through sociopolitical struggles and cultural politics."[43] Where some assume that the secular and the religious are given quantities that stand opposed, Casanova shows that the boundary between them is constantly renegotiated.

Along similar lines, Talal Asad argues that the secular and the religious were invented together to serve political ends.[44] He writes, "In this movement we have the construction of religion as a new historical object: anchored in personal experience, expressible as belief-statements, dependent on private institutions, and practiced in one's spare time. This construction of religion ensures that it is part of what is inessential to our common politics, economy, science, and morality."[45] Where it is tempting to treat the category of religion as if its significance were timeless and universal, Asad claims that it too is a recent construct – one that is designed to exclude it from mechanisms of power. For this reason, Asad sees the distinction between the secular and the religious as unstable. He writes, "The secular, I argue, is neither continuous with the religious that supposedly preceded it (that is, it is not the latest phase of a sacred origin) nor a simple break from it (that is, it is not the opposite, an essence that excludes the sacred)."[46] Asad and Casanova agree that there is some sense in which ours is a secular age, but their work demonstrates that secularization remains bound up with a religious heritage.

---

[40] José Casanova, "The Secular, Secularizations, Secularisms," in *Rethinking Secularism*, ed. Craig J. Calhoun, Mark Juergensmeyer, and Jonathan VanAntwerpen (New York: Oxford University Press, 2011), 56; cf. José Casanova, *Public Religions in the Modern World* (Chicago: University of Chicago Press, 1994).

[41] Casanova, "The Secular, Secularizations, Secularisms," 56. [42] Ibid. [43] Ibid., 63.

[44] Talal Asad, *Formations of the Secular: Christianity, Islam, Modernity* (Stanford, CA: Stanford University Press, 2003), 191–92.

[45] Asad, *Genealogies of Religion*, 207.

[46] Asad, *Formations of the Secular*, 25; cf. Mahmood, "Religious Reason and Secular Affect."

Across his corpus, Derrida frequently remarks that ostensibly secular concepts are marked by a religious heritage.[47] These comments are generally brief, but he does reflect on the theme of secularization more extensively in "Christianity and Secularization" (1996).[48] Derrida begins this essay by tracing Immanuel Kant's argument that Christianity is the only moral religion. According to Kant, this is because Christianity requires the faithful to live well regardless of the hope for a future reward – in which case, Derrida observes, the moral law supplants the authority previously identified with religion. Derrida comments, "Even if God didn't exist, it would be necessary to conduct oneself well. Consequently, this is a way of privileging Christian religion (since it is the only moral religion), and at the same time of emancipating the moral subject from religion."[49] Derrida argues that this gesture is characteristic of secularization insofar as it privileges Christian religion at the moment in which it dispenses with religion. He comments, "I have trouble with this word [secularization], precisely because it ratifies emancipation with respect to religious dogma, and at the same time it reaffirms religion within this emancipation."[50] As Derrida goes on to argue (in relation to Voltaire, Nietzsche, and others), the process of secularization is ambivalent insofar as it reinforces the influence of religion at the very moment when it promises emancipation.

Derrida's ethics of uncertainty provides a philosophical explanation for the situation that Casanova and Asad describe. As I described in Chapter 1, Derrida argues that every present element is related to what is different and that every structure is disrupted by the play of elements which elude attempts to create perfect coherence.[51] In his view, the claim to possess metaphysical certainty aims to assuage the anxiety that results from instability, but such security is unreliable.[52] According to Derrida, every

---

[47] Jacques Derrida, "Autoimmunity: Real and Symbolic Suicides," in *Philosophy in a Time of Terror: Dialogues with Jürgen Habermas and Jacques Derrida*, by Giovanna Borradori (Chicago: University of Chicago Press, 2003), 127, 130; Jacques Derrida, "Above All, No Journalists!," in *Religion and Media*, ed. Hent de Vries and Samuel Weber (Stanford, CA: Stanford University Press, 2001), 66; Jacques Derrida, "Others Are Secret Because They Are Other," in *Paper Machine* (*Cultural Memory in the Present*) (Stanford, CA: Stanford University Press, 2005), 160; Jacques Derrida, *On Cosmopolitanism and Forgiveness*, Thinking in Action (London: Routledge, 2001), 31; Jacques Derrida, "What Does It Mean to Be a French Philosopher Today?," in *Paper Machine*, Cultural Memory in the Present (Stanford, CA: Stanford University Press, 2005), 116.

[48] I have prepared a translation of this text, which will appear as "Christianity and Secularization," trans. David Newheiser, *Critical Inquiry*, forthcoming. These remarks are currently unpublished in French (Jacques Derrida, "Cristianesimo e Secolarizzazione," 1996, 219DRR/198/6, Fonds Jacques Derrida, IMEC, Saint-Germain-la-blanche herbe, Normandie). However, they have appeared in Italian (Jacques Derrida et al., "Cristianesimo e Secolarizzazione," Il Pensiero 2 [1998]: 21–42).

[49] Derrida, "Christianity and Secularization." [50] Ibid. [51] Derrida, "Différance," 13.

[52] Derrida, "Structure, Sign, and Play," 279.

thing is constituted by a complex web of relationships, leaving no stable point of reference that could ground a complete and coherent system. This suggests that the attempt to exclude religion from the public sphere is impossible in principle: where secularism assumes that the secular and the religious are strictly separated, Derrida thinks such purity is unattainable, for everything is adulterated by that which is different.

In *Specters of Marx*, Derrida draws out the implications of this impurity for the experience of time. He plays upon Marx's attentiveness to various spirits, from the specter of communism haunting Europe to the ghost of a religiosity that Marx sought to banish. The French term for "specter" is *revenant*, which serves both as the nominal form for "ghost" and as the present participle of *revenir*, to return. Accordingly, Derrida writes, "A specter is always a *revenant*. One cannot control its comings and goings because it *begins by coming back*."[53] In Derrida's treatment, the *revenant* is precisely the one who returns, who comes and goes at will, reappearing without invitation. This inflects the gesture of banishing a specter with ambivalence: although one may attempt to rid oneself of a ghost, one can never be sure that it will not inconveniently return.

Derrida suggests that this dynamic characterizes Marx's own critique of religion. Derrida writes, "[Exorcism] proceeds by formulae, and sometimes theoretical formulae play this role with an efficacity that is all the greater because they mislead as to their magical nature, their authoritarian dogmatism, the occult power they share with what they claim to combat."[54] The claim that religion is a phantasm destined to disappear thus resembles a performative incantation; its insistent repetition attempts to achieve that which it envisions. Marx criticized religion as an ideological mystification, which distracted the proletariat from the work of revolution. Yet although religion is the primal reference of ideology, Derrida notes that Marx's own project borrows a religious form. Derrida writes, "The religious also informs, along with the messianic and the eschatological ... that 'spirit' of emancipatory Marxism whose injunction we are reaffirming here, however secret and contradictory it appears."[55] Derrida is clear that Marx is nothing so simple as a religious adherent, yet (as I described in Chapter 1) he detects in Marx a certain messianic spirit. After all, Marx's dream of a specter haunting Europe invokes the prospect of apocalyptic transformation.[56]

---

[53] Derrida, *Specters of Marx*, 11. [54] Ibid., 59. [55] Ibid., 209.
[56] Compare Derrida's observation in an unpublished lecture from 1972 that Marx takes philosophy to be continuous with religion, in a certain respect, insofar as both are alienating (Jacques Derrida,

Derrida suggests that such spectrality describes what it means to inherit a tradition. He writes, "An inheritance is never gathered together, it is never one with itself. Its presumed unity, if there is one, can consist only in the *injunction* to *reaffirm by choosing.*"[57] On this view, inheritance cannot function as a given, for that which can be inherited is never monolithic. Indeed, it is this problematic and conflicted character that keeps inheritance from being entirely passive. Derrida writes, "If the readability of a legacy were given, natural, transparent, univocal...we would be affected by it as by a cause."[58] Since inheritance is obscure, requiring continuous interpretation, fidelity must be active and engaged. By the same token, however, inheritance it not entirely within our power. Derrida explains, "That we *are* heirs does not mean that we *have* or that we *receive* this or that, some inheritance that enriches us one day with this or that, but that the *being* of what we are is first of all inheritance, whether we like it or know it or not."[59] In Derrida's account, we are shaped by a past that we did not choose and of which we are not fully aware.

Responding to Risk

Derrida's affinity with recent scholarship on secularization suggests that Derrida's atheism is frequently misunderstood. Martin Hägglund has developed the most forceful and sophisticated argument in favor of the view that Derrida rejects religion, altogether and as such. Hägglund claims that religious faith is defined by the desire for immortality, whereas Derrida affirms the universality of finitude, an immanence from which there is no exception.[60] In his reading, "For Derrida, there is only one realm – the infinite finitude of *différance.*"[61] For this reason, when Derrida refers to democracy to come, Hägglund argues that this does not mean that democracy is a desirable ideal. Hägglund writes, "Democracy to come does not designate a utopian hope for a democracy that will come one day and

"Religion et Philosophie," 1972, 5, 219DRR/224/6, Fonds Jacques Derrida, IMEC, Saint-Germain-la-blanche herbe, Normandie).
[57] Derrida, *Specters of Marx*, 18. This echoes Kathryn Tanner's elegant account of tradition in "Postmodern Challenges to 'Tradition,'" *Louvain Studies* 28 (2003): 175–93. For my own treatment of tradition (which owes a great deal to Tanner), see David Newheiser, "Sexuality and Christian Tradition: Innovation and Fidelity, Ancient and Modern," *Journal of Religious Ethics* no. 43 (2015): 122–145; and David Newheiser, "Conceiving Transformation without Triumphalism: Joachim of Fiore against Gianni Vattimo," *Heythrop Journal*, no. 55 (2014): 650–662.
[58] Derrida, *Specters of Marx*, 18. [59] Ibid., 68.
[60] Martin Hägglund, *Radical Atheism: Derrida and the Time of Life* (Stanford, CA: Stanford University Press, 2008), 3. Emphasis original.
[61] Ibid., 4.

bring about a just society. It is not an ideal, and it cannot serve to justify any political commitment."⁶² According to Hägglund, for Derrida the future signifies susceptibility to change, but it has nothing to do with hope.

Hägglund's reading corrects a common misconstrual of Derrida's ethics. Where John Caputo claims that "alterity refers to the victims not the victimizers,"⁶³ Hägglund observes that "in Derrida 'the other' does not primarily designate another human being."⁶⁴ Because what is to come is entirely unpredictable, Hägglund is right that Caputo makes alterity seem safer than it actually is. Derrida explains, "Pure hospitality consists in leaving one's house open to the unforeseeable arrival, which can be an intrusion, even a dangerous intrusion, liable eventually to cause harm."⁶⁵ Since the other is unforeseeable, openness is dangerous, and so Hägglund concludes that such hospitality is far from ideal. He writes, "If I did not discriminate between what I welcome and do not welcome ... it would mean that I had opened myself without reservations to whatever is violently opposed to me and can extinguish everything that is mine."⁶⁶ This position is certainly sensible; the problem is that it inverts the significance of Derrida's account of alterity.

Although Derrida says that hospitality is dangerous, he does not conclude that it must be abandoned. On the contrary, he writes that "hospitality is not simply some region of ethics, let alone ... the name of a problem in law or politics: it is ethicity itself, the whole and the principle of ethics."⁶⁷ Insofar as it constitutes a welcome to the other, Derrida argues that hospitality is essential to ethical relation. In his account, the danger of hospitality marks the distinction between ethics and the realm of law and politics. He writes, "This pure hospitality ... has a role in ordinary life: when someone arrives, when love arrives, for example, one takes a risk, one is exposed. To understand these situations, it is necessary to maintain this horizon without horizon, this unlimitedness of unconditional hospitality, even while knowing that one cannot make it a political or juridical concept."⁶⁸ Just as Derrida's democracy to come should not be equated with any existent system, he claims that hospitality cannot be realized in a legal regime.⁶⁹ Because pure hospitality would entail allowing anything at all, it would be both impossible and unwise to instantiate it as such.

---

⁶² Ibid., 171.   ⁶³ Caputo, *The Weakness of God*, 137.   ⁶⁴ Hägglund, *Radical Atheism*, 75.
⁶⁵ Derrida, *For What Tomorrow*, 59.   ⁶⁶ Hägglund, *Radical Atheism*, 103.
⁶⁷ Jacques Derrida, *Adieu to Emmanuel Levinas*, Meridian: Crossing Aesthetics (Stanford, CA: Stanford University Press, 1999), 50.
⁶⁸ Derrida, *For What Tomorrow*, 60.   ⁶⁹ Ibid., 59.

However, Derrida is clear that hospitality may nevertheless be pursued, for desire is not restricted to that which is safe.

Hägglund complains that "the command to 'respect' the alterity of the other does not make any sense if the other wants to destroy me."[70] This is a sensible position, but it is one that Derrida does not share. Derrida writes,

> What I am interested in is the experience of the desire for the impossible. That is, the impossible as the condition of desire ... We do not give up the dream of the pure gift, in the same way that we do not give up the idea of pure hospitality. Even if we know it is impossible and that it can be perverse ... Despite this perversion, despite this impossibility, we go on dreaming or thinking of pure hospitality, of pure gift.[71]

As Hägglund recognizes, there is something peculiar about pursuing something that may be destructive, but Derrida is not deterred. Pure hospitality cannot be instantiated, and for this reason it is impossible. However, in Derrida's account, impossibility functions not to exclude desire, as Hägglund would have it, but to inflame passion all the more.

Where Hägglund attempts to limit desire to what is immanent, Derrida dreams, desires, and hopes for the beyond. Hägglund writes, "That we desire the impossible does not mean that we desire something above or beyond the possible. On the contrary, it means that whatever we desire is constituted by temporal finitude."[72] This claim is true insofar as Derrida's project entails that no desire is free from the pull of finitude, but it is false insofar as Hägglund assumes that desire is limited to that which is possible. Far from finitude constituting an insurmountable constraint, the impossible that Derrida describes operates on another level entirely. Since, Derrida says, the impossible "marks an absolute interruption in the regime of the possible,"[73] it allows for a hope that is not limited by prudential judgment.

Negative Atheology

Hägglund claims that "the logic of negative theology and the logic of deconstruction are diametrically opposite."[74] However, in "Sauf le nom" (1993) Derrida comments that "deconstruction has often been defined as the very experience of the (impossible) possibility of the impossible," and

---

[70] Hägglund, *Radical Atheism*, 100. [71] Derrida and Marion, "On the Gift," 72.
[72] Hägglund, *Radical Atheism*, 121. [73] Derrida, "Sauf Le Nom (Post Scriptum)," 43.
[74] Hägglund, *Radical Atheism*, 5.

he associates this impossibility with negative theology.⁷⁵ In this passage, Derrida is discussing Angelus Silesius, a Renaissance poet deeply influenced by the Dionysian tradition. Silesius describes union with God in terms that are, Derrida says, "more impossible still than the impossible."⁷⁶ Derrida comments, "This 'more,' this beyond, this *hyper* (*über*) obviously introduces an absolute heterogeneity in the order and in the modality of the possible."⁷⁷ As I discussed in Chapter 4, Derrida sometimes worries that the *hyper-* of negative theology betrays the tradition's apparent negativity by asserting an ultimate affirmation. As I observed, the prefix *hyper-* can mean both "above" and "against;" here Derrida notes that, on the second of these readings, the excessive character of Dionysian negative theology interrupts the authority of possibility.

Where Hägglund writes that "negative theology says no to what deconstruction affirms,"⁷⁸ Derrida goes on to associate negative theology with an affirmation of impossibility that is essential for loving life. He writes in relation to the concept of detachment developed by Meister Eckhart, "Why not recognize there love itself, that is, this infinite renunciation which somehow surrenders to the impossible?"⁷⁹ On this reading, the negativity of negative theology functions to preserve alterity while allowing for an affirmation that exceeds what can be achieved. Although such vulnerability is dangerous, Derrida recognizes that it may be endured. It is for this reason that, as I argued in Chapter 3, Derrida exemplifies a hopeful persistence. From this perspective, Hägglund's hostility toward religion and his insistence upon reasonable self-protection are both born from despair

This is the context in which Derrida uses the phrase "radical atheism." Although Hägglund takes this phrase as the title of his book, what Derrida describes is the opposite of what Hägglund has in mind. Derrida comments on Silesius, "The desire of God, God as the other name of desire, deals in the desert with radical atheism."⁸⁰ As Derrida observes, the insistence upon divine transcendence in the tradition of negative theology comes to resemble atheism. As we have seen, Dionysius denies that God exists, that God is good, and that God is divine. Insofar as negative theology requires the double movement of renunciation and affirmation that Derrida takes to characterize love, he suggests that its very aridity is paradigmatic of hyperbolic desire. Derrida writes, "If on the one hand

---

[75] Derrida, "Sauf Le Nom (Post Scriptum)," 43.   [76] Ibid.   [77] Ibid.
[78] Hagglund, *Radical Atheism*, 117.   [79] Derrida, "Sauf Le Nom (Post Scriptum)," 74.
[80] Ibid., 80.

apophasis inclines almost toward atheism, can't one say that, on the other hand or thereby, the extreme and most consequent forms of declared atheism will have always testified to the most intense desire of God?"[81] Just as negative theology is surprisingly close to atheism, Derrida suggests that some forms of atheism signal a passionate preoccupation with the divine.

As I have shown throughout this book, although Derrida is an atheist (of a sort), he draws on religious traditions with a sensitivity and intensity that can be seen as a form of fidelity. In contrast, Hägglund's atheism depends upon a concept of religion that is staggeringly simplistic. Hägglund claims that "the common denominator for religions is thus that they promote absolute immunity as the supremely desirable."[82] This provides the foil required by his claim that it is only possible to desire that which is mortal. However, the haste with which Hägglund characterizes religion – always and as such – ought to inspire suspicion. Hägglund never discusses Islam, his sole reference to Judaism is embedded in a quotation in a footnote, and he does not explain whether he sees traditions such as Taoism, Buddhism, and Shinto as "religious" in his sense of the term. He claims that "the reference to Augustine has served as the main evidence in the attempt to turn Derrida into a religious thinker,"[83] but this ignores the extensive and varied theological resonances across Derrida's oeuvre: his repeated references to circumcision, his reflections upon the tallith, his readings of Genesis and the Gospel of John, his consistent interest in messianism, and his sustained engagement with negative theology.[84] For his part, Derrida recognizes that the term "religion" has a history (formed by its complicated relationship with Christianity) that means it must be handled with care.[85]

---

[81] Ibid., 36.   [82] Hagglund, *Radical Atheism*, 8.   [83] Ibid., 146.
[84] Ibid., 237, n. 61. See, for instance, Jacques Derrida, "Circumfession," in *Jacques Derrida*, by Geoffrey Bennington and Jacques Derrida, Religion and Postmodernism (Chicago: University of Chicago Press, 1993), 3–315; Jacques Derrida, "Of an Apocalyptic Tone Newly Adopted in Philosophy," in *Derrida and Negative Theology*, ed. Harold G. Coward and Toby A. Foshay (Albany: State University of New York Press, 1991), 25–72; Jacques Derrida, "Des Tours de Babel," in *Acts of Religion*, ed. Gil Anidjar (New York: Routledge, 2002), 102–35.
[85] Derrida writes, "The word 'religion' ... is a Latin word (naturally) that has imposed itself on universal discourse (through the schemas of globalization which we must question) as naming a large number of phenomena that may not correspond to what the word religion means. In other words, ... we could track what I have tried to call globalatinization [*mondialatinisation*], which is to say an imposition (at the scale of humanity and the planet) of the Christian word religion (as it has been christianized and romanized) in order to cover a large number of phenomena that may not fall under religion" (Derrida, "Christianity and Secularization").

With staggering speed, Hägglund refers to Augustine's claim that immutability is preferable to mutability and asserts on this basis that "all religious conceptions of the highest good ... hold out such an absolute immunity."[86] Given the diversity of religious traditions, it is indefensible to suggest that Augustine's construal of incorruptibility characterizes religion as such, but the claim is false even with respect to Christianity. As I argued in Chapter 3, where some theorists claim that religious hope provides a false comfort that distracts from life here and now, Dionysius demonstrates that Christianity can acknowledge the constraints of finitude. Dionysius does affirm the hope for eternal life – to this extent Hägglund is correct – but because his hope acknowledges its vulnerability to disappointment, it does not negate the possibility of loss, nor does it suppose that this is a state that can be realized (or even imagined). Contra Hägglund, Dionysius demonstrates that Christian hope can intensify attention to mortal life.

Where secularists and traditionalists both treat religion as a univocal source of dogmatic authority, Derrida recognizes that religious traditions are diverse and multivalent. He observes, "Just as there is a negative theology, there is a negative atheology. An accomplice of the former, it still pronounces the absence of a center, when it is play that should be affirmed."[87] The irony of Hägglund's atheism is that, although he recognizes that Derrida disavows purity, he attempts to purify Derrida of any association with religion. Hägglund claims that Derrida uses apparently religious terminology only "in order to read messianism against itself," but Derrida works within religious texts rather than against them.[88] Rather than seeking to exorcise religion once and for all, Derrida draws constructively upon religious traditions. In seeking to preclude a theological reading of Derrida, Hägglund attempts to restrict the play of meaning, both within Derrida's texts and between Derrida and the religious texts that he reads. For this reason, Hägglund's argument is antithetical to the key themes of Derrida's work.[89]

---

[86] Hagglund, *Radical Atheism*, 8.   [87] Derrida, "Ellipsis," 297.
[88] Hagglund, *Radical Atheism*, 132.
[89] Hägglund dismisses Kevin Hart's reading of Derrida, but I think Hart is right: "Deconstruction offers a critique of theism, to be sure, but it is directed to the 'ism' rather than the 'theos'; that is, it offers a critique of the use to which 'God' is put, but does not make any claim whatsoever about the reality of God. In fact, to the extent to which deconstruction is a critique of theism it is also a critique of any discourse which denies there is a God" (Hart, *The Trespass of the Sign*, 27).

Folded Identities

In contrast to the picture that Hägglund presents, Derrida's relation to religion is complex. As a young man, he read religious writers including Simone Weil, Gabriel Marcel, and René le Senne, and his student essays are deeply marked by the Christian existentialism that was current at the time.[90] At the age of twenty-one, in a letter to his friend Michel Monory (a practicing Catholic), Derrida provides a poignant response to Michel's plan to visit an abbey on retreat: "I would love to imitate you. But I cannot. First, because a certain religious 'condition' forbids me; second and above all because I would be too weak as well, if I am not overly anxious, to avoid interrupting prayer, silence, steady peace, hope, and contemplation."[91] This expression of anxiety, along with Derrida's repeated requests that Michel "pray for me,"[92] suggests that (at this point, at least) Derrida desired a faith from which he felt alienated. Derrida's interest in Christianity persisted: although some suppose that Derrida took interest in religion only toward the end of his career, his published work contains theological references from the very start, and one of his earliest lecture courses (from 1961 to 62) spends weeks in a careful exegesis of medieval theologians such as Thomas Aquinas and William of Auxerre.[93] These biographical details do not determine the significance of Derrida's work, but they do suggest that his sustained engagement with religious texts is not an aberration that can be dismissed.

In one of his last published essays, "Abraham, the Other" (2003), Derrida suggests that the key themes of his work respond to this ambivalent heritage. He writes, "My suffering as a persecuted young Jew ... has no doubt killed in me an elementary confidence in any community, in any fusional gregariousness, whatever its nature."[94] As we have seen, a practice of painstaking interpretation is integral to Derrida's thought: "as if," he says, "I only learned how to read – others would say, how to

---

[90] Edward Baring's account of Derrida's intellectual genesis is invaluable; see Edward Baring, *The Young Derrida and French Philosophy, 1945–1968* (Cambridge: Cambridge University Press, 2011).
[91] Lettre de Derrida à Michel Monory, sans date (été 1951), quoted in Benoît Peeters, *Derrida* (Paris: Flammarion, 2010), 70. The translation is my own.
[92] Quoted in ibid., 64, 70.
[93] In 1963, for instance, in one of his first publications, Derrida associates modern uncertainty with "the absence of the Jewish God" (Jacques Derrida, "Edmond Jabès and the Question of the Book," in *Writing and Difference*, trans. Alan Bass [Chicago: University of Chicago Press, 1978], 10). Jacques Derrida, "Le Sens Du Transcendental (Enseignement à la Sorbonne)," 1961, 219DRR/219/13, Fonds Jacques Derrida, IMEC, Saint-Germain-la-blanche herbe, Normandie.
[94] Ibid., 15. In this essay, Derrida sometimes capitalizes the words "Jew" and "Jewish," and sometimes he doesn't. I have followed his usage in the quotations presented here.

'deconstruct' – because of having first learned to read, to deconstruct even, anti-Semitism."⁹⁵ Derrida suggests that the abstraction of his ethics owes to this history:

> It is certain that without this experience I would not have had the same access, nor perhaps any access at all, to the ethico-political motifs that have occupied me since long ago around what I have called a "new International," ... or around what I have named the desert in the desert, *khōra,* messianicity without messianism, or the im-possible as the only possible event, for example, in the un-conditionality of the gift, of forgiveness, of testimony, of hospitality, etc.⁹⁶

Derrida argues that each of these categories (messianicity, gift, forgiveness, etc.) cannot be identified in particular instances, but he admits that his understanding of them is formed by his experience of belonging to a particular community. Instead of rejecting religious commitment, then, Derrida's very suspicion of religious faith stems from a religious heritage.

Derrida describes a double movement, "a retreat outside of all community, including the one that was called my own, a merciless withdrawal that I felt already, and that I still feel, *at once, at the same time,* as less jewish *and* more jewish than the Jew, as scarcely Jewish and as superlatively Jewish as possible, more than Jew, exemplarily Jew, but also hyperbolically Jew, when I was honing its cultivation to the point of mistrusting even the *exemplarist* temptation."⁹⁷ Every nationalism, Derrida says, asserts for itself a universal exemplarity, a significance for all and everywhere, and Jewishness in particular has sometimes been seen as such. Rather than cementing Derrida's Jewish identity in a reactive gesture, the suspicion of community set in motion by Derrida's encounter with anti-Semitism led him to suspect Judaism itself. This might suggest that Derrida forswears his Jewish identity, but Derrida observes that the very distinction between inside and out is troubled here. He writes, "This experience has sharpened my reasoned mistrust of borders and oppositional distinctions (whether

---

⁹⁵ Ibid.
⁹⁶ Ibid., 21. This confession is all the more striking in contrast to Derrida's reserve, for much of his career, in relation to Judaism. See, for instance, this comment, in a note to a 1986 lecture: "If one day I had to tell my story, nothing in this narrative would start to speak of the thing itself if I did not come up against this fact: for lack of capacity, competence, or self-authorization, I have never yet been able to speak of what my birth, as one says, should have made closest to me: the Jew, the Arab" (Derrida, "How to Avoid Speaking: Denials," 135).
⁹⁷ Derrida, "Abraham, the Other," 16. Some years earlier, Derrida put the point more bluntly: "Nothing for me matters so much as my Jewishness, which, however, in so many ways matters so little in my life" (Derrida, *For What Tomorrow,* 112).

conceptual or not),"⁹⁸ and this includes the very distinction between Jew and non-Jew. Derrida's ambivalent relation to Judaism blurs the boundary between within and without.

Derrida is caught without being able to decide between two possibilities: either being-Jew is an example of a more general contamination of the authentic by the inauthentic, or it is the experience called "being-Jew" that troubles the distinction between authenticity and inauthenticity. But this alternative (whether the abstract or the particular has priority) breaks down in turn. Derrida writes, "The memory or the hope that would constitute jewishness seems to be able to emancipate itself, indeed, from tradition, from the promise and the election proper to judaism."⁹⁹ Just as Derrida is inclined to purify messianicity from the particular hopes of a determinate messianism, here he suggests that the hope of Judaism entails its self-criticism. However, he immediately adds, "Whether or not one would have to do so, it will always be possible to re-root the very idea and movement of this emancipation, the desire of this emancipation … in a given of Judaism."¹⁰⁰ That is to say, whereas it is possible to abstract the preoccupations of Derrida's work from the tradition of Judaism, this very movement of abstraction depends upon that tradition.

Derrida's conflicted relation to Judaism exemplifies the ambivalence of secularization. He writes, "This inheritance is uneffaceable, and it endorses even the experience of effacement, of emancipation, of disavowal."¹⁰¹ This describes Derrida's relation to Judaism, but (as I have described) it also clarifies the character of inheritance more generally. He explains, "One could at once and successively accredit two contradictory postulates: on the one hand, it is (from a historical, ethical, political perspective, etc.) the condition that one emancipate oneself from every dogma of revelation and of election; on the other hand, this emancipation can be interpreted as the very content of the revelation or of the election, their very idea."¹⁰² As Derrida describes it, his distance from religious belonging stems in part from his suspicion at its tendency to exclusion; however, at the same time he acknowledges that this very emancipation from religion may be grounded in the heritage of a particular tradition (such as Christianity or

---

[98] Derrida, "Abraham, the Other," 17.   [99] Ibid., 32.   [100] Ibid.
[101] Ibid., 33. There is a great deal more to say about Derrida's relation to Judaism. See, for instance, Gideon Ofrat, *The Jewish Derrida*, 1st ed. (Syracuse, NY: Syracuse University Press, 2001); Hélène Cixous, *Portrait of Jacques Derrida as a Young Jewish Saint* (New York: Columbia University Press, 2003); Sarah Hammerschlag, *The Figural Jew: Politics and Identity in Postwar French Thought* (Chicago: University of Chicago Press, 2010), 201–60.
[102] Derrida, "Abraham, the Other," 33.

Judaism). As I described earlier in this chapter, Derrida observes that Camus, Hobbes, and others remain indebted to religious forms of thought even when they are their most thoroughly secular. In his view, this ambivalent relation to a religious heritage characterizes life in a secular age whether one identifies as religious or not.

Instability, Anxiety, and Hope

I have argued that Derrida's understanding of the differential play of meaning entails that the secular cannot successfully exclude its religious other (because nothing can), and his treatment of tradition helps explain why traditions remain influential even when they have been explicitly rejected. In response to a polemical atheism, Derrida's immoderate hope opens the possibility of productive exchange at the intersection of the secular and the religious. Some political theorists claim that religious discourse should be excluded from the public sphere because it violates the strictures of "public" or "secular" reason. Derrida's account of democracy implies that it is inappropriate to predetermine deliberation through a rule of this kind. Where secularism seeks to ensure the safety of the public sphere, Derrida's messianic politics demonstrates that another disposition toward danger is possible.[103] In my view, Derrida's work suggests that the epistemological question concerning the justification for political arguments is secondary to the ethical challenge posed by our vulnerability to danger.

According to Lilla, the problem with religion is not simply that it is a source of authority that is inaccessible to some citizens. Like Hobbes, Lilla believes that religion carries an emotional power – born from fear and exhilaration – that destabilizes individual lives and, through them, the world. He writes, "Hobbes ... was not wrong to think that messianic passions can destroy the religious and political lives of those subject to them."[104] Lilla argues that, once redemption is promised, the results are unpredictable; however circumspect official doctrine might be, eschatological passion will unleash violence. He explains, "Eschatological language breeds eschatological politics, no matter what dogmatic limits theologians try to impose on it."[105] According to Lilla, theological reflection on politics is a danger even when it is private, for it unleashes passions that refuse to be contained by ordered rationality.

---

[103] See Jeffrey Stout, *Democracy and Tradition* (Princeton, NJ: Princeton University Press, 2004), 80.
[104] Lilla, *The Stillborn God*, 2007, 243.   [105] Lilla, *The Stillborn God*, 2008, 285.

Hobbes defines religion as "*feare* of power invisible," and he recognizes that fear is an unpredictable force.[106] To mitigate its danger, Hobbes insists upon the priority of unambiguous rationality. He writes, "The Light of humane minds is Perspicuous Words, but by exact definitions first snuffed, and purged from ambiguity; Reason is the *pace*; Encrease of *Science*, the *way*; and the Benefit of man-kind, the *end.*"[107] On this view, linguistic ambiguity is the source of conflict and rebellion, and so anything less than perfect clarity is politically perilous. Hobbes continues, "And on the contrary, Metaphors, and senslesse and ambiguous words, are like *ignes fatui*; and reasoning upon them, is wandering amongst innumerable absurdities; and their end, contention, and sedition, or contempt."[108] In order to preserve the priority of calculative rationality, Hobbes excludes a gratuity that surpasses self-interest, a justice that exceeds contractual obligation, and a faith that transcends comprehension.[109] Derrida agrees that love, justice, and transcendence are dangerous, but he does not conclude that they must therefore be abandoned.

Lilla observes that "fragility is a disturbing prospect," and surely he is right.[110] Insofar as the desire to find a stable basis for political life responds to this experience, secularism addresses a genuinely distressing anxiety. However, where Lilla assumes that we must choose between security and violence, Derrida describes a different response to fragility. Instead of insisting upon rational stability, he affirms a hope that endures uncertainty for the sake of future transformation. Because hope exceeds the limits of reason, it should be handled with care, but Derrida claims that this instability is best embraced to preserve the possibility of a justice that transcends our present understanding. Derrida's work suggests that the reason religion is dangerous is the reason it is indispensable: it opens imagination to a future that has not yet come into view.

---

[106] Hobbes, *Leviathan*, 42. [107] Ibid., 36. [108] Ibid. [109] Ibid., 23, 59, 64, 91, 105.
[110] Lilla, *The Stillborn God*, 2007, 6.

CHAPTER 6

Negative Political Theology

In the previous chapter I argued, drawing on Derrida, that it is both impossible and unnecessary to exclude religion from the public sphere. In this chapter I will argue, drawing on Dionysius, that theological reflection can contribute to democratic politics by modeling a bold circumspection that sustains action in the face of uncertainty. Because complacency and despair pose a danger for groups as well as for individuals, I believe the hope I describe in this book is politically indispensable.

Like religious faith, support for a political cause can harden into a rigid adherence that is impervious to other possibilities. Conversely, political movements that critique the status quo sometimes find it easier to resist power than to exercise it. Although Dionysius does not directly address democratic politics, his account of *apophasis* demonstrates that a commitment to radical transformation does not rule out the compromise required to enact concrete policies in the present. Insofar as he describes a hopeful affirmation that incorporates self-critique, Dionysius indicates that political movements can affirm realistic proposals in hope while subjecting them, at the same time, to utopian critique.

Reflection on political theology is urgently important because, as I argued in Chapter 5, religion continues to influence secular politics. Although modern democracies no longer locate authority in a monarch modeled on the divine, they practice rituals centered on sites of extraordinary significance – the flag, the founding, the constitution, the nation. These things are sacred insofar as they inspire reverence and are valued for their own sake rather than for their utility. As scholars such as Robert Bellah have argued (with Jean-Jacques Rousseau and Émile Durkheim in the background), civil society is held together by beliefs and practices that constitute a civil religion informed by, but distinct from, religious traditions such as Christianity.[1]

---

[1] Robert N. Bellah, "Civil Religion in America," *Daedalus* 96, no. 1 (1967): 1–21; Jean-Jacques Rousseau, *The Social Contract: And, the First and Second Discourses*, ed. Susan Dunn (New Haven,

When individuals, texts, and institutions are invested with special significance, they may energize political movements and inspire sacrifice for the sake of a greater good. They create a sense of shared meaning, which situates democratic contestation within a given community. However, the sacred is also dangerous. Reverence may strengthen support for a leader's ideals, but it can also crowd out criticism of their shortcomings. Zeal for national greatness can fuel hostility toward others, and it makes it harder to reckon with national guilt. To honor something as sacred entails horror at its desecration, but this leads some to label any dissent as sacrilege. There is therefore reason to worry that the sacred subverts the struggle for justice.

The work of Giorgio Agamben has done a great deal to highlight the problem of sacred politics and the sources from which it stems. Against those who assume that modern politics is thoroughly secular, Agamben argues that the sacred continues to influence democratic societies, but in his view its influence is nefarious. According to Agamben, modern governmental power is modeled on the relation between divine transcendence and God's work in the world. On his account, both Christian theology and modern democracies reinforce mundane government by investing it with glory. Because Agamben thinks the sacred functions to neutralize resistance, he concludes that profanation is politically urgent.

I agree that the sacred poses a problem for politics, but I think Agamben underestimates its critical potential. Agamben claims that Christian theologians sacralize governmental power by investing it with the glory of transcendent sovereignty. Dionysius plays a pivotal role in this argument: as Agamben observes, Dionysius describes an ornately stratified order, which stretches from heaven, through various angelic ranks, and down to the structure of the church. Since this hierarchy is only authoritative insofar as it mediates the unknowable God, Agamben concludes that Dionysian mysticism reinforces ecclesiastical bureaucracy. In Agamben's reading, Dionysius exemplifies the way in glory sacralizes governmental power. In my view, however, Dionysius develops a negative political theology that desacralizes every authority, including its own.

Agamben correctly identifies the central tension in the Dionysian corpus, but I think he misunderstands its significance. In Chapter 2

CT; London: Yale University Press, 2002); Émile Durkheim, *The Elementary Forms of Religious Life*, trans. Karen E. Fields (New York: Free Press, 1995). In addition to these sources, my understanding of the role of the sacred in secular politics is informed by Kahn, *Political Theology*; Ted Smith, *Weird John Brown: Divine Violence and the Limits of Ethics* (Stanford, CA: Stanford University Press, 2014); and Harald Wydra, *Politics and the Sacred* (New York: Cambridge University Press, 2015).

I argued in response to Stathis Gourgouris that Dionysius does not exempt Christian practice from apophatic dispossession. Where Gourgouris's argument focused on ethics, this chapter elaborates the political implications of the account of hope developed throughout this book. In my reading, Dionysius's understanding of divine transcendence entails that Christian discourse and practice are provisional and therefore subject to revision. Rather than investing worldly government with transcendent glory, Dionysius subjects every order to unstinting critique. Where Agamben inadvertently sacralizes the profane, Dionysius desacralizes the sacred, affirming some things as sacred while submitting them to critique. In this way, I argue, Dionysius offers a compelling response to the problem of sacred politics.

Although Dionysius is an unlikely resource for modern politics, he models a self-critical commitment that is politically potent. In my reading, Dionysian *apophasis* resists hegemonic power without falling into an unsustainable anarchy, affirming imperfect structures while opening them to transformation. By construing Christian faith as an affirmation that is necessarily uncertain, Dionysius demonstrates that it is not necessary to abandon the sacred in order to resist its dangerous effects. On the contrary, he suggests that the sacred can encourage the hopeful pursuit of particular goals while opening politics to unpredictable transformation.

Glory and Government

In *The Kingdom and the Glory*, Agamben argues that modern governmental power derives from a theological paradigm. In support of this claim, he traces a series of attempts by early Christian theologians to relate God's transcendent nature (what they called in Greek *theologia*) to God's immanent ordering of the world (i.e., *oikonomia*, or economy). Where their gnostic opponents claimed that a transcendent God could not intervene in human affairs, theologians such as Irenaeus of Lyons linked the economic relations among the three persons of the Trinity to the economy of salvation.[2] According to Agamben, this avoided dividing an inactive God from an active demiurge, but it introduced a break within the divine between God's being and God's praxis.[3] Some theologians sought to

---

[2] Giorgio Agamben, *The Kingdom and the Glory: For a Theological Genealogy of Economy and Government*, Meridian: Crossing Aesthetics (Stanford, CA: Stanford University Press, 2011), 50–51.
[3] Ibid., 53, 140.

resolve this rupture through the doctrine of providence, which grounds God's temporal action in God's timeless being; this link was later elaborated in terms of ministering angels who mediate God's will.[4] According to Agamben, this providential–economic structure provides the model of the modern state, which legitimates the intimate management of individuals by gesturing toward a distant and impersonal sovereignty.[5]

By means of this genealogy, Agamben aims to clarify the insidious power of government. On his account, just as medieval theology presents the angelic hierarchies as the expression of God's will, modern political thought assumes that the administrative state simply expresses legislative authority.[6] In Agamben's view, however, it is a mistake to assume that economic management is grounded in a sovereignty that precedes it. He explains, "What our investigation has shown is that the real problem, the central mystery of politics is not sovereignty, but government; it is not God, but the angel; it is not the king, but ministry; it is not the law but the police – that is to say, the governmental machine that they form and support."[7] According to Agamben, in both theology and politics, transcendent sovereignty legitimates a governmental system that is, in fact, primary. Where earlier commentators on political theology focused on the sovereign power personified in the monarch, Agamben argues that the key issue is bureaucracy.

The name Agamben gives to this legitimation is glory. Agamben observes that Christians direct praise and adoration toward the immanent Trinity (i.e., God in Godself) in response to the economic Trinity (i.e., God's work in the world).[8] In similar fashion, Agamben says, the acclamations offered to Roman emperors connected the rule of particular individuals to the glory of imperial sovereignty.[9] Likewise, modern democracies sustain the government of life by drawing on the glory of transcendent sovereignty. Agamben explains, "At each turn, [the modern democratic state] wears the regal clothes of providence, which legislates in a transcendent and universal way, but lets the creatures it looks after be

---

[4] Ibid., 141, 158.   [5] Ibid., 135.   [6] Ibid., 276.
[7] Ibid. Agamben is building on the genealogy of governmental power developed by Michel Foucault (cf. Michel Foucault, *The Birth of Biopolitics: Lectures at the Collège De France, 1978–79*, ed. Michel Senellart, trans. Graham Burchell [Basingstoke, UK; New York: Palgrave Macmillan, 2008]). I have argued elsewhere that Foucault's analysis is more circumspect and convincing (David Newheiser, "Foucault, Gary Becker and the Critique of Neoliberalism," *Theory, Culture & Society* 33, no. 5 [2016]: 3–21).
[8] Agamben, *The Kingdom and the Glory*, 209.
[9] Ibid., 178. On Agamben's account, this affinity between religious and political ceremony is not accidental; as he describes, each was modeled on the other (190).

free, and the sinister and ministerial clothes of fate, which ... confines the reluctant individuals within the implacable connection between the immanent causes and between the effects that their very nature has contributed to determining."[10] This ambivalence, by which the state promises freedom to individuals whom it manages in myriad ways, is the central object of Agamben's anxiety. Secular politics claims to exclude the sacred, but Agamben concludes that it relies on glory to legitimate the extension of economy.

Agamben argues that glory invests economic management with a transcendent significance that is, in fact, illusory. He writes, "Government glorifies the Kingdom, and the Kingdom glorifies Government. But the center of the machine is empty, and glory is nothing but the splendor that emanates from this emptiness, the inexhaustible *kabhod* that at once reveals and veils the central vacuity of the machine."[11] According to Agamben, the reciprocity between Kingdom and Government – *theologia* and *oikonomia*, transcendent sovereignty and economic order – obscures the fact that there is nothing at the heart of this circular system. He explains, "Just as liturgical doxologies produce and strengthen God's glory, so the profane acclamations are not an ornament of political power but found and justify it."[12] Although glorification presents itself as a response to a glory that is prior, Agamben claims that the act of glorification produces the glory toward which it is directed. For this reason, he concludes that the function of glory is to reinforce mundane power.

In Agamben's reading, Dionysius exemplifies this structure.[13] As he observes, Dionysius invented the term hierarchy – Greek for "holy order" or "sacred power" – and the bulk of his corpus is taken up by two treatises on the topic, *The Celestial Hierarchy* and *The Ecclesiastical Hierarchy*. Agamben comments, "It is a case, on the one hand, of placing the angels in a hierarchy, arranging their ranks according to a rigidly bureaucratic order and, on the other hand, of angelifying the ecclesiastical hierarchies,

---

[10] Agamben, *The Kingdom and the Glory*, 142.   [11] Ibid., 211.
[12] Ibid., 230; cf. ibid., 199, 224, 226.
[13] Although Agamben's engagement with Dionysius in *The Kingdom and the Glory* is relatively brief, Dionysius plays a pivotal role in his overall argument. He explains elsewhere, "It is within the reflection on angelic hierarchies as a model of ecclesiastic hierarchies that, starting with the Pseudo-Dionysius (whose work should not be read, following the equivocation that has dominated its reception in the West, in a mystical way, but as an attempt to found the sacredness of power and of ecclesiastic hierarchies on the Trinity and the angelic hierarchies), the first legitimization of the Church as a 'worldly' structure of the government of souls takes shape" ("Angels," trans. Lorenzo Chiesa, *Angelaki* 16, no. 3 [September 1, 2011]: 121).

by distributing them according to an essentially sacred gradation."[14] According to Agamben, Dionysius projects a bureaucratic order onto the angels and in this light interprets the ecclesial order as sacred. Agamben writes, "The central idea that runs throughout the Dionysian corpus is that what is sacred and divine is hierarchically ordered, and its barely disguised strategy aims ... at the sacralization of power."[15] Insofar as he invests mundane government with celestial glory, Dionysius exemplifies the providential-economic paradigm that Agamben describes.

As Agamben points out, in apparent contradiction to Dionysius's claim that every attempt to talk about God must be negated, he insists on perpetual praise. Agamben comments, "That apophatic theology has here the function of cover and serves, in fact, to found a governmental hierarchy is evident in the function of acclamation and liturgy that belongs to the divine names, with which the ineffable god must – in apparent contrast with his unsayability – ceaselessly be celebrated and his praises sung."[16] Because Dionysius says a great deal about the unsayable, Agamben concludes that *apophasis* is only a ruse. In his reading, mystical silence intensifies hierarchical power by amplifying its sacred aura. He comments, "Ineffable sovereignty is the hymnological and glorious aspect of power."[17] On this reading, Dionysian mysticism strengthens governmental power by investing it with glory.

Whereas many readers assume that this mystical silence is apolitical, Agamben argues that it reinforces governmental power. He explains, "According to the postulate of the governmental machine with which we are now familiar, an absolutely transcendent thearchy beyond every cause acts in truth as a principle of immanent order and government."[18] On Agamben's reading, negative theology exhibits the circular link between transcendent sovereignty and economic order. In his view, just as glory legitimates imperial power by making the emperor more than a man, reverence for divine transcendence invests ecclesial bureaucracy with

---

[14] Agamben, *The Kingdom and the Glory*, 152.
[15] Ibid., 154. Agamben associates glorious acclamation with the sacred, which he analyzed in *Homo Sacer: Sovereign Power and Bare Life* (trans. Daniel Heller-Roazen [Stanford, CA: Stanford University Press, 1998], 9; *The Kingdom and the Glory*, 188). Colby Dickinson comments on the earlier work: "Politics is therefore nothing less than a human situatedness founded upon a notion of sacrality which, though religion appears to many to be fading from popular acceptance in the West, cannot ever be fully effaced from what constitutes the basis for all personal and social identities formed in a sense that conveys political meaning" (*Agamben and Theology* [London: T & T Clark International, 2012], 75).
[16] Ibid., 155; cf. ibid., 224.   [17] Ibid., 156; cf. ibid., 242.   [18] Ibid., 155.

glorious authority. If Agamben is right, resisting governmental power requires undoing Dionysius's legacy.

Ambivalent *Apophasis*

I agree with Agamben that the Dionysian corpus is destabilized by a profound ambivalence. As I described in Chapter 2, Dionysius argues that, because God transcends creation, God is beyond proclamation, beyond mind, and beyond reason.[19] He writes, "Nothing that is or is known can proclaim that hiddenness beyond every mind and reason of the transcendent Godhead which transcends every being."[20] Dionysius argues that, because human language is derived from the created realm, the creator lies beyond the scope of speech. Thus, although he says that "goodness" is the name for God "which is most revered," he insists that it too is inadequate: "There is no name for [God] nor expression. We cannot follow it into its inaccessible dwelling place so far above us and we cannot even call it by the name of goodness."[21] Since even the best name for God fails, Dionysius concludes that theology requires apophatic critique.

At the same time, Dionysius describes a hierarchical structure that depends upon the immediate relation between the highest angels and God. The difficulty is that his account of divine transcendence suggests that this proximity is impossible. Whereas Dionysius sometimes says that the highest angels are like God, elsewhere he writes that "no being can in any way or as a matter of right be named like to [the Godhead]."[22] Although he says that some angels see and know God, elsewhere he claims that "the divinity is not only invisible and incomprehensible, but also 'unsearchable and inscrutable.'"[23] If unmediated access to God is impossible for every created being (including the angels), it follows that the process of hierarchical mediation can never begin. Conversely, if God is known through Christian worship, it would seem that God is not unknowable after all.

As Agamben observes, Dionysius's description of the angelic hierarchies is inseparable from his understanding of the church, and the same problem recurs here as well. *The Mystical Theology* ends in a frenzy of negation, but it opens with prayer and describes an ascent that mirrors the movements of Christian liturgy. Dionysius's central concern with respect to theological

---

[19] DN 981A, 129. [20] DN 981A, 129. [21] DN 981A, 129.
[22] CH 208C, 163; CH 293B, 176. [23] DN 588C, 50.

language is to praise God appropriately; *hymneō*, the term Dionysius often uses for talk about God, connotes a liturgical song rather than a declarative statement.[24] Whereas *apophasis* indicates that God is radically elusive, Dionysius's account of hierarchy suggests that ecclesial structures provide reliable access to the divine.

Some specialist interpreters agree with Agamben that Dionysian *apophasis* reaffirms the authority of the church. As Charles Stang observes, earlier interpreters divided the *theologia* of *The Divine Names* and *The Mystical Theology* from the *oikonomia* of the hierarchical works, but recent scholarship tends to interpret the theological treatises through the lens of hierarchy.[25] The current consensus is that Dionysius's affirmation of Christian worship brackets his apparent negativity. According to Andrew Louth and Alexander Golitzin, the unknowing that Dionysius describes actually refers to the knowledge of God that is available within the church. If these interpreters are correct, Agamben is right that the function of Dionysian mysticism is to sacralize ecclesial structures.

In my reading, *apophasis* cannot reinforce the affirmation of ecclesial hierarchy, for it calls every affirmation into question. This point is clear from one of the texts Louth and Golitzin offer in support of their reading. Dionysius writes:

> Then he [Moses] breaks free of them, away from what sees and is seen, and he plunges into the truly mysterious darkness of unknowing [*ton gnophon tēs agnōsias*]. Here, renouncing all that the mind may conceive … he belongs completely to him who is beyond everything. Here, being neither oneself nor someone else [*oute heautou oute heterou*], one is supremely united to the completely unknown by an inactivity [*anenergēsia*] of all knowledge, and knows beyond the mind by knowing nothing [*tō mēden ginōskein hyper noun ginōskōn*].[26]

Golitzin and Louth observe that this passage echoes the movements of the liturgy that Dionysius would have known (with Moses typifying the bishop). However, this does not entail (as they claim) that this darkness reinforces the authority of Christian worship.[27] On the contrary, Dionysius's negativity is unstinting: Moses abandons what is seen, renounces what can be conceived, and knows nothing. On Dionysius's terms, if

---

[24] E.g. DN 597C, 58.
[25] Stang, *Apophasis and Pseudonymity in Dionysius the Areopagite: "No Longer I,"* 7–8.
[26] MT 1.3 1001A, 137.
[27] Alexander Golitzin, *Mystagogy: A Monastic Reading of Dionysius Areopagita.*, ed. Bogdan Bucur (Collegeville, MN: Liturgical Press, 2014); Andrew Louth, *Denys the Areopagite* (London: Continuum, 1989), 30–31.

union with God were to occur, it could neither be described nor identified. (If one truly "knows beyond the mind by knowing nothing," then one could not know that it has happened.) For this reason, Dionysius precludes any certainty concerning whether the church provides access to God.[28]

Where Louth and Golitzin claim that Dionysius's affirmation of the church constrains his negativity, I think the coherence of the Dionysian corpus cuts in the other direction. As I argued in Chapter 2, Dionysius presents his affirmation of ecclesial hierarchy as a hope that is necessarily uncertain. He associates "hierarchical traditions" with the "now" in which we "learn these things in the best way we can," but their authority is relativized by the fact that union with God remains for the "time to come" that remains "beyond understanding."[29] Agamben assumes that Dionysius's affirmation of Christian commitment circumscribes his negativity, but I have argued that Dionysian *apophasis* juxtaposes affirmation and negation in order to indicate that neither is adequate to the divine. Rather than sacralizing the *oikonomia* of the church by associating it with the *theologia* of divine transcendence, Dionysius desacralizes every claim to access the divine.[30]

Profanation and Play

Although Agamben intends to dissolve Dionysius's legacy, Dionysian *apophasis* resembles Agamben's own attempts to disrupt the link between glory and government. Agamben argues that human life has an undetermined character that he calls impotentiality, "being able to not do."[31] He claims that, unlike animals (which are ruled by biological necessity), "human life is inoperative and without purpose."[32] This freedom from

---

[28] In light of this reading of Dionysius, I have argued elsewhere that it is inappropriate to appeal to spiritual practices to draw a sharp distinction between Christian theology and secular thought ("Theology and the Secular," *Political Theology* 17, no. 4 [2016]: 378–89).

[29] DN 592B, 52–53. Translation modified.

[30] In his novel *Silence*, Shusaku Endo writes in a different idiom but to similar effect: "The priest raises his foot. In it he feels a dull, heavy pain. This is no mere formality. He will now trample on what he has considered the most beautiful thing in his life, on what he has believed most pure, on what is filled with the ideals and the dreams of man. How his foot aches! And then the Christ in bronze speaks to the priest: 'Trample! Trample! I more than anyone know of the pain in your foot. Trample! It was to be trampled on by men that I was born into this world. It was to share men's pain that I carried my cross'" (Shusaku Endo, *Silence* [London: Quartet Books, 1978], 259).

[31] Giorgio Agamben, *Nudities*, trans. David Kishik and Stefan Pedatella (Stanford, CA: Stanford California Press, 2011), 43.

[32] Agamben, *The Kingdom and the Glory*, 245; cf. Giorgio Agamben, *The Coming Community* (Minneapolis: University of Minnesota Press, 2009), 42.

teleological determination does not entail that humans ought to do nothing; instead, Agamben's point is that the ability to not do is required for action to be free. On his account, when democratic subjects are alienated from their impotentiality, they are rendered docile, directed by governmental power toward activities that serve the state.[33] Since government operates by putting its members to work – with rather than against their consent – impotentiality threatens governmental power. Agamben explains, "We can now begin to understand why doxology and ceremonials are so essential to power. What is at stake is the capture and inscription in a separate sphere of the inoperativity that is central to human life."[34] On this view, glory captures the capacity to not do within a particular sphere in order to prevent it from disrupting governmental order.[35]

It is for this reason that Agamben presents profanation as a political task. He writes, "Profanation ... neutralizes what it profanes. Once profaned, that which was unavailable and separate loses its aura and is returned to use."[36] Agamben explains that, in contrast to secularization (which displaces sacrality from heavenly to earthly sovereignty), profanation neutralizes the sacred, thereby releasing a given object from the religious norms that bind it.[37] Where profanation opens the possibility of a new use, Agamben claims that religion aims to circumscribe inoperativity through the figure of glory. He writes, "Glory is what must cover with its splendor the unaccountable figure of divine inoperativity ... [The] typical form [of the *theologia gloriae*] is that of mysticism, which – in the face of the glorious figure of power – can do nothing except fall silent."[38] In his view, by localizing inoperativity within a particular domain, mysticism precludes profanation by encouraging silent compliance.

My reading of Dionysius demonstrates that this is an unjustified stereotype. As I argued in Chapter 2, Dionysian mysticism is not simply

---

[33] Agamben explains, "Separated from his impotentiality, deprived of the experience of what he can not do, today's man believes himself capable of everything, and he repeats his jovial 'no problem' ... precisely when he should instead realize that he has been consigned in unheard of measure to forces and processes over which he has lost all control" (*Nudities*, 44).

[34] Agamben, *The Kingdom and the Glory*, 245. He comments elsewhere: "All apparatuses of power are always double: they arise, on the one hand, from an individual subjectivizing behavior and, on the other, from its capture in a separate sphere ... We must always wrest from the apparatuses – from all apparatuses – the possibility of use that they have captured" (Giorgio Agamben, *Profanations*, trans. Jeff Fort [London: Zone Books, 2007], 91–92).

[35] Elsewhere he writes, "Glory is nothing other than the separation of inoperativity into a special sphere: that of worship or liturgy" (Agamben, *Nudities*, 101; cf. Giorgio Agamben, *The Use of Bodies*, trans. Adam Kotsko, 2016, 265).

[36] Agamben, *Profanations*, 77.   [37] Ibid., 73.   [38] Agamben, *The Kingdom and the Glory*, 163.

silent; on the contrary, Dionysius insists that the mystery of God ought to inspire proliferating speech. In an echo of Agamben's profanation, Dionysius says that scandalous names for God are preferable to those that are pleasant since they disturb pious inertia.[39] He writes that people call God "good, beautiful, wise, beloved, ... sun, star, and fire, water, wind, and dew," but they must also speak "of his anger, grief, and rage, of how he is said to be drunk and hungover, of his oaths and curses, of his sleeping and waking."[40] Because Dionysius worries that theology will provide false assurance, he argues that it must make affirmations that destabilize a complacent security.[41]

Against the assumption that theology runs along paths predetermined by pious authorities, Dionysius frequently displays a striking creativity. In a dense meditation on biblical references to God as "fire," he ruminates that fire "is undetectable and becomes evident only through its own workings on matter"; that "wherever it is, it changes things toward its own activity"; that "with kindling warmth it causes renewal"; and that "it appears suddenly, naturally and of itself, and soon it rises up irresistibly and, losing nothing of itself, it communes joyfully with everything."[42] These are not self-evident attributes of fire, nor is their theological application obvious, but Dionysius draws surprising significance from unusual imagery. In this way, rather than repeating familiar propositions, Dionysius suggests that Christian thought ought to be radically inventive.

In similar fashion, Dionysius suggests that "each of the many parts of the human body can provide us with images which are quite appropriate to the powers of heaven"[43] – including "eyes, ears, hair, face, and hands, back, wings, and arms, a posterior, and feet."[44] Against this background, he explains how God is like sight, smell, taste, touch, teeth, adolescence, eyelids, eyebrows, shoulders, and arms.[45] Dionysius notes that "[God] is represented [in the Bible] as drinking, as inebriated, as sleeping, as

---

[39] CH 141B, 150.   [40] DN 596B, 55–56; MT 1033B, 139.
[41] CH 141B, 150. Agamben takes the oath to be the sacrament of power, which guarantees the connection between words and things. He writes, "To pronounce the name of God means to understand it as that experience of language in which it is impossible to separate name and being, words and things" (Giorgio Agamben, *The Sacrament of Language: An Archaeology of the Oath*, trans. Adam Kotsko [Stanford, CA: Stanford University Press, 2011], 52). On this basis, he claims that "the age of the eclipse of the oath is also the age of blasphemy, in which the name of God breaks away from its living connection with language and can only be uttered 'in vain'" (71; cf. 2, 40–41). Insofar as Dionysius divides strictly between the names of God (which must be plural) and divine transcendence (which is neither a being nor a thing), he suggests that the prevalence of blasphemy is not unique to modernity. In fact, it was never possible to avoid taking God's name in vain.
[42] CH 15.2 329B, 184.   [43] CH 15.3 329D, 185.   [44] DN 597B, 57.   [45] CH 332A, 185.

Hope in a Secular Age

someone hung-over."[46] Although these passages are potentially scandalous, Dionysius claims that they signify "that incomprehensible superabundance [*hyperochēn*] of God by virtue of which his capacity to understand transcends any understanding or any state of being understood."[47] Rather than foreclosing speech, Dionysius expands incongruous connections in an effort to explode every preconception concerning the divine.[48]

Dionysius's theological method opens Christian discourse to unpredictable play, but play is a feature that Agamben identifies as a prime example of profanation. According to Agamben, when a cat toys with a ball of yarn and when a child plays with a toy car, they deactivate characteristic behaviors (such as driving and predation) in order to open them to a new use.[49] Agamben assumes that such play is the opposite of religion; the Latin term *religio* stems, he says, from anxious scrupulosity in relation to prescribed forms of observance. Against this view, Dionysius suggests that Christian thought contains a critical principle that opens it to playful expansion. Agamben assumes that mysticism consists in a glorious silence that circumscribes possibility, but Dionysius argues that divine hiddenness entails that speech should proliferate without restriction. On his terms, Christian discourse and practice are constitutively open to new use, for their present condition is only provisional.

I think the ambivalence that perplexes readers of Dionysius is also an advantage. Where many interpreters treat *apophasis* as if it is an intellectual exercise, I have argued that Dionysius juxtaposes affirmation and negation in order to underscore that there is no grasping God, and this tension functions as an ethical discipline that is oriented toward future transformation. Where Agamben claims that theologians elide the distinction between God's (objective) glory and the (subjective) glorification of worship, Dionysius insists upon the gap between the present practice of Christian life and union with God (which remains yet to come).[50] Against both complacency and despair, Dionysius suggests that Christian faith is sustained by an uncertain hope, which in turn encourages the playful creativity of his theological method. In contrast to Agamben, who resolves this tension by pitting profanation against the sacred, Dionysius affirms some things as sacred while resisting its appropriation as a tool of legitimation.

---

[46] CH 1105B, 282. [47] CH 1112C, 287; cf. Ep. 9 1112, 287.
[48] The disorienting effect of divine superabundance [*hyperochēn*] exemplifies the way in which, as I argued in Chapter 4, the prefix *hyper-* (for beyond) is simultaneously intensifying and contrastive.
[49] Agamben, *Profanations*, 76. [50] Agamben, *The Kingdom and the Glory*, 200, 214.

Principled Ambivalence

My argument undercuts Agamben's claim that modern governmental power, with all its nefarious effects, is the legacy of Christian theology.[51] Some theologians legitimate mundane power by appropriating celestial glory, but Agamben is wrong to claim that Dionysius is one of them. On the contrary, Dionysius argues that any theology of this kind misconstrues the hopeful character of Christian commitment. Although Derrida does not share Dionysius's vision of sacred politics, he rebuts Agamben's account from the other direction. As I argued in Chapter 3, he and Dionysius share a hope inflected with negativity. This enables him to see the ambivalence of religious traditions as a resource rather than supposing that they must simply be rejected.

Like many readers, Agamben assumes that Derrida aims to overcome metaphysics, and he complains that Derrida fails to do so.[52] However, as I argued in Chapter 1, Derrida does not think it is possible to purify philosophy in this way.[53] Rather than stigmatizing his interlocutors, Derrida tends to work within their texts, exploring internal tensions in order to open unexamined possibilities. This interpretive method is possible because, in Derrida's view, every conceptual or political structure is disrupted by the play of elements that preclude perfect coherence. Where some interpreters associate deconstruction with total play, Derrida argues that such indeterminacy is not a state that a person can sustain. Instead, he describes an ethics that acknowledges uncertainty while taking responsibility for particular judgements. As I have argued, insofar as he models an affirmation that persists without assurance, Derrida exemplifies the discipline of hope.

---

[51] Ibid., 276.

[52] Agamben writes, "Although we must certainly honor Derrida as the thinker who has identified with the greatest rigor ... the original status of the gramma and of meaning in our culture, it is also true that he believed he had opened a way to surpassing metaphysics, while in truth he merely brought the fundamental problem of metaphysics to light" (*Language and Death: The Place of Negativity* [Minneapolis: University of Minnesota Press, 2007], 39).

[53] Thomas Baldwin refers to "Derrida's rejection of Platonism, and indeed his rejection of 'metaphysics' in general" ("Death and Meaning: Some Questions for Derrida," in *Arguing with Derrida*, ed. Simon Glendinning [Oxford; Malden, MA: Blackwell, 2001], 92). Derrida responds: "I have insisted again and again that I am not rejecting metaphysics. I do not 'reject' metaphysics. Not even Platonism. Indeed, I think there is an unavoidable necessity of re-constituting a certain Platonic gesture ... I am not 'rejecting' anything, certainly not metaphysics and certainly not Plato" ("Response to Baldwin," in *Arguing with Derrida*, ed. Simon Glendinning [Oxford; Malden, MA: Blackwell, 2001], 105).

Hope in a Secular Age 145

Agamben sometimes seems nostalgic for a pure profanation that preceded the emergence of religion, but Dionysius and Derrida suggest (in different ways) that things are more complicated.[54] (For one thing, as Derrida observes, the genealogies that Agamben develops often seem unreliable.[55]) Like Dionysius, Derrida situates his work within the tension between imperfect affirmations and the negativity required by that which remains radically elusive. Much as Dionysius subjects the things he says are sacred to desacralizing critique, Derrida holds particular concepts and practices as extraordinarily significant while insisting that they must remain subject to revision. Where Agamben pits profanation against the sacred, Derrida and Dionysius show that it is possible to draw upon symbols that possess special significance while maintaining a critical practice that loosens their authority.

Derrida's sympathetic engagement with religious traditions exhibits this principled ambivalence. In an interview from 2002, Derrida reflects on a line he wrote a decade earlier: "if you knew, G., my experience of prayers, you would know everything."[56] Derrida comments,

> My way of praying, if I pray, has more than one edge ... If I gather images from my childhood, I find images of God as a Father – a severe, just Father with a beard – and also, at the same time, images of a Mother who thinks I am innocent, who is ready to forgive me ... There is another layer, of course, which involves my culture, my philosophical experience, my experience of a critique of religion that goes from Feuerbach to Nietzsche. This is the experience of a nonbeliever, someone who is constantly suspicious of the child, someone who asks, "To whom am I praying? Whom am I addressing? Who is God?"[57]

In this passage, Derrida describes a practice of prayer that is internally conflicted. On the one hand, he links prayer to anthropomorphic images – a man with a beard, a forgiving mother, and so forth. On the other hand, Derrida is drawn by the critique of religion developed by nineteenth-

---

[54] Agamben, *Profanations*, 74, 86; Agamben, *Nudities*, 111; Giorgio Agamben, "What Is a Destituent Power?," *Environment and Planning D: Society and Space* 32, no. 1 (2014): 65–74.

[55] Jacques Derrida, *The Beast and the Sovereign Vol. I*, ed. Michel Lisse, Marie-Louise Mallet, and Ginette Michaud, trans. Geoffrey Bennington (Chicago, IL: University of Chicago Press, 2009), 92. In my view, Agamben's genealogies are often illuminating, but they tend to rely on a dubious reconstruction of the original meaning of the concepts and practices in question (Giorgio Agamben, "What Is an Apparatus?," in *What Is an Apparatus? and Other Essays*, 2010, 8; Agamben, *The Sacrament of Language*, 65–66; cf. Leland de la Durantaye, "Homo Profanus: Giorgio Agamben's Profane Philosophy," *Boundary 2* 35, no. 3 [2008]: 29, 30, 32).

[56] Derrida, "Circumfession," 188.

[57] Jacques Derrida, "Epoché and Faith: An Interview with Jacques Derrida," in *Derrida and Religion: Other Testaments*, ed. Yvonne Sherwood and Kevin Hart (New York: Routledge, 2005), 30.

century atheists such as Nietzsche and Feuerbach. These critics pose pointed questions that unveil the extent to which the object of prayer is uncertain, and they call into question whether prayer amounts to anything more than a projection of the subject or the community. However, rather than rejecting prayer in light of this critique, Derrida describes a way of praying that holds the two together.

As the interview continues, Derrida connects this conflicted prayer to the tradition of negative theology. He explains, "When I pray, I am thinking about negative theology, about the unnamable, the possibility that I might be totally deceived by my belief, and so on. It is a very skeptical – I don't like this word, 'skeptical,' but it will have to do – prayer ... Instead of 'skepticism,' I could talk of epoché, meaning by that the suspension of certainty, not of belief. This suspension of certainty is part of prayer."[58] Once again, Derrida draws upon negative theology to describe the possibility of a faith that foreswears certainty. Rather than obliterating belief, this skepticism functions to distinguish belief from knowledge; it constitutes a critical perspective on a commitment that one continues to hold. As Derrida explains a few lines later, if prayer were grounded in certain knowledge, it would simply be an order – "just as though I were ordering a pizza!"[59] Once again, Derrida relates this uncertain affirmation to hope: "I think this hopelessness is a part of what prayer should be. Yet I know there is hope, there is calculation."[60] Derrida suggests that prayer is characterized by a hope against hope, which incorporates both affirmation and negativity.

Derrida acknowledges that this could seem perplexing. He comments, "I know that this appears negative, but it isn't; it is a way of thinking when praying that does not simply negate prayer. It is a way of asking all the questions that we are posing at this conference, all of them. These questions are a part of my experience of prayer."[61] Although some commentators assume that religion is antithetical to critique, Derrida does not.[62] On the contrary, in an essay from 1996 he suggests that disenchantment is itself a resource for the religious.[63] He explains,

> A certain interruptive unraveling is the condition of the "social bond" ... The hypersanctification of this non-relation or of this transcendence would come about by way of desacralization rather than through secularization or laicization, concepts that are too Christian; perhaps even by way of a certain

---

[58] Ibid., 30–31. [59] Ibid., 31. [60] Ibid. [61] Ibid., 30.
[62] See, for instance, my response to Stathis Gourgouris in Chapter 1.
[63] Derrida, "Faith and Knowledge," 99.

"atheism," in any case by way of a radical experience of the resources of "negative theology" – and going beyond even this tradition.[64]

Here Derrida draws upon the arguments of Emmanuel Levinas, who argued that holiness is strictly distinct from the sacred. Derrida describes this gesture – sanctifying the gap between oneself and the other – as desacralizing. Crucially, however, he observes that desacralization does not exclude holiness, nor does the atheism he has in mind exclude religion. As Derrida recognizes, insofar as negative theology incorporates self-critique, disenchantment may operate within religious traditions. As I argued in Chapter 4, Derrida is drawn to negative theology because he recognizes that it opens the possibility of unforeseen transformation.

Desacralizing Authority

Although it is not immediately obvious, the Dionysian corpus is profoundly political. When Dionysius speaks of union with God, he writes not in the singular but in the first person plural. Elsewhere he explains that the individual's union with God depends upon the unity that exists in the body of the church. He writes, "It is not possible to be gathered together toward the One and to partake of peaceful union with the One while divided among ourselves."[65] In contrast to "that fragmentation of desire which is the source of corporeal and impassioned hostility between equals,"[66] the worshipping congregation is unified by the exchange of peace that forms part of the Eucharistic liturgy. Dionysius explains, "This, it seems to me, is the united and undivided life prescribed for us by the kiss of peace as it joins like to like and turns the fragmented away from the divine and unique visions."[67] On his account, this moment in the church's worship heals fragmentation, purifying desire by enacting communal unity. This is the subtext of Dionysius's insistence upon hierarchical mediation, which knits together all reality in a cooperative harmony directed toward the creator.

Dionysius sometimes draws conclusions from his understanding of hierarchy that appear authoritarian. He writes, "Even if disorder and confusion should undermine the most divine ordinances and regulations, that still gives no right, even on God's behalf, to overturn the order which God himself has established. God is not divided against himself. Otherwise, how could his kingdom stand?"[68] This implies that an individual's

---

[64] Ibid.   [65] CH 6.1 200C, 160.   [66] CH III.III.9 437A, 218.   [67] CH III.III.9 437A, 218.
[68] Ep. 8.1 1088C, 272.

status in the hierarchy sanctifies any behavior whatsoever. This text does contain the suggestion that a person's position in the hierarchy may be lost if it is exercised unworthily, and it is framed by a demand for mercy that culminates in a vision in which the failure of compassion is portrayed as an act of violence toward Jesus himself.[69] Despite these mitigating factors, I do not intend to endorse the political positions that Dionysius himself held. However, insofar as the structure Dionysius describes entails that every authority is only provisional, the implication of his argument is anti-authoritarian.

Because the purpose of hierarchical division is "to achieve a proportion appropriate to sacred objectives and so as to bring all the elements together in order into a cohesive and harmonious communion," the harmonious well-being of all provides a rationale for opposing the abuse of hierarchical power.[70] Indeed, two words Dionysius uses for the Eucharist – *synaxis* for "gathering" and *koinōnia* for "communion" – underscore the intimate relation between communal unity and union with God. He writes, "Every sacredly initiating operation draws our fragmented lives together into a one-like divinization. It forges a divine unity [*theōsin synagousēs*] out of the divisions within us. It grants us communion [*koinōnian*] and union with the One."[71] According to Dionysius, the Christian liturgy of Communion fosters communion with God by gathering together a diverse community. In this view, right relation with God depends upon right relation with others, and the church's worship is caught up in this interplay, healing hostility through a harmony that serves as the condition for the uplifting of each to the divine.

Dionysius does not directly address politics in the modern sense of the term, but there is a democratizing force to the structure he describes. Agamben notes that Dionysius refers to the Trinity with the term *thearchia* (a compound term for divine order or rule), and he claims in this light that Dionysius's politics is theocratic.[72] On this reading, Dionysius exemplifies the danger of sacred politics, foreclosing critique by identifying a given political arrangement with divine authority. However, this is precisely the opposite of what Dionysius is doing. Dionysius argues that the divine cannot be appropriated in discourse or practice, and so thearchy cannot be identified with any political system. Where Agamben claims that "the providential *oikonomia* is fully translated into a hierarchy," I have argued

---

[69] Ep. 8.2 1092B, 274, Ep. 8.6 1000C, 280. I am grateful to Kathryn Tanner for pointing this out to me in private conversation.
[70] EH 5.2 504A, 235.   [71] EH 3.1 424C, 209.   [72] Agamben, *The Kingdom and the Glory*, 155.

that Dionysian *apophasis* preserves the radical distinction between divine transcendence and earthly order.[73] Insofar as it is unknowable, thearchy undermines every attempt to institute theocracy, including (above all) within the church. Instead, Dionysius describes a communal enterprise in which every authority is questionable.[74]

Rather than precluding contestation, Dionysius echoes Agamben's vision of an undetermined politics. Agamben writes,

> One can therefore understand the essential function that the tradition of Western philosophy has assigned to contemplative life and to inoperativity: properly human praxis is sabbatism that, by rendering the specific functions of the living inoperative, opens them to possibility. Contemplation and inoperativity are, in this sense, the metaphysical operators of anthropogenesis, which, by liberating the living man from his biological or social destiny, assign him to that indefinable dimension that we are accustomed to call "politics."[75]

On Agamben's account, contemplation frees people from teleological determination, thereby opening the space for politics (which is free from necessity). Agamben goes on to claim, once again, that this inoperativity is antithetical to religion, but I have argued that this reading is wrong. Dionysius suggests that, on the terms of Christian thought, comportment toward the sacred should not constrain impotentiality. In my view, the discipline of *apophasis* is paradigmatically political, for its aim is to open an undetermined future.[76]

Negativity and Politics

I think Agamben identifies an important problem. Political action is often directed toward identifiable ends, but it is inspired by commitments that transcend the pursuit of individual interests. This is especially clear in moments of national crisis, when citizens are driven to extraordinary sacrifice on behalf of the nation, but even everyday politics is charged by values such as justice, freedom, and equality that go beyond particular

---

[73] Ibid., 154.
[74] It is for this reason, I think, that Dionysius often invites correction on the part of his interlocutors (e.g., CH 308B, 181).
[75] Agamben, *The Kingdom and the Glory*, 251.
[76] Agamben writes, "While humans have reflected for centuries on how to preserve, improve, and ensure their knowledge, we lack even the elementary principles of an art of ignorance" (Agamben, *Nudities*, 113–14). However, such an art (sometimes called *docta ignorantia*, *"learned ignorance"*) has been developed with a high degree of sophistication within Christian thought.

policy goals. Such commitments constitute a faith that exceeds the calculation of cause and effect, and they are sustained by symbols that carry special significance.[77] Political communities are often motivated by appeals to revered individuals (such as Ronald Reagan or Martin Luther King, Jr.), documents (such as the U.S. Constitution or the Universal Declaration of Human Rights), and institutions (such as the judiciary or the military). The danger, as Agamben observes, is that holding such things as sacred can function as an obstacle to political imagination, freezing a given configuration of power through unquestioned reverence.

Like Agamben, many commentators assume that the function of political theology is to sacralize power. Carl Schmitt argues that politics depends upon an exceptional authority that finds its model in the miraculous power of God.[78] Erik Peterson accepts this understanding of political theology, but he claims that Christian trinitarian theology precludes any neat association between human and divine authority – and so he concludes that Christianity cannot have a political theology.[79] Contra Peterson, Stathis Gourgouris claims that political theology is essentially monarchical, even when it is trinitarian in form; in his view, religion is inevitably idolatrous, elevating some things as sacred to conceal the groundless character of human existence.[80] These theorists differ over whether political theology is a good or bad thing, but they agree that it sacralizes worldly power. Against this consensus, I have argued that Dionysius develops a negative political theology that desacralizes every assertion of power.[81]

Some suppose that *apophasis* leaves us with nothing to say in relation to issues that require a decisive response, but this is a misunderstanding. As I have argued, Dionysian *apophasis* is not simply negative. Instead, it holds

---

[77] Stephen Bush's analysis of the function of the sacred in debates over torture is helpful. Bush argues that the sacredness of human life does not supply independent reasons for prohibiting torture, but it can support the prohibition of torture through its emotional force ("Torture and the Politics of the Sacred," *Soundings: An Interdisciplinary Journal* 97, no. 1 [2014]: 85–87, 95).

[78] Schmitt, *Political Theology*, 47.

[79] Erik Peterson, "Monotheism as a Political Problem: A Contribution to the History of Political Theology in the Roman Empire," in *Theological Tractates*, trans. Michael J. Hollerich (Stanford, CA: Stanford University Press, 2011), 102–5.

[80] Stathis Gourgouris, "Political Theology as Monarchical Thought," *Constellations* 23, no. 2 (2016): 145–59; cf. Gourgouris, *Lessons in Secular Criticism*. I discussed Gourgouris's argument at greater length in Chapter 2.

[81] The term "negative political theology" has a short history, which I address in David Newheiser, "Why the World Needs Negative Political Theology," *Modern Theology*, forthcoming. I take the term to mean something different than what my predecessors describe, in large part because I understand the tradition of negative theology differently than they do.

affirmation and negation together in tension in order to open the possibility of unpredictable development. This requires self-critique, to be sure, but it also encourages bold affirmation. By foreclosing false certainty, *apophasis* entails that every commitment is a risk for which each person bears responsibility. Its aim is not simply to insist upon circumspection; as I have described, it encourages a riotous creativity premised upon free experimentation. Although Dionysius offers little guidance about what positions a democratic citizen ought to hold, he models political askesis that sustains the pursuit of aims that are fragile and uncertain. Rather than insisting upon a silence that would still say too much, Dionysius demonstrates that it is possible to affirm particular aims provisionally while simultaneously subjecting them to critique. In this way, Dionysius describes an uncertain hope that avoids the oscillation between presumption and despair.

Sacrality is a source of power, and power is dangerous – but power is also the precondition for political action.[82] The sacred establishes community, holding together a fractious collective through shared sites of special significance. Although it sometimes numbs political imagination, it can also encourage proliferating interpretation of shared points of reference. Symbols of common identity give a group something to argue over, and they situate disagreement within a shared enterprise. The sacred brings bodies together within rites of communal identity: singing a hymn or the national anthem, eating the Eucharistic host or a piece of apple pie, processing on Palm Sunday or in a Pride parade.[83] Such collective action has a performative power that opens political possibilities.[84] For this reason, despite its danger, the sacred remains an indispensable resource for a politics in pursuit of justice. What is needed, I think, is to draw power from the sacred without allowing it to harden into myopia, insisting upon a justice to come while pursing particular improvements on the level of law. Dionysius suggests that this is possible through a circumspect hope.

---

[82] Cf. Michel Foucault, "On the Genealogy of Ethics: An Overview of Work in Progress," in *Michel Foucault: Beyond Structuralism and Hermeneutics*, ed. Paul Rabinow and Hubert Dreyfus (Chicago: University of Chicago Press, 1983), 256.

[83] In response to an earlier draft of this chapter, William Cavanaugh pressed me to specify the difference between the Eucharist and apple pie. I think it is appropriate to discriminate between the various signs that lay claim to the sacred, but my argument operates in a different register. For the purposes of this chapter, I do not assume that the sacraments of Christian worship are efficacious signs of grace, nor do I exclude that possibility.

[84] Judith Butler, *Notes toward a Performative Theory of Assembly* (Cambridge, MA: Harvard University Press, 2015).

Throughout this book I have argued that Dionysius and Derrida share a hope of this kind. It could seem that practices directed toward God differ from those directed toward immanent ends, but Derrida argues that politics is motivated by objects (such as justice and democracy) that exceed any effort to specify them (in principle or in practice). On this view, justice and democracy must be filled out with concrete content to be politically effective, but any judgment concerning them should be held open to future revision. Because Derrida, despite his atheism, shares an uncertain hope with Dionysius, this suggests that a negative political theology may be broadly useful, and not only for religious believers.[85]

It could seem tempting to reject sacred politics altogether, but my argument suggests that this gesture allows sacrality to persist undetected. Democratic societies are divided by hierarchies of race, class, and culture, and those who claim that equality is achieved only obscure persistent injustice. For this reason, a sustainable politics requires both the affirmation of particular structures and suspicion of those same arrangements. Dionysius shows that, rather than choosing between dogmatic adherence and pure profanation, it is possible to inhabit a middle space in which we affirm some things as sacred while holding them open to development. Against a politics of purity, Dionysius shows that it is possible to pursue particular ends without relinquishing utopian critique.

In the wake of the Great Recession of 2007, a range of movements emerged around the world to resist racial and economic injustice, from Occupy to Syriza and the "Arab Spring." The energy that animated these groups was inspiring, but they struggled to transition from opposition to sustainable power.[86] Where protest movements pursue the purity of

---

[85] Compare Robert Bellah's comment: "The religious dimension in political life as recognized by [U.S. President John F.] Kennedy not only provides a grounding for the rights of man which makes any form of political absolutism illegitimate; it also provides a transcendent goal for the political process" ("Civil Religion in America," 4). I think William Cavanaugh is right to claim that "Christianity . . . thus serves a democratic order by relativizing any claim to justice and truth" (*Migrations of the Holy: God, State and the Political Meaning of the Church* [Grand Rapids, MI: Eerdmans, 2011], 134). However, I think he is wrong to oppose Christian worship to secular liturgies (which are, he suggests, inevitably idolatrous; 120–22). If Dionysius is right that Christian worship is not immune to idolatry, then it is not unique after all. On the contrary, as I have argued, both religious and political reverence may attend to transcendence through a disciplined negativity.

[86] On this point, Slavoj Zizek is uncharacteristically lucid: "Echoing the rise of big popular protests in the last years, with hundreds of thousands assembling in public places (from New York, Paris and Madrid to Athens, Istanbul and Cairo), 'assemblage' . . . became a popular topic of theory. One should retain a sceptical distance towards this topic: whatever its merits, it leaves untouched the key problem of how to pass from assembling protest to the imposition of a new power, of how this new power will function in contrast to the old one" (Slavoj Zizek, *The Courage of Hopelessness* [London: Allen Lane, 2017]).

justice, the work of governing must reckon with ambiguity and compromise. Both relation and negation are needed, but – as I discussed in relation to Rita Felski and Eve Kosofsky Sedgwick in Chapter 1 – it is difficult to maintain these affective registers at once. In my view, Dionysius and Derrida demonstrate (in different idioms) that this discipline is not impossible. In contrast to an unmodulated negation that simply obliterates its object, they describe a negativity that holds affirmation open to future revision. Against both complacency and despair, they point to a politics of hope.

Conclusion

If someone commends hope without reservation, you ought to be suspicious. Hope connotes positivity and light. It is directed toward that which one desires, and its fulfillment is a cause for rejoicing. It often refers to everyday desires, as in the hope for good weather or for good traffic on the way to work. Under duress, hope can seem like the last anchor to life, as when the hope for a cure encourages someone unwell to struggle toward health. Hope is often prescribed in difficult times. "Keep hope," one's friends may say by way of encouragement – or, if they're especially worried, "Don't lose hope." Hope enables people to stave off the darkness, holding on to the promise of better things.

At the same time, hope has darkness at its heart. Because concerns what may be rather than what is, hope is fundamentally uncertain. In contrast to optimism, hope possesses no confidence concerning its fulfillment – on my account, it may persist even when one thinks the outcome is impossible. Hope concerns what is to come, which is necessarily unknown. For this reason, although the term "hope" has a positive valence, it is frequently the source of suffering. It is painful to maintain a desire that is continually frustrated; under such circumstances, despair may feel like relief. Hope presses into the unknown, and so it is dangerous.

This danger provides hope its potency. Because hope is not determined by the rational calculation of probabilities, it can sustain commitment even when the situation is bleak. Through the extra-rational tenacity of hope, religious and political movements can keep faith in the face of disappointment. Persistence can be good or bad depending on its object, and hope (in itself) cannot discriminate between them. As resolute desire, hope is therefore a risk, but it is one worth running, for our lives would otherwise be constrained by the scope of our certainties.

My account of hope is wagered on the suspicion that people feel the force of the future even when they act as if things are secure. Although it is good to contemplate the lilies of the field, anxiety is understandable when one does not know how to find food and shelter. In less extreme circumstances, people are sometimes confronted with their fragility even if they generally distract themselves with other concerns. We cannot be sure that our loves will endure, that our projects will succeed, or that we stand on the side of justice and truth. It is tempting to dissimulate these difficulties – and indeed some try – but hope allows us instead to face them. Between false confidence and paralyzing despair, hope persists without assurance.

Over the course of this book, I have described the discipline of hope in conversation with deconstruction and negative theology. If I am right that Dionysius and Derrida are, despite their differences, surprisingly close, my argument suggests that Christian thought and contemporary theory may look to each other to illuminate questions of common concern. Although Derrida is an atheist (of a sort), my reading suggests that he is more useful as a resource for religious reflection than many suppose. By the same token, whereas some philosophers are squeamish about theology, Dionysius contributes to conversations that interest contemporary theorists – concerning consciousness and temporality, the persistence of sacrality, and the politics of critique. Insofar as my account undermines the hackneyed distinction between "natural" and "supernatural" hope, it suggests that theologians, philosophers, and political theorists may borrow freely from one another.

Hope of this kind requires a bold humility, but humility is harder than it seems. Those who claim that one must submit to the Lord frequently appropriate divine authority for themselves; supposing themselves to have achieved such modesty, they assert that their beliefs are molded to the mind of God. Conversely, the loudest critics of religion oppose dogmatism, but in foreclosing faith they invest a contestable decision with incontrovertible authority. Whereas apparent self-abnegation is sometimes subtle self-assertion, hope requires reflexive critique. Insofar as Derrida and Dionysius insist that our judgments inevitably remain our own, the decision in favor of an apophatic hope is (like everything else) uncertain. But where negation alone is a sort of assertion, holding affirmation and negation together in tension indicates that provisional efforts in the present are qualified by the unforeseeable future.

Since complacency is a constant danger – precisely where we least expect it – continual vigilance is required. "It was said of Abbot Agatho that for three years he carried a stone in his mouth until he learned to be silent."[1]

---

[1] Thomas Merton, ed., *The Wisdom of the Desert: Sayings from the Desert Fathers of the Fourth Century* (New York: New Directions, 1970), 30.

I have sought to suggest that hope is a discipline of this kind. Whereas it seems to some that Derrida and Dionysius are primarily concerned with language and reference, I have argued that their discursive negativity functions as an ethical practice of openness to the unexpected. *Apophasis* reminds us that the beyond can be captured neither in a discursive description, nor in a political system, nor in ritual practice (whether religious or not). In my understanding, hope does not preclude such efforts – as if the stone were large enough to exclude speech altogether – but it sits like a pebble tucked into one's cheek, reminding its practitioner that there is always more to be said.

Bibliography

Aberth, John. "Pseudo-Dionysius as Liberator: The Influence of the Negative Tradition on Late Medieval Female Mystics." *Downside Review* 114, no. 395 (April 1996): 96–115.

Agamben, Giorgio. "Angels." Translated by Lorenzo Chiesa. *Angelaki* 16, no. 3 (September 1, 2011): 117–23.

The Coming Community. Minneapolis: University of Minnesota Press, 2009.

Homo Sacer: Sovereign Power and Bare Life. Translated by Daniel Heller-Roazen. Stanford, CA: Stanford University Press, 1998.

The Kingdom and the Glory: For a Theological Genealogy of Economy and Government. Meridian: Crossing Aesthetics. Stanford, CA: Stanford University Press, 2011.

Language and Death: The Place of Negativity. Minneapolis: University of Minnesota Press, 2007.

Nudities. Translated by David Kishik and Stefan Pedatella. Stanford, CA: Stanford University Press, 2011.

Profanations. Translated by Jeff Fort. Brooklyn: Zone Books, 2007.

The Sacrament of Language: An Archaeology of the Oath. Translated by Adam Kotsko. Stanford, CA: Stanford University Press, 2011.

The Use of Bodies. Translated by Adam Kotsko. Stanford, CA: Stanford University Press, 2016.

"What Is a Destituent Power?" *Environment and Planning D: Society and Space* 32, no. 1 (February 1, 2014): 65–74.

"What Is an Apparatus?" In *What Is an Apparatus? And Other Essays*, 1–24. Stanford, CA: Stanford University Press, 2010.

Ahbel-Rappe, Sara. "Damascius on the Third Hypothesis of the Parmenides." In *Plato's Parmenides and Its Heritage*, Vol. 2, edited by John Douglas Turner and Kevin Corrigan, 143–56. Atlanta: Society of Biblical Literature, 2010.

Alighieri, Dante *The Divine Comedy. 1, Inferno*. Translated by Robin Kirkpatrick. London; New York: Penguin Books, 2010.

Aristotle. *The "Art" of Rhetoric*. Translated by John Henry Freese. London: Heinemann, 1926.

Arthur, Rosemary A. *Pseudo-Dionysius as Polemicist: The Development and Purpose of the Angelic Hierarchy in Sixth Century Syria*. Ashgate New Critical

Thinking in Religion, Theology and Biblical Studies. Aldershot, UK; Burlington, VT: Ashgate, 2008.
Asad, Talal. *Formations of the Secular: Christianity, Islam, Modernity*. Stanford, CA: Stanford University Press, 2003.
——— *Genealogies of Religion: Discipline and Reasons of Power in Christianity and Islam*. Baltimore: Johns Hopkins University Press, 1993.
Audi, Robert. *Religious Commitment and Secular Reason*. Cambridge; New York: Cambridge University Press, 2000.
Baldwin, Thomas. "Death and Meaning: Some Questions for Derrida." In *Arguing with Derrida*, edited by Simon Glendinning, 89–101. Oxford; Malden, MA: Blackwell, 2001.
Baring, Edward. *The Young Derrida and French Philosophy, 1945–1968*. Cambridge: Cambridge University Press, 2011.
Barry, Peter. *Beginning Theory: An Introduction to Literary and Cultural Theory*. Manchester: Manchester University Press, 1995.
Bellah, Robert N. "Civil Religion in America." *Daedalus* 96, no. 1 (1967): 1–21.
Berger, Peter L. "Secularism in Retreat." *The National Interest* 46 (1996): 3–12.
——— *The Sacred Canopy: Elements of a Sociological Theory of Religion*. Garden City, NY: Doubleday, 1967.
Berlant, Lauren. *Cruel Optimism*. Durham, NC: Duke University Press, 2011.
Borges, Jorge Luis. "On Exactitude in Science." In *Collected Fictions*, translated by Andrew Hurley, 325. New York: Viking, 1998.
Bradley, Arthur. "Without Negative Theology: Deconstruction and the Politics of Negative Theology." *Heythrop Journal* 42, no. 2 (2001): 133–47.
Brainard, F. Samuel. *Reality and Mystical Experience*. University Park: Pennsylvania State University Press, 2000.
Bush, Stephen S. "Torture and the Politics of the Sacred." *Soundings: An Interdisciplinary Journal* 97, no. 1 (February 21, 2014): 75–99.
Butler, Judith. *Notes toward a Performative Theory of Assembly*. Cambridge, MA: Harvard University Press, 2015.
Calhoun, Craig J., Mark Juergensmeyer, and Jonathan VanAntwerpen. "Introduction." In *Rethinking Secularism*, edited by Craig J. Calhoun, Mark Juergensmeyer, and Jonathan VanAntwerpen, 3–30. New York: Oxford University Press, 2011.
Calvino, Italo. *Invisible Cities*. Translated by William Weaver. New York: Harcourt Brace Jovanovich, 1978.
Camus, Albert. *The Myth of Sisyphus, and Other Essays*. New York: Knopf, 1955.
Caputo, John D. "Apostles of the Impossible." In *God, the Gift, and Postmodernism*, edited by John D. Caputo and Michael J. Scanlon, 185–222. Bloomington: Indiana University Press, 1999.
——— *Hoping against Hope: Confessions of a Postmodern Pilgrim* (Minneapolis: Fortress Press, 2015), 10–21, 96–102.
——— *More Radical Hermeneutics: On Not Knowing Who We Are*. Studies in Continental Thought. Bloomington: Indiana University Press, 2000.
——— *Philosophy and Theology*. Horizons in Theology. Nashville, TN: Abingdon Press, 2006.

"On the Power of the Powerless: Dialogue with John D. Caputo." In *After the Death of God*, edited by Jeffrey W. Robbins, 114–62. New York: Columbia University Press, 2007.

The Prayers and Tears of Jacques Derrida: Religion without Religion. Bloomington: Indiana University Press, 1997.

The Weakness of God: A Theology of the Event. Bloomington: Indiana University Press, 2006.

Carabine, Deirdre. *The Unknown God: Negative Theology in the Platonic Tradition, Plato to Eriugena.* Louvain Theological and Pastoral Monographs 19. Louvain: Peeters Press, 1995.

Carlson, Thomas. *Indiscretion: Finitude and the Naming of God.* Chicago: University of Chicago Press, 1999.

Casanova, José. *Public Religions in the Modern World.* Chicago: University of Chicago Press, 1994.

"The Secular, Secularizations, Secularisms." In *Rethinking Secularism*, edited by Craig J. Calhoun, Mark Juergensmeyer, and Jonathan VanAntwerpen, 54–74. New York: Oxford University Press, 2011.

Casanova, José, Michael Kessler, John Milbank, and Mark Lilla. "A Conversation: José Casanova, Michael Jon Kessler, John Milbank, and Mark Lilla." In *Political Theology for a Plural Age*, by Michael Kessler, 12–40. New York: Oxford University Press, 2013.

Cavanaugh, William T. *Migrations of the Holy: God, State and the Political Meaning of the Church.* Grand Rapids, MI: Eerdmans, 2011.

The Myth of Religious Violence: Secular Ideology and the Roots of Modern Conflict. Oxford: Oxford University Press, 2009.

Cixous, Hélène. *Portrait of Jacques Derrida as a Young Jewish Saint.* New York: Columbia University Press, 2003.

Collins, Guy. "Defending Derrida: A Response to Milbank and Pickstock." *Scottish Journal of Theology* 54, no. 3 (2001): 344–65.

"Thinking the Impossible: Derrida and the Divine." *Literature and Theology* 14, no. 3 (September 1, 2000): 313–34.

Coole, Diana H. *Negativity and Politics: Dionysus and Dialectics from Kant to Poststructuralism.* London; New York: Routledge, 2000.

Crosby, Christina. *A Body, Undone: Living on after Great Pain.* New York: New York University Press, 2017.

Cunningham, Conor. *A Genealogy of Nihilism: Philosophies of Nothing and the Difference of Theology.* London; New York: Routledge, 2002.

Darley, Alan Philip. "'We Know in Part': How the Positive Apophaticism of Aquinas Transforms the Negative Theology of Pseudo-Dionysius." *Heythrop Journal*, 2011. DOI: 10.1111/j.1468-2265.2010.00658.x.

Derrida, Jacques. "Above All, No Journalists!" In *Religion and Media*, edited by Hent de Vries and Samuel Weber, 56–93. Stanford, CA: Stanford University Press, 2001.

"Abraham, the Other." In *Judeities: Questions for Jacques Derrida*, edited by Bettina Bergo, Joseph D. Cohen, and Raphael Zagury-Orly, 1–35. New York: Fordham University Press, 2007.

Adieu to Emmanuel Levinas. Meridian: Crossing Aesthetics. Stanford, CA: Stanford University Press, 1999.
Without Alibi. Translated by Peggy Kamuf. Meridian: Crossing Aesthetics. Stanford, CA: Stanford University Press, 2002.
Aporias. Meridian: Crossing Aesthetics. Stanford, CA: Stanford University Press, 1993.
"Of an Apocalyptic Tone Newly Adopted in Philosophy." In *Derrida and Negative Theology*, edited by Harold G. Coward and Toby A. Foshay, 25–72. Albany, NY: State University of New York Press, 1991.
"Autoimmunity: Real and Symbolic Suicides." In *Philosophy in a Time of Terror: Dialogues with Jürgen Habermas and Jacques Derrida*, by Giovanna Borradori, 85–126. Chicago: University of Chicago Press, 2003.
The Beast and the Sovereign, Vol. 1. Translated by Geoffrey Bennington. Chicago: University of Chicago Press, 2009.
The Beast and the Sovereign, Vol. I. Edited by Michel Lisse, Marie-Louise Mallet, and Ginette Michaud. Translated by Geoffrey Bennington. Chicago: University of Chicago Press, 2009.
"Christianity and Secularization," trans. David Newheiser, *Critical Inquiry*, forthcoming.
"Circumfession." In *Jacques Derrida*, by Geoffrey Bennington and Jacques Derrida, 3–315. Religion and Postmodernism. Chicago: University of Chicago Press, 1993.
On Cosmopolitanism and Forgiveness. Thinking in Action. London: Routledge, 2001.
"Cristianesimo e Secolarizzazione," 1996. 219DRR/198/6. Fonds Jacques Derrida, IMEC, Saint-Germain-la-blanche herbe, Normandie.
The Death Penalty, Vol. 1. Edited by Geoffrey Bennington, M. Crépon, and Thomas Dutoit. Translated by Peggy Kamuf. Chicago: University of Chicago Press, 2014.
"Deconstruction and the Other." In *Debates in Continental Philosophy: Conversations with Contemporary Thinkers*, by Richard Kearney, 139–56. London: Fordham University Press, 2004.
"The Deconstruction of Actuality." In *Negotiations: Interventions and Interviews, 1971–2001*, edited by Elizabeth Rottenberg. Cultural Memory in the Present. Stanford, CA: Stanford University Press, 2002.
"Derrida's Response to Jean-Luc Marion." In *God, the Gift, and Postmodernism*, edited by John D. Caputo and Michael J. Scanlon, 42–47. Bloomington: Indiana University Press, 1999.
"Différance." In *Margins of Philosophy*, translated by Alan Bass, 1–28. Chicago: University of Chicago Press, 1982.
Dissemination. Chicago: University Press, 1981.
"Edmond Jabès and the Question of the Book." In *Writing and Difference*, translated by Alan Bass, 64–78. Chicago: University of Chicago Press, 1978.

"Ellipsis." In *Writing and Difference*, translated by Alan Bass, 295–300. Chicago: University of Chicago Press, 1978.

"Epoché and Faith: An Interview with Jacques Derrida." In *Derrida and Religion: Other Testaments*, edited by Yvonne Sherwood and Kevin Hart, 27–52. New York: Routledge, 2005.

"Events? What Events?" In *Negotiations: Interventions and Interviews, 1971–2001*, edited by Elizabeth Rottenberg, 74–76. Cultural Memory in the Present. Stanford, CA: Stanford University Press, 2002.

"The Eyes of Language: The Abyss and the Volcano." In *Acts of Religion*, edited by Gil Anidjar, 189–227. New York: Routledge, 2002.

"Faith and Knowledge: The Two Sources of 'Religion' at the Limits of Reason Alone." In *Acts of Religion*, edited by Gil Anidjar, 40–101. New York: Routledge, 2002.

"Force of Law: The 'Mystical Foundation of Authority.'" In *Acts of Religion*, edited by Gil Anidjar, 228–98. New York: Routledge, 2002.

"On Forgiveness: A Roundtable Discussion with Jacques Derrida." In *Questioning God*, edited by John D. Caputo, Mark Dooley, and Michael J. Scanlon. Bloomington: Indiana University Press, 2001.

The Gift of Death. Chicago: University of Chicago Press, 1995.

The Gift of Death and Literature in Secret. 2nd ed. Religion and Postmodernism. Chicago: University of Chicago Press, 2008.

"Globalization, Peace, and Cosmopolitanism." In *Negotiations: Interventions and Interviews, 1971–2001*, edited by Elizabeth Rottenberg, 371–86. Cultural Memory in the Present. Stanford, CA: Stanford University Press, 2002.

Of Grammatology. 1st American ed. Baltimore: Johns Hopkins University Press, 1976.

"'I Have a Taste for the Secret.'" In *A Taste for the Secret*, by Maurizio Ferraris and Jacques Derrida, 1–92. Edited by Giacomo Donis and David Webb, translated by Giacomo Donis. Cambridge: Polity, 2001.

"How to Avoid Speaking: Denials." In *Derrida and Negative Theology*, edited by Harold G. Coward and Toby A. Foshay, 73–142. Albany, NY: State University of New York Press, 1991.

"How to Avoid Speaking: Denials." In *Psyche: Inventions of the Other, Volume II*, edited by Peggy Kamuf and Elizabeth Rottenberg, 143–95. Stanford, CA: Stanford University Press, 2008.

"L'argument Ontologique et Autres Preuves de l'existence de Dieu," March 1962. 219DRR/220/6. Fonds Jacques Derrida, IMEC, Saint-Germain-la-blanche herbe, Normandie.

Le Problème De La Genèse Dans La Philosophie De Husserl. 1re éd. Epiméthée. Paris: Presses Universitaires de France, 1990.

"Le Sens Du Transcendental," 1961. 219DRR/337/3. Fonds Jacques Derrida, IMEC, Saint-Germain-la-blanche herbe, Normandie.

"Letter to John P. Leavey." *Semeia* 23 (1982): 61–62.

"L'idée de Simplicité," 1952. DRR 222. Fonds Jacques Derrida, IMEC, Saint-Germain-la-blanche herbe, Normandie.

Limited Inc. Evanston, IL: Northwestern University Press, 1988.
"L'Une des pires oppressions: L'Interdiction d'une langue." Interview by Aïssa Khelladi. *Algérie Littérature Action* 9 (March 1997): 105–16.
"A Madness Must Watch over Thinking." In *Points ...: Interviews, 1974–1994*, 339–64. Meridian: Crossing Aesthetics. Stanford, CA: Stanford University Press, 1995.
Marges De La Philosophie. Collection "Critique." Paris: Éditions de Minuit, 1972.
Monolingualism of the Other, or, The Prosthesis of Origin. Cultural Memory in the Present. Stanford, CA: Stanford University Press, 1998.
"A Number of Yes." In *Psyche: Inventions of the Other, Volume II*, edited by Peggy Kamuf and Elizabeth Rottenberg, 231–40. Stanford, CA: Stanford University Press, 2008.
"Negotiations." In *Negotiations: Interventions and Interviews, 1971–2001*, edited by Elizabeth Rottenberg, 11–40. Cultural Memory in the Present. Stanford, CA: Stanford University Press, 2002.
"Not Utopia, the Im-Possible." In *Paper Machine*, 121–35. Cultural Memory in the Present. Stanford, CA: Stanford University Press, 2005.
"The Original Discussion of 'Différance.'" In *Derrida and Différance*, by David Wood and Robert Bernasconi. Evanston, IL: Northwestern University Press, 1988.
"Others Are Secret Because They Are Other." In *Paper Machine*, 136–63. Cultural Memory in the Present. Stanford, CA: Stanford University Press, 2005.
Paper Machine. Cultural Memory in the Present. Stanford, CA: Stanford University Press, 2005.
"Politics and Friendship." In *Negotiations: Interventions and Interviews, 1971–2001*, edited by Elizabeth Rottenberg, 147–98. Cultural Memory in the Present. Stanford, CA: Stanford University Press, 2002.
"Qual Quelle." In *Margins of Philosophy*, translated by Alan Bass, 273–306. Chicago: University of Chicago Press, 1982.
"Recherches Sur L'Hellenisme," 1949. 219DRR/336/7. Fonds Jacques Derrida, IMEC, Saint-Germain-la-blanche herbe, Normandie.
"Religion et Philosophie," 1972. 219DRR/224/6. Fonds Jacques Derrida, IMEC, Saint-Germain-la-blanche herbe, Normandie.
"Response to Baldwin." In *Arguing with Derrida*, edited by Simon Glendinning, 102–8. Oxford; Malden, MA: Blackwell, 2001.
"From a Restricted to a General Economy." In *Writing and Difference*, translated by Alan Bass, 251–77. Chicago: University of Chicago Press, 1978.
Rogues: Two Essays on Reason. Meridian: Crossing Aesthetics. Stanford, CA: Stanford University Press, 2005.
"Sauf Le Nom (Post Scriptum)." In *On the Name*, edited by Thomas Dutoit, 35–88. Meridian: Crossing Aesthetics. Stanford, CA: Stanford University Press, 1995.
Specters of Marx: The State of the Debt, the Work of Mourning, and the New International. New York: Routledge, 1994.

"Structure, Sign, and Play in the Discourse of the Human Sciences." In *Writing and Difference*, translated by Alan Bass, 278–94. Chicago: University of Chicago Press, 1978.

"Taking Sides for Algeria." In *Negotiations: Interventions and Interviews, 1971-2001*, edited by Elizabeth Rottenberg, 117–24. Cultural Memory in the Present. Stanford, CA: Stanford University Press, 2002.

"Terror, Religion, and the New Politics." In *Debates in Continental Philosophy: Conversations with Contemporary Thinkers*, by Richard Kearney, 3–14. London: Fordham University Press, 2004.

"Théologico-Politique: Nationalité et Nationalisme Philosophique," 1986. 219DRR/175/1. Fonds Jacques Derrida, IMEC, Saint-Germain-la-blanche herbe, Normandie.

On Touching, Jean-Luc Nancy. Meridian: Crossing Aesthetics. Stanford, CA: Stanford University Press, 2005.

The Truth in Painting. Chicago: University of Chicago Press, 1987.

"Violence and Metaphysics: An Essay on the Thought of Emmanuel Levinas." In *Writing and Difference*, translated by Alan Bass, 79–153. Chicago: University of Chicago Press, 1978.

"What Does It Mean to Be a French Philosopher Today?" In *Paper Machine*, 112–20. Cultural Memory in the Present. Stanford, CA: Stanford University Press, 2005.

"What Remains by Force of Music." In *Psyche: Inventions of the Other, Vol. I*, 81–89. Meridian: Crossing Aesthetics. Stanford, CA: Stanford University Press, 2007.

For What Tomorrow: A Dialogue. Cultural Memory in the Present. Stanford, CA: Stanford University Press, 2004.

Derrida, Jacques, and Jean-Luc Marion. "On the Gift: A Discussion Between Jacques Derrida and Jean-Luc Marion." In *God, the Gift, and Postmodernism*, edited by John D. Caputo and Michael J. Scanlon, 54–78. Bloomington: Indiana University Press, 1999.

Derrida, Jacques, Gianni Vattimo, Vincenzo Vitiello, and Maurizio Ferraris. "Cristianesimo e Secolarizzazione." *Il Pensiero* 2 (1998): 21–42.

Dickinson, Colby. *Agamben and Theology*. London: T & T Clark International, 2012.

Dionysius the Areopagite, Pseudo-. *OEuvres Complètes Du Pseudo-Denys l'Aréopagite*. Translated by Maurice de Gandillac. Bibliothèque Philosophique. Paris: Aubier, Editions Montaigne, 1943.

The Works of Dionysius the Areopagite, Translated by John Parker. Merrick, NY: Richwood, 1976.

The Divine Names and Mystical Theology. Translated by John D. Jones. Milwaukee, WI: Marquette University Press, 1980.

Pseudo-Dionysius: The Complete Works, The Classics of Western Spirituality. Translated by Colm Luibheid. New York: Paulist Press, 1987.

Corpus Dionysiacum I. Edited by Beate Regina Suchla. Berlin: De Gruyter, 1990.

Corpus Dionysiacum II. Edited by Günter Heil and Adolf Martin Ritter. Berlin: De Gruyter, 1991.

Durantaye, Leland de la. "Homo Profanus: Giorgio Agamben's Profane Philosophy." *Boundary 2* 35, no. 3 (August 1, 2008): 27–62.

Durkheim, Émile. *The Elementary Forms of Religious Life*. Translated by Karen E. Fields. New York: Free Press, 1995.

Eagleton, Terry. *Hope without Optimism*. New Haven, CT; London: Yale University Press, 2017.

Elliot, David. *Hope and Christian Ethics*. New York: Cambridge University Press, 2017.

Endō, Shūsaku. *Silence*. London: Quartet Books, 1978.

Felski, Rita. *The Limits of Critique*. Chicago: University of Chicago Press, 2015.

Fiddes, Paul. *The Promised End: Eschatology in Theology and Literature*. Oxford; Malden, MA: Blackwell Publishers, 2000.

Fiskå Hägg, Henny. *Clement of Alexandria and the Beginnings of Christian Apophaticism: Knowing the Unknowable*. New York: Oxford University Press, 2006.

Foucault, Michel. "On the Genealogy of Ethics: An Overview of Work in Progress." In *Michel Foucault: Beyond Structuralism and Hermeneutics*, edited by Paul Rabinow and Hubert Dreyfus, 229–52. Chicago: University of Chicago Press, 1983.

The Birth of Biopolitics: Lectures at the Collège de France, 1978–79. Edited by Michel Senellart. Translated by Graham Burchell. Basingstoke, UK; New York: Palgrave Macmillan, 2008.

Fukuyama, Francis. *The End of History and the Last Man*. London: Penguin, 1992.

Furey, Constance M. "Discernment as Critique in Teresa of Avila and Erasmus of Rotterdam." *Exemplaria* 26, no. 2–3 (June 1, 2014): 254–72.

Golitzin, Alexander. *Et Introibo Ad Altare Dei: The Mystagogy of Dionysius Areopagita with Special Reference to Its Predecessors in the Eastern Christian Tradition*. Thessaloniki: Patriarchikon Idruma Paterikōn Meleton, 1994.

"Hierarchy versus Anarchy? Dionysius Areopagita, Symeon the New Theologian, Nicetas Stethatos, and Their Common Roots in Ascetical Tradition." *St. Vladimir's Theological Quarterly* 38 (1994): 131–79.

Mystagogy: A Monastic Reading of Dionysius Areopagita. Edited by Bogdan Bucur. Collegeville, MN: Liturgical Press, 2014.

"The Mysticism of Dionysius Areopagita: Platonist or Christian?" *Mystics Quarterly* 19, no. 3 (1993): 98–114.

"'On the Other Hand' (A Response to Fr Paul Wesche's Recent Article on Dionysius)." *St. Vladimir's Theological Quarterly* 34, no. 4 (1990): 305–23.

"Review Essay: *Pseudo-Dionysius: A Commentary on the Texts and an Introduction to Their Influence*, by Paul Rorem." *Mystics Quarterly* 21, no. 1 (March 1994): 28–38.

Gourgouris, Stathis. "Every Religion Is Idolatry." *Social Research* 80, no. 1 (2013): 101–28.

Lessons in Secular Criticism. New York: Fordham University Press, 2013.

"Political Theology as Monarchical Thought." *Constellations* 23, no. 2 (June 1, 2016): 145–59.

Gregory of Nyssa. *The Life of Moses*. New York: Paulist Press, 1978.

Griffiths, A. Phillips. "Certain Hope." *Religious Studies* 26, no. 4 (1990): 453–61.

Habermas, Jürgen. *The Philosophical Discourse of Modernity: Twelve Lectures.* Cambridge, MA: MIT Press, 1987.

Habermas, Jürgen, and Jacques Derrida. *Philosophy in a Time of Terror: Dialogues with Jürgen Habermas and Jacques Derrida.* Edited by Giovanna Borradori. Chicago: University of Chicago Press, 2003.

Hadot, Pierre. *Philosophy as a Way of Life: Spiritual Exercises from Socrates to Foucault.* Edited by Arnold Davidson. Malden, MA: Blackwell, 1995.

Hägglund, Martin. *Radical Atheism: Derrida and the Time of Life.* Meridian. Stanford, CA: Stanford University Press, 2008.

Hammerschlag, Sarah. *The Figural Jew: Politics and Identity in Postwar French Thought.* Chicago: University of Chicago Press, 2010.

Hans, James. *The Play of the World.* Amherst: University of Massachusetts Press, 1981.

Hart, Kevin. *The Trespass of the Sign: Deconstruction, Theology, and Philosophy.* 1st paperback ed. New York: Cambridge University Press, 1991.

Hartman, Geoffrey. *Saving the Text: Literature, Derrida, Philosophy.* Baltimore: Johns Hopkins University Press, 1981.

Hathaway, Ronald F. *Hierarchy and the Definition of Order in the Letters of Pseudo-Dionysius: A Study in the Form and Meaning of the Pseudo-Dionysian Writings.* The Hague: Nijhoff, 1969.

Hector, Kevin. "Apophaticism in Thomas Aquinas: A Re-reformulation and Recommendation." *Scottish Journal of Theology* 60, no. 04 (2007): 377–93.

Hobbes, Thomas. "Behemoth: The History of the Causes of the Civil Wars of England." In *The English Works of Thomas Hobbes, Vol. 6 (Dialogue, Behemoth, Rhetoric)*, edited by William Molesworth, 161–418. Aalen: Scientia-Verl., 1839.

———. *Leviathan.* Edited by Richard Tuck. Cambridge; New York: Cambridge University Press, 1991.

Hollywood, Amy. *Acute Melancholia and Other Essays.* New York: Columbia University Press, 2016.

Horton, Michael. "Eschatology after Nietzsche: Apollonian, Dionysian or Pauline?" *International Journal of Systematic Theology* 2, no. 1 (March 1, 2000): 29–62.

Hughes, Kevin. "The Crossing of Hope, or Apophatic Eschatology." In *The Future of Hope: Christian Tradition amid Modernity and Postmodernity*, edited by Miroslav Volf and William Katerberg, 101–24. Grand Rapids, MI: William B. Eerdmans Pub. Co., 2004.

Husserl, Edmund. *Analyses Concerning Passive and Active Synthesis: Lectures on Transcendental Logic.* Dordrecht; Boston: Kluwer Academic Publishers, 2001.

———. *Cartesian Meditations: An Introduction to Phenomenology.* The Hague: M. Nijhoff, 1960.

Ivanovic, Filip. "The Ecclesiology of Dionysius the Areopagite." *International Journal for the Study of the Christian Church* 11, no. 1 (February 2011): 27–44.

Jones, John D. "The Divine Names in John Sarracen's Translation: Misconstruing Dionysius's Language about God?" *American Catholic Philosophical Quarterly* 82, no. 4 (Fall 2008): 661–82.

Jones, John N. "Sculpting God: The Logic of Dionysian Negative Theology." *Harvard Theological Review* 89, no. 4 (1996): 355–71.
Jones, Tamsin. *A Genealogy of Marion's Philosophy of Religion: Apparent Darkness*. Bloomington: Indiana University Press, 2011.
Kahn, Paul W. *Political Theology: Four New Chapters on the Concept of Sovereignty*. New York: Columbia University Press, 2011.
Kearney, Richard. *The God Who May Be: A Hermeneutics of Religion*. Bloomington: Indiana University Press, 2001.
Kearney, Richard, and Jens Zimmermann, eds. *Reimagining the Sacred: Richard Kearney Debates God with James Wood, Catherine Keller, Charles Taylor, Julia Kristeva, Gianni Vattimo, Simon Critchley, Jean-Luc Marion, John Caputo, David Tracey, Jens Zimmermann, and Merold Westphal*. New York: Columbia University Press, 2016.
Kharlamov, Vladimir. *The Beauty of the Unity and the Harmony of the Whole: The Concept of Theosis in the Theology of Pseudo-Dionysius the Areopagite*. Eugene, OR: Wipf & Stock Publishers, 2008.
Knepper, Timothy D. "Three Misuses of Dionysius for Comparative Theology." *Religious Studies* 45, no. 2 (June 2009): 205–21.
Koch, Hugo. "Der Pseudo-Epigraphische Character Der Dionysischen Schriften." *Theologische Qartalschrift* 77 (1895): 353–421.
Latour, Bruno. "Why Has Critique Run out of Steam? From Matters of Fact to Matters of Concern." *Critical Inquiry* 30, no. 2 (January 1, 2004): 225–48.
Leitch, Vincent B. "Late Derrida: The Politics of Sovereignty." *Critical Inquiry* 33, no. 2 (2007): 229–47.
Levinas, Emmanuel. *Time and the Other and Additional Essays*. Pittsburgh, PA: Duquesne University Press, 1987.
Liddell, Henry George. *A Greek–English Lexicon*. Rev. and augm. throughout. Oxford: Clarendon Press, 1996.
Light, Aimee. "Sculpting God: An Exchange (1)." *Harvard Theological Review* 91, no. 2 (1998): 205–6.
Lilla, Mark. "Coping with Political Theology." *Cato Unbound*, October 8, 2007. http://www.cato-unbound.org/2007/10/08/mark-lilla/coping-political-theology.
——— "Extremism's Theological Roots." *The Jerusalem Post*, October 8, 2001.
——— *The Reckless Mind: Intellectuals in Politics*. New York: New York Review of Books, 2001.
——— *The Stillborn God: Religion, Politics, and the Modern West*. New York: Knopf, 2007.
——— *The Stillborn God: Religion, Politics, and the Modern West*. New York: Vintage, 2008.
Lossky, Vladimir. *The Mystical Theology of the Eastern Church*. London: J. Clarke, 1957.
Louth, Andrew. *Denys the Areopagite*. London: Continuum, 1989.
——— "Pagan Theurgy and Christian Sacramentalism in Denys the Areopagite." *Journal of Theological Studies* 37, no. 2 (1986): 432–38.
Luther, Martin. *Luther's Works, Vol. 36: Word and Sacrament II*. Edited by Abdel Ross Wentz. Philadelphia: Fortress Press, 1959.

Mahmood, Saba. *Politics of Piety: The Islamic Revival and the Feminist Subject.* Princeton, NJ: Princeton University Press, 2005.
  "Religious Reason and Secular Affect: An Incommensurable Divide?" *Critical Inquiry* 35, no. 4 (2009): 836–62.
Marcel, Gabriel. *Homo Viator: Introduction to the Metaphysic of Hope.* South Bend, IN: St. Augustine's Press, 2010.
Marion, Jean-Luc. *God without Being: Hors-Texte.* Religion and Postmodernism. Chicago: University of Chicago Press, 1991.
  The Idol and Distance: Five Studies. Perspectives in Continental Philosophy no 17. New York: Fordham University Press, 2001.
  "In the Name." In *God, the Gift, and Postmodernism*, edited by John D. Caputo and Michael J. Scanlon, 20–42. Bloomington: Indiana University Press, 1999.
Martin, Adrienne. *How We Hope: A Moral Psychology.* Princeton: Princeton University Press, 2013.
Martinich, Aloysius. *The Two Gods of Leviathan: Thomas Hobbes on Religion and Politics.* Cambridge; New York: Cambridge University Press, 1992.
Marx, Karl. *Critique of Hegel's "Philosophy of Right."* Translated by Joseph O'Malley. Cambridge: Cambridge University Press, 1970.
Mazzucchi, Carlo Maria. "Damascio, Autore Del Corpus Dionysiacum, e Il Dialogo 'Peri Politikes Epistemes.'" *Aevum: Rassegna Di Scienze Storiche Linguistiche e Filologiche* 80, no. 2 (2006): 299–334.
Merton, Thomas, ed. *The Wisdom of the Desert: Sayings from the Desert Fathers of the Fourth Century.* New York: New Directions, 1970.
Migliore, Daniel L. *Faith Seeking Understanding: An Introduction to Christian Theology.* Grand Rapids, MI: Eerdmans Publishing, 1991.
Milbank, John. "The Sublime in Kierkegaard." In *Post-Secular Philosophy: Between Philosophy and Theology*, edited by Phillip Blond, 61–81. London; New York: Routledge, 1998.
  Theology and Social Theory: Beyond Secular Reason. 2nd ed. Oxford; Malden, MA: Blackwell Publishing, 2006.
  Truth in Aquinas. London; New York: Routledge, 2001.
Mittleman, Alan. *Hope in a Democratic Age: Philosophy, Religion, and Political Theory.* Oxford: Oxford University Press, 2009.
Mortley, Raoul. *From Word to Silence.* 2 vols. Theophaneia 30. Bonn: Hanstein, 1986.
Newheiser, David. "Conceiving Transformation without Triumphalism: Joachim of Fiore against Gianni Vattimo." *Heythrop Journal* 55 (2014): 650–62.
  "Derrida and the Danger of Religion." *Journal of the American Academy of Religion* 86, no. 1 (2018): 42–61.
  "Desacralizing Political Theology: Dionysius the Areopagite and Giorgio Agamben." *Modern Theology*, DOI:10.1111/moth.12506.
  "Eckhart, Derrida, and the Gift of Love." In *Desire, Faith, and the Darkness of God: Essays in Honor of Denys Turner*, edited by David Newheiser and Eric Bugyis, 430–56. Notre Dame, IN: University of Notre Dame Press, 2015.

"Foucault, Gary Becker and the Critique of Neoliberalism." *Theory, Culture & Society* 33, no. 5 (2016): 3–21.

"Sexuality and Christian Tradition: Innovation and Fidelity, Ancient and Modern," *Journal of Religious Ethics* no. 43 (2015): 122–145.

"Theology and the Secular." *Political Theology* 17, no. 4 (July 3, 2016): 378–89.

"Tradition, Novelty, and the Need for Discernment." *The Living Church*, January 29, 2012, 19–22.

"Why the World Needs Negative Political Theology." *Modern Theology*, forthcoming.

Ofrat, Gideon. *The Jewish Derrida*. 1st ed. Syracuse, NY: Syracuse University Press, 2001.

O'Rourke, Fran. *Pseudo-Dionysius and the Metaphysics of Aquinas*. Studien Und Texte Zur Geistesgeschichte Des Mittelalters, Bd. 32. Leiden; New York: E. J. Brill, 1992.

Packer, George. "Dark Hours: Violence in the Age of Terror." *The New Yorker* (July 20, 2015): 72–75.

Palmer, D. W. "Atheism, Apologetic, and Negative Theology in the Greek Apologists of the Second Century." *Vigiliae Christianae* 37, no. 3 (1983): 234–59.

Perl, Eric David. *Theophany: The Neoplatonic Philosophy of Dionysius the Areopagite*. Albany: State University of New York Press, 2007.

Peterson, Erik. "Monotheism as a Political Problem: A Contribution to the History of Political Theology in the Roman Empire." In *Theological Tractates*, translated by Michael J. Hollerich, 68–105. Stanford, CA.: Stanford University Press, 2011.

Pickstock, Catherine. *After Writing: On the Liturgical Consummation of Philosophy*. Challenges in Contemporary Theology. Oxford; Malden, MA: Blackwell Publishers, 1998.

"Reply to David Ford and Guy Collins." *Scottish Journal of Theology* 54, no. 3 (2001): 405–22.

Pieper, Josef. *On Hope*. San Francisco: Ignatius Press, 1986.

Plato. *Plato 4: Cratylus, Parmenides, Greater Hippias, Lesser Hippias*. Translated by Harold North Fowler. Cambridge. MA; London: Harvard University Press, 1939.

Rapaport, Herman. *The Theory Mess: Deconstruction in Eclipse*. New York: Columbia University Press, 2001.

"The Idea of Public Reason Revisited." *University of Chicago Law Review* 64, no. 3 (Summer 1997): 756–807.

Rawls, John. *Political Liberalism*. New York: Columbia University Press, 1993.

Rist, John M. "A Note on Eros and Agape in Pseudo-Dionysius." *Vigiliae Christianae* 20, no. 4 (1966): 235–43.

Roberts, Tyler. *Encountering Religion: Responsibility and Criticism After Secularism*. New York: Columbia University Press, 2013.

Roques, René. "Introduction." In *La Hiérarchie Céleste*, by Pseudo-Dionysius, translated by Maurice de Gandillac. Sources Chrétiennes, no 58. Paris: Éditions du Cerf, 1958.

L'univers Dionysien; Structure Hiérarchique Du Monde Selon Le Pseudo-Denys. Théologie 29. Paris: Aubier, 1954.

"Pierre l'Ibérien et Le 'Corpus' Dionysien." *Revue de l'histoire Des Religions* 145, no. 1 (1954): 69–98.

Rorem, Paul. *Pseudo-Dionysius: A Commentary on the Texts and an Introduction to Their Influence.* New York: Oxford University Press, 1993.

Rorty, Richard. *Consequences of Pragmatism: Essays, 1972–1980.* Minneapolis: University of Minnesota Press, 1982.

Rousseau, Jean-Jacques. *The Social Contract: And, the First and Second Discourses.* Edited by Susan Dunn. New Haven, CT; London: Yale University Press, 2002.

Royle, Nicholas. *After Derrida.* Manchester: Manchester University Press, 1995.

Rubenstein, Mary-Jane. "Dionysius, Derrida, and the Critique of 'Ontotheology.'" *Modern Theology* 24, no. 4 (2008): 725–41.

Saffrey, Henri Dominique. "Nouveaux Liens Objectifs Entre Le Pseudo-Denys et Proclus." *Revue Des Sciences Philosophiques et Théologiques* 63, no. 1 (January 1979): 3–16.

"Un Lien Objectif Entre Le Pseudo-Denys et Proclus." In *Studia Patristica*, 9 (1966): 98–105.

Schmitt, Carl. *Political Theology: Four Chapters on the Concept of Sovereignty.* Cambridge, MA: MIT Press, 1985.

Scott, Joan Wallach. "Against Eclecticism." *Differences* 16, no. 3 (December 1, 2005): 114–37.

Searle, John R. "The Word Turned Upside Down." *New York Review of Books* (October 27, 1983): 74–79.

Sedgwick, Eve Kosofsky. *Touching Feeling: Affect, Pedagogy, Performativity.* Durham, NC; London: Duke University Press, 2006.

Seesengood, Robert Paul. *Paul: A Brief History.* Chichester, UK; Malden, MA: Wiley-Blackwell, 2010.

Seung T. K. *Structuralism and Hermeneutics.* New York: Columbia University Press, 1984.

Shaw, Gregory. "Neoplatonic Theurgy and Dionysius the Areopagite." *Journal of Early Christian Studies* 7, no. 4 (Winter 1999): 573–99.

Smith, James K. A. "Determined Hope: A Phenomenology of Christian Expectation." In *The Future of Hope: Christian Tradition amid Modernity and Postmodernity*, edited by Miroslav Volf and William Katerberg, 200–27. Grand Rapids, MI: William B. Eerdmans Pub. Co., 2004.

Smith, Ted. *Weird John Brown: Divine Violence and the Limits of Ethics.* Stanford, CA: Stanford University Press, 2014.

Spinoza, Benedict de. *Ethics.* Translated by E. M. Curley. London; New York: Penguin Books, 1996.

Stang, Charles M. *Apophasis and Pseudonymity in Dionysius the Areopagite: "No Longer I."* Oxford: Oxford University Press, 2012.

Stiglmayr, Josef. "Der Neuplatoniker Proclus Als Vorlage Des Sogen. Dionysius Areopagiten in Der Lehre Vom Übel." *Historisches Jahrbuch* 16 (1895): 721–48.

"Die Eschatologie Des Pseudo-Dionysius." *Zeitschrift Für Katholische Theologie* 23 (1899): 1–21.
Stout, Jeffrey. *Democracy and Tradition*. Princeton, NJ: Princeton University Press, 2004.
Tanner, Kathryn. "Postmodern Challenges to 'Tradition.'" *Louvain Studies* 28 (2003): 175–93.
Taylor, Charles. *A Secular Age*. Cambridge, MA: Belknap Press of Harvard University Press, 2007.
Thomas Aquinas. *The Summa Theologica*, 2nd rev. ed. Translated by Fathers of the English Dominican Province. 1920. http://www.newadvent.org/summa/.
"Doctrine in a Radically Apophatic Register." *Scottish Journal of Theology* 69, no. 2 (May 2016): 123–39.
Ticciati, Susannah. *A New Apophaticism: Augustine and the Redemption of Signs*. Leiden: Brill, 2015.
The Darkness of God: Negativity in Christian Mysticism. Cambridge: Cambridge University Press, 1995.
Turner, Denys. *Faith, Reason, and the Existence of God*. Cambridge; New York: Cambridge University Press, 2004.
"How to Read the Pseudo-Denys Today?" *International Journal of Systematic Theology* 7, no. 4 (2005): 428–40.
Julian of Norwich, Theologian. New Haven, CT: Yale University Press, 2011.
Vanneste, Jan. "Is the Mysticism of Pseudo-Dionysius Genuine?" *International Philosophical Quarterly* 3, no. 2 (1963): 286–307.
Warren, Calvin L. "Black Nihilism and the Politics of Hope." *CR: The New Centennial Review* 15, no. 1 (April 1, 2015): 215–48.
Wear, Sarah Klitenic, and John M. Dillon. *Dionysius the Areopagite and the Neoplatonist Tradition: Despoiling the Hellenes*. Ashgate Studies in Philosophy and Theology in Late Antiquity. Aldershot, UK; Burlington, VT: Ashgate, 2007.
Webster, John. "Eschatology, Anthropology and Postmodernity." *International Journal of Systematic Theology* 2, no. 1 (2000): 13–28.
Williams, Janet. "The Apophatic Theology of Dionysius the Pseudo-Areopagite." *Downside Review* 117, no. 408 (1999): 157–72.
Williams, Rowan. *Faith in the Public Square*. London; New York: Bloomsbury, 2012.
The Tragic Imagination. Oxford: Oxford University Press, 2016.
Winters, Joseph Richard. *Hope Draped in Black: Race, Melancholy, and the Agony of Progress*. Durham, NC: Duke University Press, 2016.
Wydra, Harald. *Politics and the Sacred*. New York: Cambridge University Press, 2015.
Zahavi, Dan. *Self-Awareness and Alterity: A Phenomenological Investigation*. Evanston, IL: Northwestern University Press, 1999.
Zizek, Slavoj. *The Courage of Hopelessness*. London: Allen Lane, 2017.

Subject Index

absence and presence, Derrida on, 22–37
affirmation and negativity, coexistence of
   in deconstruction, 18–19, 21, 30, 37–39
   in negative theology, 40–41, 43–45, 47, 54, 58, 95, 143, 150
Agamben, Giorgio, 14, 133–43, 145, 148–50.
   See also negative political theology
   Homo Sacer, 137n15
   The Kingdom and the Glory, 134
   Language and Death, 144n52
   Profanations, 141n34
   The Use of Bodies, 141n35
Agatho, Abbot, 155
Algeria, Derrida on, 113–14
alterity and otherness
   Derrida's ethics regarding, 122–23
   negative theology and deconstruction both moved by desire for, 87
Althusser, Louis, 17
anxiety, Hobbes's attribution of religious belief to, 111–12
apophasis, 11, 40–42, 44–45, 47–48, 102n84, 106, 138–40, 149–51
apophatic theology. *See* negative theology
aporia, 29, 100
Arab Spring, 152
Aristotle, 63, 78, 81n68
Arthur, Rosemary, 43n9
Asad, Talal, 4n5, 118
atheism
   Derrida and, 109, 124–26, 144
   of Gourgouris, versus Dionysius's self-critical faith, 55–57
Augustine of Hippo, 125

Baldwin, Thomas, 144n53
Barry, Peter, 20n9
Bataille, Georges, 92n28
Beckett, Samuel, 71n32
Bellah, Robert, 132, 152n85
Berlant, Lauren, 83

Borges, Jorge Luis, 12
Borne, Etienne, 91
Bradley, Arthur, 105n96
Bush, Stephen, 150n77

calculative judgment. *See* law/calculative judgment
Calvino, Italo, *Invisible Cities*, 1–2, 4
Camus, Albert
   critique of hope by, 5–6, 13, 63–67, 70, 71n32, 73, 82
   on death penalty debate, 114
   The Myth of Sisyphus, 64
   secularization, religious elements in description of, 115n25
capital punishment (death penalty), religious and secular debates about, 114
Caputo, John, 10–11, 14, 74, 77, 85–89, 92, 98, 100–1, 105–6, 122–23
   Prayers and Tears of Jacques Derrida, 86
Casanova, José, 117–18
Cavanagh, William, 151n83, 152n85
Christianity. *See also* religion and secular politics
   Derrida on, 115
   desire of Derrida for faith from which he felt alienated, 127–30
   Enlightenment viewed as phenomenon of, 115
   eschatology/messianism in, 3
   hope, Christian/Dionysian concept of, 66–71
   oikonomia and *theologia*, linking of, 134, 136
Cicero, 82
Clement of Alexandria, 102n84
Coole, Diana, 45n15
cosmic hierarchy, mediation of, 41–42, 48–50, 58, 133, 136, 138, 147–49
creative interpretation of texts, 11–13
critique and self-criticism
   atheism of Gourgouris versus self-critical faith of Dionysius, 55–57
   of deconstruction, 18–19, 30n53, 33–37
   Derrida's understanding of, 30n53

Subject Index

critique and self-criticism (cont.)
  discipline of the will, self-critical, hope as, 7–9, 79, 82, 84, 155
  of hope, 2–5, 14, 63–66
  negative theology and self-critical nature of faith, 55–58
  profanation and descralization, political/religious task of, 140–43, 145

Damascus, 71n27
dangerousness
  eschatology/messianism, political dangers of, 110
  of hope, 82–84
  of religion, 110–13
Dante, *Inferno*, 80
death penalty, religious and secular debates about, 114
deconstruction, 13, 17–39
  affirmation and negativity, coexistence of, 18–19, 21, 30, 37–39
  critiques of, 18–19, 30n53, 33–37
  defined and described, 18–19
  as ethics of uncertainty, 19–22, 32, 37, 103–4, 144
  faith and, 9–11
  of law/calculative judgment, 30–33
  Marion's treatment of, 93–97, 101
  negative theology and, 10, 14, 85, 89–93. *See also* relationship between deconstruction and negative theology
  negativity, Derrida's politics inflected by, 30–33
  philosophy as conceptual system, problem of, 19–22
  political commitment and, 28–30
  subjective certainty, destabilization of, 22–37
  time and justice, understanding of, 25–28
democracy, Derrida on, 32–33, 76, 121, 130
Derrida, Jacques
  apocalyptic privilege, on assertion of, 94–101
  atheism and, 109, 117–26, 146
  Caputo elided with, 89n12
  Caputo's treatment of, 85–89, 92, 100–1
  on Christianity, 115
  comparison of Dionysius and Derrida on hope, 72–74, 151, 155
  on content of hope, 77
  on creative interpretation of texts, 11–12, 28n43
  critique, understanding of, 30n53
  deconstruction and, 13. *See also* deconstruction
  on democracy, 32–33, 76, 121, 130
  desire for faith from which he felt alienated, 127–30
  différance, concept of, 23–24, 32, 35, 88–89, 98, 101
  Dionysius compared, 9, 14, 85, 152, 155
  Dionysius considered by, 91
  on eschatology/messianism, 9, 38, 72–75, 87, 113, 125–26
  on faith, 9–11, 73
  hope, concept of, 8–9, 13, 63–64, 71–74, 82, 144
  hospitality, on risks of, 122–23
  hyperousios/superessentiality, problem of, 97–99
  on the impossible, 123–24
  Judaism and, 9, 87, 105, 127–30
  Marion on, 93–97, 101
  on mystical negativity and pursuit of justice, 105
  negative political theology of, 144–47
  play, concept of, 20–22, 27
  on political commitments and religious faith, 14
  on prayer, 145–46
  on radical elusiveness of justice, 75–76
  on rationality/transcendence of hope, 79, 81
  risk, on acceptance of, 109–23
  on secularism/secularization, 119–21
  separation of religion and politics, rebuttal to, 109–10, 113–17
  speech/knowledge about the hyperessential, on problem of, 99–101
Derrida, Jacques, works
  "Abraham, the Other," 127
  "Deconstruction and the Other," 72n33
  "Différance," 19, 22–25, 32, 72, 88–89, 91, 98
  Dissemination, 92
  "Edmond Jabès and the Question of the Book," 91, 127n93
  "Ellipsis," 92
  "Faith and Knowledge," 115n28
  "Force of Law," 19, 25–30, 32, 35n79, 72
  "From a Restricted to a General Economy," 92
  The Gift of Death, 129n102
  "How to Avoid Speaking: Denials," 37n91, 89–91, 97, 128n96
  "The Idea of Simplicity," 17
  "Negotiations," 36n84
  "Of an Apocalyptic Tone," 100
  Of Grammatology, 22n17, 28n43
  La Problème de la Genèse dans la Philosophie de Husserl (thesis), 97
  "Qua Quelle," 92
  Rogues, 19, 31–33, 72, 81n67

Subject Index

"Sauf le nom," 104
Specters of Marx, 37, 76, 120
"Structure, Sign, and Play," 19–22, 24–25, 30–31, 71
A Taste for the Secret, 74
"Terror, Religion, and the New Politics," 76n44
The Truth in Painting, 92
"Violence and Metaphysics," 91, 95n46
"What Remains by Force of Music," 92
Dickinson, Colby, 137n15
différance, Derridean concept of, 23–24, 32, 35, 88–89, 98, 101
Dionysius the Areopagite
 Agamben's engagement with, 136–39, 148
 biographical information, 41
 Christian/Dionysian concept of hope, 66–71
 comparison of Dionysius and Derrida on hope, 72–74, 151, 155
 on content of hope, 77
 on creative interpretation of texts, 11–12
 Derrida compared, 9, 14, 85, 151, 155
 Derrida considering, 91
 eschatological reading of, 60n82, 68–69, 70n26, 76
 faith and, 9–11
 on hierarchy and mediation, 41–42, 48–50, 58, 133, 136, 138, 147–49
 hope, concept of, 9–13, 63–64, 66–71, 82
 hyperousios/superessentiality, problem of, 87, 90n14, 91–92, 96–102
 on incarnation, 70
 Marion's treatment of, 93–97, 101
 mysticism and, 54–55, 61, 76, 137–38, 141
 negative political theology of, 132–34, 147–49. *See also* negative political theology
 negative theology of, 13, 40–45. *See also* negative theology
 Neoplatonism of, 13, 42
 Paul (apostle) and, 12–13, 115
 political instincts of, 105
 on praise, 93–96, 137
 pseudonym used by, 12, 41
 radical atheism of Derrida compared to negative theology of, 124
 on rationality/transcendence of hope, 79, 81
 on resurrection and afterlife, 67–68
 Thomas Aquinas compared, 45–47
Dionysius the Areopagite, works
 The Celestial Hierarchy, 44n14, 57, 136
 The Divine Names, 61, 95n48, 139
 The Ecclesiastical Hierarchy, 57, 60n82, 95n48, 136
 Epistles, 70, 71n27, 95n48
 The Mystical Theology, 42, 44n14, 46n23, 47, 54–55, 95n48, 99–100, 138
discipline of the will, self-critical, hope as, 7–9, 83–84, 155
dogmatic idolatry, problem of, in negative theology, 51–53
Durkheim, Émile, 132

Eagleton, Terry, 81
Meister Eckhart, 45, 87, 92n28, 124
Elliot, David, 5
Endo, Shusaku, *Silence*, 140n30
Enlightenment, viewed as Christian phenomenon, 115
eschatology/messianism
 apocalyptic privilege, Derrida on assertion of, 90–101
 in Christianity, 3
 Derrida on, 9, 38, 72–75, 87, 113, 125–26
 Dionysius, eschatological reading of, 60n82, 68–69, 70n26, 76
 Marx and, 120
 political dangers of, 110
 specific hope contents of particular traditions of, 74
ethics
 affinity between negative theology and deconstruction at level of, 102–4
 deconstruction as ethics of uncertainty, 19–22, 32, 37, 103–4, 144
 of negative theology, 47–48, 103, 143
 risk, Derrida on acceptance of, 122–23
Eucharistic liturgy, Dionysius on, 147–48
evil
 as malformed desire for the good, 48
 nothingness of, 43n9

faith and hope, 9–11, 73
Felski, Rita, 13, 18, 33–36, 152
Feuerbach, Ludwig, 146
Fiddes, Paul, 77n47
fire, Dionysius on biblical references to God as, 142
Foucault, Michel, 135n7
Freud, Sigmund, 25
Furey, Constance M., 30n53

Gandillac, Maurice de, 97–98
glory, Agamben on legitimation of government by, 135–38, 140–41

Gnostics, 134
Golitzin, Alexander, 11, 53–54, 60n82, 139–40
Gourgouris, Stathis, 40, 51–57, 145, 150
Great Recession (2007), 152

Habermas, Jürgen, 20–21
Hägglund, Martin, 10–11, 14, 121–26
Hans, James, 20n9
Hart, Kevin, 21n12, 73n37, 92n28, 98n65, 126n89
Hartman, Geoffrey, 20n11
Hathaway, Ronald, 41n1
Hector, Kevin, 46n23
hierarchy, cosmic, mediation of, 41–42, 48–50, 58, 133, 136, 138, 147–49
Hierotheus (teacher of Dionysius), 55n62
Hobbes, Thomas, 109, 111–13, 116–17, 130–31
Leviathan, 112
Hollywood, Amy, 44n12
hope, 1–16, 63–84, 154–56
  Christian concepts of, 66–71
  the comfortable and familiar, orientation away from, 16
  comparison of Dionysius and Derrida on, 72–74, 155
  content of, 74–77
  creative interpretation of texts and, 11–13
  critiques of, 5–7, 14, 63–66
  darkness at heart of, 154
  defined and described, 64, 82
  Derrida's concept of, 8–9, 13, 63–64, 71–74, 82, 144. See also Derrida, Jacques
  difficulty/indispensability of, 1–3
  Dionysius's concept of, 9–13, 63–64, 66–71, 82. See also Dionysius the Areopagite
  as discipline of the will requiring self-critical stance, 7–9, 83–84, 155
  faith and, 9–11, 73
  future, orientation toward, 16
  negative political theology and, 151–53
  prayer, Derrida on, 146
  rationality/transcendence of, 4, 77–82
  religion and secular politics, as response to danger/fragility of, 130–31
  Romans 8:24-25 on, 6
  in a secular age, 3–5, 66
  suffering and danger, as source of, 82–84
Horton, Michael, 89n12
hospitality, Derrida on risks of, 122–23
Hughes, Kevin, 74, 76
Hugo, Victor, 114
Husserl, Edmund, 24
hyperousios/superessentiality, 87, 90n14, 91–92, 96–102

the impossible, Derrida on, 123–24
incarnation, Dionysius on, 70
Irenaeus of Lyons, 134

Jews and Judaism
  Derrida and, 9, 87, 105, 127–30
  hope and, 3
John Scotus Eriugena, 90n18, 91
Jones, John N., 44n14, 46n23
justice
  law/calculative judgment and, 27–28
  mystical negativity and pursuit of, 104–5
  radical elusiveness of, in Derrida's thought, 75–76
  time and, Derridean understanding of, 25–28

Kahn, Paul, 29n44, 115n26
Kearney, Richard, 102n84
Kennedy, John F., 152n85
khōra, 32n65, 104, 128
Kierkegaard, Søren, 67
King, Martin Luther, Jr., 150
Knepper, Timothy, 44n14
Koch, Hugo, 42n3

Latour, Bruno, 18, 33–34, 58
law/calculative judgment
  deconstruction of, 30–33
  as interpretive and provisional, 28–30
  justice and, 27–28
  violence/force, association with, 31
le Senne, René, 127
Levinas, Emmanuel, 25, 102n84, 147
Lévi-Strauss, Claude, 36
Light, Aimee, 44n14
Lilla, Mark, 28–29, 109–17, 130–31
  The Stillborn God, 110n4
liturgy. See worship
Louth, Andrew, 11, 139–40
Luther, Martin, 42n4

Mahmood, Saba, 36
Marcel, Gabriel, 67–68, 127
Marion, Jean-Luc, 10–11, 14, 85–86, 93–97, 101, 104–5
  The Idol and Distance, 93
  "In the Name," 94
Martin, Adrienne, 9, 69, 79, 80n60, 81, 82n69
Marx, Karl, and Marxism, 6, 37–38, 74n39, 120
Mary (mother of Jesus), 55n62
Mazzucchi, Carlo, 71n27
mediation of cosmic hierarchy, 41–42, 48–50, 58, 133, 136, 138, 147–49
messianism. See eschatology/messianism

Subject Index

Milbank, John, 17n2
Mittleman, Alan, 71n32, 80
Monory, Michael, 127
Mortley, Raoul, 71n27
mysticism
    Agamben on glory and, 141
    defined, 76
    Dionysius and, 54–55, 61, 76, 137–38, 141
    negative theology and, 54–55, 61
    pursuit of justice and mystical negativity, 104–5

negative political theology, 14, 132–53
    Agamben and, 14, 133–44, 148–50
    apophasis of Dionysius and, 138–40, 150
    cosmic hierarchy of Dionysius and, 133, 136, 138, 147–49
    Derrida and, 144–47
    of Dionysius, 132–34, 147–49
    glory, Agamben on legitimation of government by, 135–38, 140–41
    government versus sovereignty, primacy of, 135
    hope and, 151–53
    oikonomia and *theologia*, early Christian linking of, 134, 136
    profanation and descralization, task of, 140–43, 145
    religion/secular politics and, 132–33
    sacralization of political power, avoiding, 149–50
    the sacred, using performative power of, 150–51
negative theology, 13, 40–61
    affirmation and negativity, coexistence of, 40–41, 43–45, 47, 54, 58, 95, 143, 151
    apophasis, 11, 40–42, 44–45, 102n84, 106
    Caputo on Derrida and, 85–89, 92, 100–1
    cosmic hierarchy and mediation in, 41–42, 48–50, 58
    deconstruction and, 10, 14, 85, 89–93. *See also* relationship between deconstruction and negative theology
    defined and described, 40–45
    Derrida's views on, 89–93
    discipline of hope and, 7
    dogmatic idolatry, problem of, 51–53
    ecclesial and cosmic hierarchies, parallels between, 51–52, 60
    ecclesial worship practices and, 53–54
    ethics of, 47–48, 103, 143
    faith and, 9–11
    the impossible, Derrida's discussion of, 123
    Marion's treatment of, 93–97, 101
    mysticism and, 54–55, 61
    possibility of human knowledge of God in, 45–58
    prayer, Derrida on, 146
    radical atheism associated with Derrida and, 109, 117–26
    self-critical nature of faith and, 55–58
    as term, 8n16
    Thomas Aquinas and Dionysius compared, 45–47
    time in, 58–61
negativity, deconstructive. *See* deconstruction
negativity and affirmation, coexistence of
    in deconstruction, 18–19, 21, 30, 37–39
    in negative theology, 40–41, 43–45, 47, 54, 58, 95, 143, 150
negativity of evil, 43n9
Neoplatonism, 13, 42, 71n27, 87
Nicholas of Cusa, 90n18, 91
Nietzsche, Friedrich, 146

Occupy movement, 152
oikonomia and *theologia*, early Christian linking of, 134, 136
O'Rourke, Fran, 46n23
otherness and alterity
    Derrida's ethics regarding, 122–23
    negative theology and deconstruction both moved by desire for, 87

Packer, George, 33
Parain, Brice, 98
Paul (apostle)
    conversion of, 71
    Derrida on Christianity and, 115
    Dionysius the Areopagite and, 12–13, 115
    negative theology of, 41
    Romans 8:24–25 on hope, 6
Peterson, Erik, 150
Philo of Alexandria, 90n18, 91
philosophy as conceptual system, problem of, 19–22
Pieper, Josef, 83n73, 83
Plato and Platonism, 91, 144n53
Parmenides, 71n27
play
    Agamben on, 143
    Derridean concept of, 20–22, 27
    in Dionysian theological method, 143
Plotinus, 42n6, 90n18, 91
politics. *See also* justice; law/calculative judgment; negative political theology; religion and secular politics
    critique, critique of, 18–19, 30n53, 33–37
    deconstruction and, 28–30

politics. (cont.)
  democracy, Derrida on, 32–33, 76, 121, 130
  Dionysius, political instincts of, 105
  glory, Agamben on legitimation of government by, 135–38, 140–41
  government versus sovereignty, primacy of, 135
  mystical negativity and pursuit of justice, 104–5
  negativity, Derrida's politics inflected by, 30–33
  religious faith and, 12
  speech/knowledge about the hyperessential, problem of, 100
  time and justice, understanding of, 25–28
postmodernism, 70n26
praise, Dionysius on, 93–96, 137
prayer, Derrida on, 145–46
presence and absence, Derrida on, 22–37
Proclus, 42n3
Pseudo-Dionysius. See Dionysius the Areopagite

rationality/transcendence of hope, 4, 77–82
Rawls, John, 108n2
Reagan, Ronald, 150
relationship between deconstruction and negative theology, 85–105
  apocalyptic privilege, Derrida on assertion of, 90–101
  Derrida's views on negative theology, 89–93
  ethics, 102–4
  hope as alternative to, 102
  hyperousios/superessentiality, problem of, 87, 90n14, 91–92, 96–102
  Marion's treatment of Dionysius, deconstruction, and negative theology, 93–97, 101
  mystical negativity and pursuit of justice, 104–5
  praise, Dionysius interpreted by Marion through lens of, 93–97
  predication, Marion's move away from, 93
  secularism/secularization, concept of, 109n3, 117–21
  speech/knowledge about the hyperessential, problem of, 99–102
religion. See also Christianity; Jews and Judaism
  concept of, 4n5, 115n27
religion and secular politics, 14, 108–31
  Agamben on, 133–34
  arguments on dangerousness of religion and need for separation of, 110–13
  concept of secularism/secularization, 109n3, 117–21
  conflicted identity of Derrida and, 127–30

  Derrida's rebuttal to separation of, 109–10, 113–17
  Hobbes on, 109, 111–13, 116–17, 130–31
  hope as response to danger/fragility of, 130–31
  impossibility/lack of necessity in excluding religion from public life, 109, 114–16
  Lilla on separation of, 109–17
  modernity, unease about place of religion in, 108–9
  negative political theology and, 132–33
  radical atheism associated with Derrida and, 109, 117–26
  risk, Derrida on acceptance of, 109–23
Roberts, Tyler, 30n53
Romans 8:24–25 on hope, 6
Roques, René, 60n82
Rorty, Richard, 20–21
Rousseau, Jean-Jacques, 132
Royle, Nicholas, 20n11
Rubenstein, Mary-Jane, 89, 93n32
Russell, Bertrand, 71n32

Saffrey, Henri Dominique, 42n3
Sarracen, John, 46n23
Saul (Paul), conversion of, 71
Saussure, Ferdinand de, 23, 36
scandalous names for God, Dionysius on, 142
Schmitt, Carl, 29n44, 116n32, 150
Sea of Faith network, 43n9
Searle, John R., 20n9
secular politics and religion. See religion and secular politics
secularism/secularization, concept of, 109n3, 117–21
Sedgwick, Eve Kosofsky, 13, 18, 33–34, 36, 152
self-criticism. See critique and self-criticism
separation of religion and politics. See religion and secular politics
signs and signification, 22–23
Silesius, Angelus, 124
Smith, James K. A., 74n39, 89n12
Spinoza, Baruch, 78, 83
Stang, Charles, 139
Stiglmayr, Josef, 42n3
suffering and danger, hope as source of, 82–84
superessentiality/*hyperousios*, 87, 90n14, 91–92, 96–102
Syriza, 152

Tanner, Kathryn, 121n57
Taylor, Charles, *A Secular Age*, 3–4, 108n1, 116n30
Thomas Aquinas, 45–47, 96, 99, 127
Ticciati, Susannah, 48n28

time
    deconstruction and Derridean understanding of justice, 25–28
    in negative theology of Dionysius, 58–61
Timothy, Dionysius's *The Mystical Theology* addressed to, 99–100
transcendence/rationality of hope, 4, 77–82
Turner, Denys, 46n23, 95n48

Warren, Calvin, 5
Webster, John, 70n26
Weil, Simone, 127

William of Auxerre, 127
Williams, Janet, 44n14
Williams, Rowan, 45n16
Winters, Joseph, 83
worship
    Eucharistic liturgy, Dionysius on, 147–48
    negative theology and ecclesial worship practices, 53–54
    praise, Dionysius on, 93–96, 137

Zahavi, Dan, 24n25